Beginning Google Web Toolkit

From Novice to Professional

■■■

Bram Smeets, Uri Boness, and
Roald Bankras

Apress®

Beginning Google Web Toolkit: From Novice to Professional

Copyright © 2008 by Bram Smeets, Uri Boness, and Roald Bankras

ISBN-13 (pbk): 978-1-4302-1031-3

ISBN-13 (electronic): 978-1-4302-1032-0

Printed and bound in the United States of America 9 8 7 6 5 4 3 2 1

Lead Editor: Steve Anglin
Technical Reviewer: Massimo Nardone
Editorial Board: Clay Andres, Steve Anglin, Ewan Buckingham, Tony Campbell, Gary Cornell,
    Jonathan Gennick, Matthew Moodie, Joseph Ottinger, Jeffrey Pepper, Frank Pohlmann,
    Ben Renow-Clarke, Dominic Shakeshaft, Matt Wade, Tom Welsh
Project Manager: Sofia Marchant
Copy Editor: Benjamin Berg
Associate Production Director: Kari Brooks-Copony
Production Editor: Kelly Winquist
Compositor: Octal Publishing, Inc.
Proofreader: Dan Shaw
Indexer: Julie Grady
Artist: Octal Publishing, Inc.
Cover Designer: Kurt Krames
Manufacturing Director: Tom Debolski

Distributed to the book trade worldwide by Springer-Verlag New York, Inc., 233 Spring Street, 6th Floor, New York, NY 10013. Phone 1-800-SPRINGER, fax 201-348-4505, e-mail orders-ny@springer-sbm.com, or visit http://www.springeronline.com.

For information on translations, please contact Apress directly at 2855 Telegraph Avenue, Suite 600, Berkeley, CA 94705. Phone 510-549-5930, fax 510-549-5939, e-mail info@apress.com, or visit http://www.apress.com.

Apress and friends of ED books may be purchased in bulk for academic, corporate, or promotional use. eBook versions and licenses are also available for most titles. For more information, reference our Special Bulk Sales–eBook Licensing web page at http://www.apress.com/info/bulksales.

The source code for this book is available to readers at http://www.apress.com.

To all my friends and family, especially my wonderful wife, Petra,
for her love and support, and my lovely sister, Sophie.
—Bram Smeets

To my amazing and beloved children, Daan and Lian, who managed
to spare quite a few playtime hours in order for me to write this book.
—Uri Boness

To Layla, who supported me throughout the book.
—Roald Bankras

Contents at a Glance

Contents

About the Authors

BRAM SMEETS is a Java architect with more than eight years' experience in developing enterprise Java applications. Currently, Bram is technical director at JTeam (www.jteam.nl), a Java software development company based in the Netherlands, and senior consultant at SpringSource (www.springsource.com). He is a regular speaker at technology-focused conferences such as The Ajax Experience and SpringOne. Using GWT, Bram has delivered several successful RIA projects at JTeam. He's also done Ajax and GWT training for several companies.

URI BONESS is a software engineer and architect with more than eight years' experience developing Java applications. Currently, Uri serves as the chief scientist at JTeam. Over the years, Uri has contributed and initiated several open source projects, including GWToolbox—a set of GWT modules to help simplify the development of GWT applications. Like Bram, Uri too delivered several GWT-based projects and gave several training sessions on the subject. His main technology interests are focused on search and RIA, which he considers to be the real backbone of the new age of enterprise applications.

ROALD BANKRAS is a software engineer and project manager with more than five years of Java experience. Roald has gathered his experience running e-Procurement and custom back-office projects for mid- and large-size companies in the Netherlands. During the last year, Roald has put his knowledge to use implementing a complete fulfillment system using GWT.

About the Technical Reviewer

 **MASSIMO NARDONE** was born under Mount Vesuvius and holds a master's degree in computing science from the University of Salerno, Italy. He works currently as IT security and infrastructure architect, security consultant, and Finnish invention development team leader (FIDTL) for IBM Finland. His main security responsibilities include IT infrastructure, security auditing and assessment, PKI/WPKI, secure tunneling, LDAP security, and SmartCard security.

With more then 13 years of work experience in mobile, security, and web technologies for both national and international projects, he's worked as a project manager, software engineer, research engineer, chief security architect, and software specialist. He's also worked as a visiting lecturer and supervisor for exercises at the Networking Laboratory of the Helsinki University of Technology (TKK) for a course on security of communication protocols.

He also works as a security application auditing expert to check on new application vulnerabilities using security standards such as ISO 17799 and ISO 27001 (formal BS7799:2).

He has researched, designed, and implemented security methodologies for different areas such as Standard BS7799, PKI and WPKI, Security Java (JAAS, JSSE, JCE), BEA Web logic Security, J2EE Security, LDAP Security, SSO, Apache Security, MS SQL Server Security, XML Security, SmartCard Security, and so on. He currently holds four International patents (in PKI, SIP, SAML, and proxy areas).

Acknowledgments

We want to thank everyone who has supported us and/or participated in writing this book. During the months of work, a lot of people kept asking about our progress, which worked as a real stimulant to finish the book. We'd like to thank all the people at Apress, Sofia Marchant in particular, for their support and making sure the book stayed on track. Furthermore, we thank Tom Welsh for putting up with us non–native English speakers and the many "keep it simple" remarks, and also Benjamin Berg for the many style and grammar suggestions. Last, we'd like to thank Steve Anglin for allowing this book to see the light and intervening whenever necessary.

We also want to thank all our colleagues at JTeam for putting up with us during the writing of this book, especially Leonard Wolters for providing us with the time to write it. Furthermore, we thank Jelmer Kuperus and Tom van Zummeren for providing valuable content for the book.

Last, we'd all like to thank our friends and families for putting up with us and supporting us.

Bram, Uri, and Roald

Introduction

Over the last couple of years, we've noticed that our customers have gotten more demanding when it comes to the usability of their web applications. Inspired by the "web 2.0" trend and applications such as Gmail and the like, we've tried many approaches to building these rich Internet applications (RIAs). But all of these had one big flaw: they required us to learn a different language, including adhering to a whole new set of conventions and best practices. Only with the introduction of Google Web Toolkit (GWT) have we begun to feel confident about building this kind of application in a maintainable fashion.

This book introduces GWT within the context just described, and will guide you through the first steps of using it to build real-world applications. The goal is to get you as a Java developer up to speed quickly by providing just enough background and a lot of hands-on code samples. During the course of the book, we'll guide you through the different aspects of GWT that we feel are important, and leave out the ones we feel are out-of-scope for beginners. Most of the code samples will gradually build to make up a real-world sample application that allows you to manage your tasks using a web application.

After reading this book, you'll be equipped with the necessary knowledge and tools to start building real-world applications using GWT.

Who This Book Is For

This book is intended for Java developers who wish to reuse their Java expertise for writing complex rich Internet applications using the GWT framework. It can also serve those developers who have extensive knowledge of other web development technologies such as JavaScript and HTML, as GWT helps abstract away one of the biggest challenges in such development: browser compatibility and client-side performance.

How This Book Is Structured

This book is divided into eight chapters:

Chapter 1 introduces the basic concepts of contemporary rich Internet application development. It walks you through the history of web application development and provides a solid basic knowledge of the technologies that drive modern Web 2.0 applications in general and GWT positioning in particular.

Chapter 2 introduces you to GWT. This chapter details the basic concepts of GWT, the problems it was designed to solve, and its inner workings. You'll learn about the anatomy of a typical GWT application, and will also be introduced to the GWTasks sample application (a task management application) you'll be developing along with the book.

Chapter 3 gives you all the tools to get started with GWT. It teaches you how to create a simple GWT project from scratch, run it, and debug it. It's highly recommended that you not skip this chapter, as the following chapters rely on the knowledge it provides.

Chapter 4 shows how to develop GWT application in more detail. It introduces the basic components that are available for you to use when creating GWT user interfaces. It introduces some of the more common widgets and panels that will be used to develop an initial version of the sample application.

Chapter 5 builds on the knowledge gained in the previous chapter and introduces more advanced UI components. Among other things, you'll learn how to create your own custom UI elements that can be reused in any application. This chapter also discusses the role of the application architecture and design from the software development perspective, and provides tools to build robust, extensible, and maintainable code bases for your application. All techniques learned in this chapter will be put to action and applied on the sample application.

Chapter 6 introduces server-side communication and how it can be done in GWT applications. It explains the basics of such communication and covers the various mechanisms supported by GWT. By the end of this chapter, the GWTasks application will be a full-blown task management application with a solid server-side back end.

Chapter 7 discusses the important role testing has in the application development process. It introduces the different types of testing, from fine-grained unit testing to full-blown functional testing using third-party tools such as Selenium.

Chapter 8 enriches your knowledge and GWT expertise by discussing some of the more advanced features GWT has to offer. Each section in this chapter is dedicated to a specific topic that will help you build better and more advanced GWT applications. As opposed to the other chapters, each section in this chapter can be read independently of the others.

This book was specially structured to get you up-to-speed with GWT in a more efficient and practical manner. The sample application plays a major role in it, as it serves as a concrete example of how the theory can be applied.

Prerequisites

We assume that you have a good understanding of the Java programming language and are at least familiar with Java 5 features such as generics, annotations, and enum types. A good understanding of basic HTML is required as well, and knowledge of JavaScript will serve as an advantage (though it's not a requirement).

Downloading the Code

The code for the examples and the sample application in this book is available to readers in the Download section of the Apress web site at http://www.apress.com. Each chapter has associated code examples and optionally a relevant sample application version. Please feel free to visit the Apress web site and download all the code there. You can also check for errata and find related titles from Apress.

CHAPTER 1

∎∎∎

Introducing Rich Internet Applications (RIAs)

The Google Web Toolkit (GWT) is an open source framework that makes building RIAs easy for Java developers. You can use your Java expertise to build "fat clients" that can be deployed as web applications. These desktop-like applications are typically written in JavaScript in order to leverage the huge installed base of web browsers. But JavaScript is quite a different language from Java (its name was chosen for marketing reasons) and therefore requires different development practices.

However, GWT allows you to develop JavaScript applications in Java! This is accomplished with the most important part of GWT, the Java-to-JavaScript compiler. This compiler translates your Java code into JavaScript that runs in the user's browser. As an added bonus, GWT copes with most browser quirks, allowing you to focus on writing code that actually does something.

This book aims to show you how to use GWT to build RIAs. But before introducing GWT in any detail, we first need to give you some historical perspective. If you're already familiar with the inner workings of the Web, and if you know about the advantages of Ajax compared with other approaches to building RIAs (such as Flex), feel free to skip this chapter and start with Chapter 2, which introduces GWT.

This chapter provides a short history of software systems, how we typically interact with them, and how we make them available to the user. We introduce different types of applications, including RIAs, and describe Ajax as an approach to building RIAs. Finally, we compare some different approaches to developing RIAs, before zooming in on one in particular in the next chapter: GWT.

A Short History

Software systems have been around for several decades, but it's only fairly recently that they started to be used by countless millions of people around the world. Only 20 years ago, the majority of software applications were used by trained professionals, whereas today most inhabitants of the world interact directly with one or more software applications every day. This enormously rapid growth in the number of people regularly using computers couldn't have taken place without the great advances in usability and user interface techniques that accompanied it.

Looking back, it's hard to believe that interacting with early computers was fun for some people (although I might get into a fight with those of you still using Vim). Most people who remember "green screen" terminals will agree that working with a command prompt is generally not the most pleasant user experience. Issuing a command using the keyboard, pressing Enter, and waiting for the output to show up on the screen hardly constitutes a rich client (although for some tasks and some users, it's still appropriate and sometimes even more productive).

In order to avoid confusion, let's explain what characterizes a rich client. The "richness" of the client is determined by the interaction model that the client offers to the user. A rich user interaction model is one that can support a variety of input methods and responds intuitively and in a timely fashion. As a rule of thumb, in order to be considered rich, the user interaction should be as good as the current generation of desktop applications, such as word processors and spreadsheets. This includes features such as providing different means of interaction (for example, using keyboard and mouse to navigate, inline editing, and drag and drop) and direct visual feedback (for example, changing the cursor shape, indications using colors, and highlighting buttons and windows).

The change from those old kinds of application to modern rich web applications that this book deals with has been a long, gradual one. Figure 1-1 provides an overview of the main stages of this change, and will serve as the basis for our short history. We can roughly distinguish four stages in the evolution of software applications. The arrow depicts the path through those stages over time.

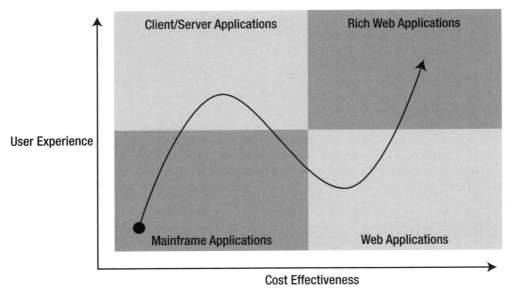

Figure 1-1. *An overview of the history of software applications*

Mainframe Applications

Starting around the 1960s, mainframe applications, whose users gained access through punch cards and lsater terminals (or terminal emulations), formed the first stage of software applications. The "green screen" terminals (the monochrome monitors of most terminals and early

PCs) provided a text-based user interface for interacting with the server-side application. Obviously a text-based user interface doesn't allow for rich interactivity such as drag and drop or instant feedback while the user types. Furthermore, terminal applications can't provide the best responsiveness, as the user input always has to be processed on the server before the user can get feedback.

From a cost effectiveness perspective, mainframe applications are often criticized for spiraling maintenance costs that are the result of a vicious circle of lack of documentation and the inability to upgrade. Applications had to be developed for the specific operating system that the application needed to be deployed on, possibly resulting in an even larger code base depending on the number of supported operating systems.

Client/Server Applications

As the personal computer became more popular, people began to have computing power on or under their desks. With this revolution came the change from a command-line UI to a more desktop-like UI, resulting from the WIMP (windows, icons, menus, and pointer device) model invented at Xerox PARC in the 1970s. Although the early adoptions by Apple and later Microsoft were poor, they allowed developers to create applications featuring richer interaction with the user. The graphical power of desktop machines helped applications become more user friendly by providing better visual feedback. However, these applications still required centralized data storage and processing, therefore needing to interact with a central server, hence the term *client/server.*

In terms of cost effectiveness, things didn't improve much, for in addition to the server side of the software, a client side also had to be developed. And as the requirements for the client side usually dictated support for more than just one OS, development and maintenance costs grew even worse. Another cost-increasing factor was that because the software didn't run in one central place but on numerous individual machines, a new version of the software required an update to all the machines that it was installed on.

Web Applications

At the same time that software applications were developed on or around a central server, the Internet and the Web were becoming more popular and more widespread. The Web was originally meant as a platform to allow people to share information by publishing documents and cross-referencing them using hyperlinks. As usage of the Web became more widespread, more and more people started having software on their computers that could interact with this document structure. The web browser provided common functionality, such as going back and forward through the navigation history and bookmarking certain pages for later retrieval. But the main advantage was that instead of software vendors needing to create specific versions of their applications for different operating systems, they had this huge installed base at their disposal. If only they could tap into that!

In order to understand the next steps in the evolution of the software application, we have to look in little more detail at the structure and inner workings of the Web. Web browsers render documents formatted using the Hypertext Markup Language (HTML) (`http://www.w3.org/HTML`). They find the document that the user wants using a uniform resource locator (URL) (`http://www.w3.org/Adressing`) and use a Hypertext Transfer Protocol (HTTP) (`http://www.w3.org/Protocols`) request to retrieve the document from a remote web server.

This is an important concept of the Web: all documents actually reside on one or more web servers, and the web browser (the client) retrieves the document from the server. It then reads the HTML document, applies the formatting rules defined in the file (as discussed later), and renders it on screen for the user to read.

The enormous popularity of the Web is largely due to the fact that it's unique; there's only one Web, wherever you go and whatever platform you use. Moreover, the Web is defined by a handful of vendor-neutral industry standards that are laid down and managed by bodies such as the World Wide Web Consortium (W3C) (http://www.w3.org) and the Internet Engineering Task Force (IETF) (http://www.ietf.org). That has prevented individual vendors, such as Microsoft, from taking over the Web by adding proprietary extensions. The Web only works because people agree on the standards that browsers can implement and that content providers and application developers can adhere to. Not only HTML, but other standards such as Cascading Style Sheets (CSS) (http://www.w3.org/Style/CSS), Document Object Model (DOM) (http://www.w3.org/DOM), Scalable Vector Graphics (SVG) (http://www.w3.org/Graphics/SVG), and Portable Network Graphics (PNG) (http://www.w3.org/Graphics/PNG) have contributed to the Web's success. Most of these standards will be discussed in the course of this book.

Instead of just using the Web to serve static HTML documents to users, someone came up with the idea of letting users request a dynamically generated document. That way, for instance, the user could take advantage of the (already installed) web browser to review real-time statistics or personalized content. This is where the web application was born. A *web application* is an application that resides on a central server and can be accessed by users through web browsers that they already have.

From a cost effectiveness perspective, this is a great way to develop software applications. You develop and deploy the applications once, and instead of having to install client applications on every user's machine, the clients already have all the necessary software preinstalled. Also, when you develop a new version of your application, you just replace the central version, and because clients interact with that central version, they will automatically receive the new version.

However, from a richness point of view, things went back to the mainframe days. Instead of having the rich user experience of the desktop application, allowing multiple means of interaction, responsiveness, and visual feedback, things went back to the issue-a-command-and-wait interaction model. Every action in a web application results in a call to the server to generate the next page or document. Therefore, as a client, you issue a command by clicking on a link or submitting a form, and then you might have to wait hundreds of milliseconds or even seconds for the entire page/document to return from the server. In the meantime, you have no way to interact with the application.

Even though there's an obvious setback in terms of usability, the greatly improved cost effectiveness has made web applications today's most popular type of software application.

Rich Web Applications

Although web applications have become the de facto standard for developing software applications, they're mostly used to develop general-purpose, publicly available applications. Still, numerous applications that depend heavily on rich user interaction to accomplish certain day-to-day tasks are developed as client/server applications. The reason for this is obvious, as the Web and its document-centric approach don't allow for rich user interaction. Imagine a spreadsheet-like web application, where every time you enter or modify data in a cell, you have to wait for the entire page to reload with recalculated values. This is even worse when the communication between client and server goes over a public network, typically leading to higher latency between requests and responses. Having too much latency for direct feedback might lead to an unresponsive application, and is therefore not suited to performing a person's everyday job. Therefore these kinds of applications, up until recently, remained in the client/server domain, leveraging the capacities of a truly rich application, but still carrying the burden of being targeted at different environments.

This is where Ajax comes in to solve this issue by allowing developers to create user-friendly applications and still reap the benefits of being able to deploy applications on the Web.

Introducing Ajax

As sketched in the previous sections, developers needed a way to develop interactive applications while still being able to deploy those applications on the web. Ajax meets exactly that need. For instance, developers can use Ajax to provide autocomplete functionality that retrieves and displays appropriate suggestions as users type into an input field. They can also write powerful, Web-based chat applications that don't need to refresh the entire page while the user is typing a new message.

Ajax does all this by using JavaScript in the browser to modify the UI directly, using the `XMLHttpRequest` object, which is discussed later, to communicate with the server without having to refresh the entire page. Then it uses the information returned from the server, usually in XML or another text format, to update the UI.

Even before the term *Ajax* was coined, developers were already developing applications like those described, using browser-specific features (such as Netscape's LiveConnect: `http://developer.mozilla.org/en/docs/LiveConnect`). But it wasn't until Jesse James Garrett coined the term in his article "Ajax: A New Approach to Web Applications" (`http://www.adaptivepath.com/publications/essays/archives/000385.php`) that this way of developing applications really took off. Although Ajax is now just a word that stands for nothing, Garrett suggested it as an acronym for *Asynchronous JavaScript and XML*. Let's first look at each of the components in this acronym in order to understand what Ajax is all about.

Asynchronous

In order to understand the main difference between Ajax's and the typical applications that were developed before Ajax, we have to look closer at how users interact with web applications. Figure 1-2 illustrates this for a typical web application. The user starts off by requesting a web page. The server processes the request and sends the result back to the browser, where it's subsequently rendered for the user. A typical web application then allows the user to do only a limited number of things. The user can provide input data by using *form widgets* (clicking on a link or button to submit the information), or by requesting a new page. The result of either action is that the user has to wait for the server to return a response. Meanwhile, the user can no longer use the application. This is called a *synchronous* interaction model. All user interaction halts until the server returns with a response, and only then can the user continue to use the application.

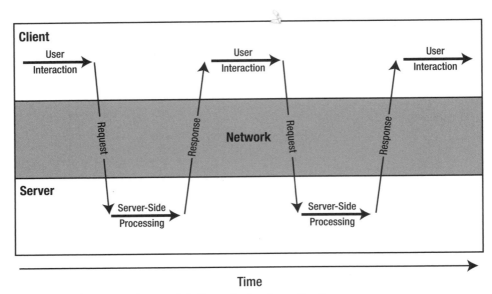

Figure 1-2. *The interaction model of a typical web application*

Although this model is acceptable for browsing through web pages (say, at a news site), it's unacceptable for more day-to-day applications, like our earlier spreadsheet example. In the case of a spreadsheet application, modifying a value and then having to wait for the server to return the recalculated outcome of a formula is unacceptable. First of all, you want to continue interacting with the spreadsheet while the result of the action is recalculated. But even more importantly, you also want to avoid having to receive and (re)render the entire page. This provides extra overhead because the server has to regenerate the entire page, the entire page is sent over the network, and the browser has to render the entire page again.

It would be so much better if we could update only the relevant cells in the spreadsheet. This is where the *asynchronous* model comes into play, taking away the gaps in the interaction and allowing the user to continue interacting with the application while previous actions are handled by the server. This model is shown in Figure 1-3.

The problem with the interaction shown in Figure 1-3 is that it breaks the classic Web model of HTTP requests for HTML pages, whose simplicity is one of its greatest strengths. The way to do this without losing more than we gain is by introducing an *Ajax engine*, a layer between the user interaction and the server communication. This engine runs inside the browser and delegates actions to the server while also handling the results. Because the engine dispatches calls to the server and pushes results to the user, the user can continue to interact with the application in the meantime. Because the engine adheres to the same standards, the Web model remains intact.

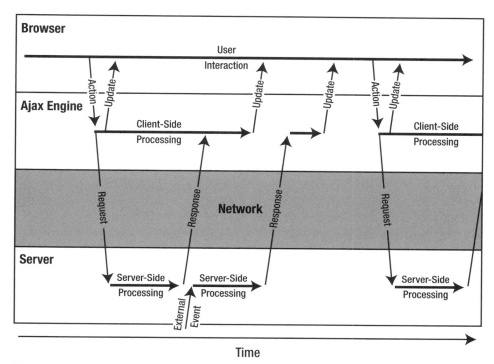

Figure 1-3. *The interaction model of an Ajax application*

To implement this asynchronous model, we need a way to send requests to the server asynchronously, without having to do a page refresh. As already mentioned, the Web was originally meant for linking documents together and navigating between them. Therefore, the Web and its standards don't directly support Ajax-style operations. However, developers are creative people, and if there's a way, it will be used to get the job done. It turned out that there was a way to do these asynchronous calls from the browser, only not in a browser-independent manner. Microsoft Internet Explorer ships with a built-in ActiveX control (XmlHttpRequest) that could be used to make an asynchronous call. Mozilla/Firefox contains its own similar mechanism, conveniently also called XmlHttpRequest, only implemented as a native object. Both mechanisms are similar in the way you use them. This allowed developers to apply this asynchronous model in applications that work in most browsers. This quickly made Ajax quite popular.

■**Note** Although the use of XmlHttpRequest, either as an ActiveX component or as a native object, is by far the most popular way to dispatch asynchronous calls to the server, there are other ways. Two examples of other remoting mechanisms are using a hidden iframe and dynamically adding a script tag in the head of the document.

JavaScript

JavaScript is a scripting language created by Brendan Eich when he was working at Netscape. Originally it was named *Mocha* and later *LiveScript*, but renamed JavaScript around 1995. Although the name suggests otherwise, the language is quite different from the Java programming language, although they share a common ancestor in the C syntax. JavaScript was probably named after the Java language as a marketing move that was part of a strategic alliance between Sun Microsystems and Netscape. Some say they used Java in the name to give JavaScript the allure of being the new "hot" web programming language. It's mostly because of the support in Netscape that JavaScript became the most widely supported scripting language in browsers. Microsoft started off with its own dialect called *JScript*, but later switched to supporting JavaScript. In 1996, JavaScript was submitted for standardization, resulting in the ECMAScript specification with JavaScript as one of its implementations, others being *ActionScript* (heavily used by Adobe) and *JScript*, which is still used for Microsoft's Active Scripting.

JavaScript is a dynamic, weakly typed, prototype-based language with first-class functions. It supports the structured programming syntax of C, including loops, switch statements, and so on. One exception is that it doesn't support block-level scoping.

In order to get a better idea of JavaScript, let's look at Listing 1-1, which shows a simple HTML page that uses JavaScript to display an alert to the user with a value that the user has supplied in an input field.

Listing 1-1. *Sample JavaScript Embedded in an HTML Page*

```
<html>
    <head>
        <title>JavaScript sample</title>

        <script type="text/javascript">
            function handleButtonClick() {
                var input = document.getElementById('query');
                alert('Query: ' + input.value);
            }
        </script>
    </head>
    <body>
        Query:
        <input id="query" type="text" value=""/>
        <button onclick="handleButtonClick()">Show</button>
    </body>
</html>
```

The JavaScript fragment in Listing 1-1 looks much like Java, and it's easy to understand what the code is trying to achieve. However, you should also note the subtle differences, such as the variable and function declarations. Luckily, as you'll see in the remainder of this chapter, you don't need to know much more about JavaScript if you want to develop RIAs using GWT.

However, if you want more information about JavaScript, try the *JavaScript 1.5 User's Guide* (`http://developer.mozilla.org/en/docs/Core_JavaScript_1.5_Guide`), *Beginning JavaScript with DOM Scripting and Ajax: From Novice to Professional* by Christian Heilmann (Apress, 2006), and *Pro JavaScript Techniques* by John Resig (Apress, 2006).

XML

Extensible Markup Language (XML) has become popular in the developer world as a means of transferring data in a language-neutral manner. Basically, a markup language is a language that employs tags to describe how its content is to be structured, laid out, or formatted. For instance, the sample XML fragment in Listing 1-2 describes the structure of a menu.

Listing 1-2. *Sample XML Describing a Menu Structure*

```
<?xml version="1.0" encoding="UTF-8"?>
<menu>
    <item id="1">
        <description>
            A menu item
        </description>
    </item>
    <item id="2">
        <description>
            Another menu item
        </description>
    </item>
</menu>
```

As you can see, the information in Listing 1-2 is structured in a hierarchical way. XML is a simplified form of the Standard Generalized Markup Language (SGML). Both SGML and XML are meta-markup languages, allowing you to define your own markup languages. One application of SGML is HTML, as depicted in Figure 1-4. Listing 1-3 shows some textual content marked up using HTML.

Listing 1-3. *Sample Content Containing HTML Markup*

```
<div>
    <h1>New version of GWT released</h1>
    <p>
        Last night, word reached us that a new version of the hugely popular
        application development framework by Google<sup>TM</sup> is released.
        <br>
        More information:
        <a href="http://code.google.com/webtoolkit">
            http://code.google.com/webtoolkit
        </a>
    </p>
    <p>Sept. 21, 2008</p>
</div>
```

Basically, HTML provides a set of predefined tags that developers can use to add markup information to content. Note that in HTML, you can't use your own tags. So for instance, changing the h1 tag to name would result in the interpreter either failing or just ignoring it.

This is where XML comes in: it allows you to define your own tags. XML allows different ways to describe your document structure by means of schemas. Different schema languages exist for XML, including the Document Type Definition (DTD), which provides a limited set of functionality, and the more powerful XML Schema. But as these document descriptions are optional, you can easily do without them. So the content from Listing 1-3 could be expressed using XML as shown in Listing 1-4.

Listing 1-4. *Content Containing XML Markup*

```
<newsitem>
    <name>New version of GWT released</name>
    <description>
        Last night, word reached us that a new version of the
        hugely popular application development framework by
        Google<sup>TM</sup> is released.
    </description>
    <link>http://code.google.com/webtoolkit</link>
    <date>Sept. 21, 2008</date>
</newsitem>
```

If you compare Listings 1-4 and 1-3, you'll note that XML adds much more semantic value to the text. As its name spells out, XML is a markup language. But unlike HTML, which uses markup for a single well-defined purpose, XML is also a language for defining markup languages. It adds semantic value by describing the content within the tags. Still, one could write an interpreter that uses the semantic information described by the tags and use that to format the information to the user.

Although it may seem so, HTML is not an extension of XML. This is because in contrast to XML, HTML allows for single tags: opening tags with no closing tags, such as the <br> in Listing 1-3. This is allowed in SGML but not in XML; in XML, each opening tag should have a corresponding closing tag or it should be an empty tag: it should be either
</br> or <br/>. In order for HTML to be more easily validated and accessible for more devices and platforms, Extensible Hypertext Markup Language (XHTML) recently has become popular. This combines the set of tags defined in HTML with the stricter syntax of XML, allowing for easier validation and interpretation. Figure 1-4 gives an overview of all the markup languages we've discussed so far.

Before we look at XML and more specifically how it's used in Ajax, let's digress for a moment. As mentioned earlier, the Web works because of standards. One of these standards is the Document Object Model (DOM): see http://www.w3.org/DOM/. This platform- and language-neutral interface allows programs and scripts to dynamically access and update the content, structure, and style of documents (for example, XML and HTML documents). The DOM represents a document as a hierarchical tree of nodes that can be accessed and manipulated. All browsers that support JavaScript use the DOM to represent and render HTML documents. This allows developers to use JavaScript to inspect and modify the document and therefore the UI. If you look back at Listing 1-1, you can see how we use the DOM to access the input field and retrieve its value. We used the JavaScript method getElementById(String) on the DOM representation of the HTML page.

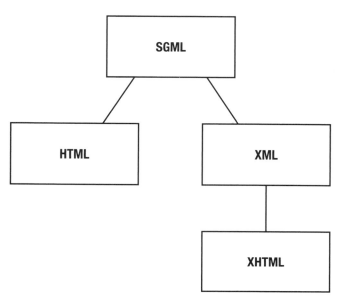

Figure 1-4. *SGML and a selection of its child languages*

As mentioned earlier, XML allows data to be transferred in an interchangeable way. This is exactly what it's used for in Ajax applications. It allows you to transfer data from the client to the server and vice versa. This makes it easy for the client-side platform to be quite different from the server-side platform. So for instance, while the client side is written in JavaScript, the server side can be written in any possible programming language. Therefore, XML seemed like an ideal data transfer format when Ajax was created. However, as we'll see in the next section, that turned out to be incorrect.

From AJAX to Ajax

So far we've discussed the major components that, in the past, made up the acronym AJAX. However, in 2006 Garrett redefined the AJAX as *Ajax* (a simple name, standing for nothing in particular).

Why did he make this change, and why is it important to discuss here? Let's first look at why he made the change. After several years of developing applications based on this new paradigm, two of the three components expanded beyond their original context. The first, *asynchronous*, remained in place, although it was more and more implemented without using the XmlHttpRequest object that had originally been one of the biggest catalysts behind the whole movement. But the other two, JavaScript and XML, were slowly being expanded. As we'll see in the next section, other approaches such as Flex use a language other than JavaScript to do their scripting in the browser environment. Flex for instance uses ActionScript for scripting (http://www.adobe.com/devnet/actionscript), but also has support for other scripting languages.

Therefore, the *JavaScript* part of the AJAX acronym was no longer valid. But even more obvious was the need for a change to the *XML* part of the acronym. XML turned out not to be the best choice for exchanging data between the client and the server. Obviously in some cases you could use XHTML to communicate the content and place it directly inside a page, but this is inconvenient when sending plain data. This is mostly because browsers tend to work differently with XML, both because APIs tend to differ, but even more importantly because the performance can be very different.

Therefore, after initially using XML, developers started to look for alternatives. Basically, they found three alternatives to XML:

- **A proprietary protocol**—either a textual or binary protocol that allows for data communication between the client and server. The advantage of a proprietary protocol is that it can easily be optimized for both size and speed.

- **JavaScript Object Notation (JSON)**—JSON is a lightweight data interchange format based on name/value pairs. Originally based on JavaScript, and implemented as a subset of it, JSON provides a good bridge between a JavaScript client and a server implementation using Java. For more information, see `http://www.json.org`.

- **Plain JavaScript**—instead of using a specific interchange protocol, you could send plain JavaScript over the wire. Although this is the most powerful and flexible option (because you can use all features and syntax provided by the language), it requires the server to generate JavaScript. As the server-side code is generally written in a language other than JavaScript, this isn't recommended. It's usually much better to use some interchange format such as JSON.

Each solution has its advantages and disadvantages, but if we look at the majority of Ajax applications today, we must conclude that XML is no longer the most widely used data transport format.

So Garrett redefined Ajax as a name rather than an acronym. He defined Ajax as an application developed for the Web, using DHTML (see sidebar) and doing some kind of remote communication with the server in an asynchronous manner. That's the kind of application that you'll learn to develop in this book.

DYNAMIC HTML (DHTML)

The term *DHTML* describes the usage of several of the previously described technologies to create interactive and animated web sites. DHTML combines a static markup language (such as HTML), a client-side scripting language (such as JavaScript), a presentation definition language (such as CSS), and the DOM. Combining these technologies allows you to dynamically change the appearance and behavior of a web page. More recently, DHTML is also referred to as *DOM Scripting*, although this somewhat narrows the meaning of the term.

Advantages and Disadvantages of RIAs

Before exploring different approaches to building rich Internet applications, let's first look at their advantages and disadvantages compared to classical and web applications. In the previous sections, we have already touched on some of these.

RIA Benefits

Next to the obvious, intrinsic benefits of building a rich Internet application, it also comes with the following additional benefits:

- **No installation required**—the application is downloaded automatically and runs inside the browser. The software that actually runs the application is already installed on the client machine.

- **Updates are automatic**—new versions of the application are also downloaded automatically by simply revisiting the application's web page.

- **Platform independent**—a rich Internet application can potentially run on every platform and operating system, as long as it has an Internet browser and connection to the Internet.

- **More secure**—applications run in the restricted environment of a web browser and are therefore much less likely to be harmful than applications that need to be installed.

- **More responsive**—because not all user actions require server communication, rich Internet applications tend to be more responsive than classic web applications.

- **More scalable**—a great part of the computational work as well as state keeping can be offloaded to the client, so the server can handle many more users. It no longer needs to maintain state, or at least not as much.

- **More network efficient**—in classical web applications, every user action requires the server to regenerate the entire page and send that over the network. In the case of a rich Internet application, the entire application UI only needs to be communicated once. All other requests to the server require only the actual data to be sent to the client.

RIA Shortcomings

With every good thing, there are some drawbacks. The same goes for Ajax and building rich Internet applications. The following are some of the limitations:

- **Requires JavaScript or specific plug-in**—because the entire application runs through the JavaScript interpreter on the client, what happens when the user has turned off JavaScript completely? Usually, the application does little or nothing. Obviously it's possible to have a backup plan for those users, but then you have to maintain two separate applications, which is far from ideal.

- **No access to system resources**—as Ajax applications run inside a browser, they're limited in the resources they can access. For instance, an Ajax application can't access the client file system.

- **Hard for search engines to index fully**—because most search engines don't (yet) support applications that do partial page updates or use specific plug-ins such as Flash, most rich Internet applications are badly indexed by search engines. The larger search engines plan to improve their support for these kinds of applications as their popularity grows, but it will always be difficult to sufficiently index them.

- **Accessibility issues**—doing partial page updates using JavaScript or a specific plug-in can break accessibility. The biggest and most notorious issue is that existing screen readers don't handle this correctly. Although screen readers will try to provide better support, application developers should always keep accessibility in mind when developing software applications, and even more when developing rich Internet applications, because accessibility is easier to break.

- **Depends on an Internet connection**—because these applications are served from the Web and run in the web browser, they require at least an initial Internet connection. But even during usage, an Internet connection is needed to communicate with the server. When the connection is (temporarily) not available, most rich Internet applications fail to function. However, there are some attempts to use local services provided by the browser for temporary storage while a connection is unavailable.

When Should You Use Ajax?

Based on the benefits and shortcomings outlined in the previous section, we strongly believe that rich Internet applications aren't suitable for every application. But there are definite guidelines as to when to build a rich Internet application and when to stick to developing classical web applications as you've probably been doing for some time. Consider the following list:

- You want to develop an application that users need on a daily basis, and they spend a lot of time using the application.

- Business tasks rely on direct feedback from the application to enhance productivity.

- Most, if not all, of the application requires user authentication and authorization, so indexability by search engines is not the top priority.

- It's safe to assume that JavaScript is turned on, or it's acceptable to require users to turn it on before using the application.

We feel that if your application meets these prerequisites, a rich Internet application should be preferred. Assuming you have such an application (at least in mind), let's look at the different approaches that are available for developing these applications.

Different Approaches to Building RIAs

To build these rich Internet applications, we need an easy way to develop the code that runs in the browser and a way to call the server remotely. Let's briefly look at the different approaches that are available. Note that this isn't meant as an exhaustive listing of all frameworks and solutions, but just a highlight of the different approaches.

Handwritten JavaScript

The first and probably most widely used way to develop Ajax applications is by taking a normal web application and adding Ajax capabilities to it by writing some JavaScript. You would usually use preexisting libraries that allow you to focus on the important stuff while reusing features such as remoting and convenience classes for manipulating the interface. In general, there are four main concerns with this approach:

- **JavaScript is not Java**—developing applications using JavaScript is totally different from developing applications in Java. It's not only a completely separate language with its own concepts and constructs, but it also requires a different tool set. And although it's nice for developers to learn a new language, that might not be the best choice from a business perspective. The obvious solution is to hire professional JavaScript developers; but really skillful JavaScript developers are hard to find.

- **Browser quirks**—the biggest challenge and probably the most time-consuming activity when developing Ajax applications is coding an application that handles all the differences between browsers and even between different versions of the same browser. A good JavaScript developer should know all these browser quirks by heart.

- **Too many libraries**—assuming you don't want to reinvent the wheel, you start looking for libraries that give you the basic features you need. But where do you start and which one do you choose for a particular project? At the time of this writing, AjaxPatterns.org listed 42 JavaScript Multipurpose frameworks and 51 Java Ajax frameworks, so in all, you have to choose from 93 frameworks for building your application.

- **Libraries only solve part of the puzzle**—choosing a library is generally not enough; they typically solve only part of the puzzle in that they only handle a certain aspect of building Ajax applications. One might contain basic functionality for remoting, while another provides widgets, and a third handles visual effects. So you end up with a number of different frameworks that you have to tie together into one application.

This approach is workable when adding limited Ajax functionality to a traditional web application. But taking into account these concerns, we don't suggest using this approach to develop the rich Internet applications that we discussed earlier.

Flex

Adobe Flex is a set of tools for developing rich Internet applications on the proprietary Adobe Flash platform. Flash itself offers a lot more than you could get from HTML in terms of real-time interactivity. However, developing rich applications in Flash is daunting and unintuitive for core developers. The Flash development tool is geared for designers, and developing on a timeline is a strange concept for applications that aren't driven by time but by user actions. Flex removes that barrier to entry by providing a programmatic way for developing RIAs. Although the Flex platform was originally developed by Macromedia in 2004 as a commercial product, Adobe made parts of it open source in 2007 after its acquisition of Macromedia.

When developing rich Internet applications using Flex, you use the tools provided by Adobe. The good thing about this is that Flex comes with a lot of built-in functionality, such as widgets, drag and drop, vector graphics, and animations. This will greatly speed up your development, especially if you're already familiar with Flash and ActionScript.

The main advantage of using Flex is that you develop your application to run inside the controlled environment of the Flash plug-in. So you don't have to take browser quirks into account. On the other hand, the client must have the plug-in installed on the client computer, which might be not the case in some locked-down environments such as schools and government agencies. Some purists also feel that Flex isn't a real Ajax application framework, as it doesn't adhere to the standards normally used for building Ajax applications, such as XHTML and JavaScript.

In February 2008, Adobe released its Adobe AIR runtime, which allows applications developed in Flex to be deployed as local desktop applications while still enjoying the benefits of Ajax, such as seamless installation and updating. The main benefit of AIR is that it gives application developers the best of both worlds: you can use the deployment model of a web application while still getting desktop integration if you need it. More in-depth coverage of Flex, and a guide on how to get up to speed, can be found in *The Essential Guide to Flex 3* by Charles E. Brown (Friends of ED, 2008).

Adobe Flex, especially since the release of Adobe AIR, is a good choice for developing rich Internet applications. Especially when you can't do without desktop integration features such as user notification, startup integration, background processes, and (most important) access to the local file system, Flex is a great option. However, remember that even though it's mostly open source, it still requires users to install a proprietary plug-in before using your applications developed in Flex.

More information about Flex can be found at `http://www.adobe.com/products/flex` and more about Adobe AIR can be found at `http://www.adobe.com/products/air`.

Java Applets and JavaFX

Another approach to building rich Internet application is using Java applets, or more recently, JavaFX. The most interesting part of JavaFX for our purposes is JavaFX Script, a scripting language for easily creating rich media and interactive content. However, it's built on the Java development platform, so if you want to deploy JavaFX applications on the Web, you're in essence deploying a Java applet, only one created with JavaFX. Therefore, we'll discuss Java applets in this section and just note that it also covers applications written in JavaFX.

The main benefit of a Java applet is that it's a Java program that runs on the client side. Although there are some obvious security restrictions when running from the browser, you can do anything you want with a Java applet, for example make connections to the originating server and spawn threads. You can even drop all security restrictions by digitally signing the application and asking the user for additional permissions, such as accessing the local file system. So if you want to build a rich Internet application, this appears to be the ideal solution. More in-depth information can be found in *JavaFX Script: Dynamic Java Scripting for Rich Internet/Client-side Applications* by James L. Weaver (Apress, 2007).

The main problem with Java applets and JavaFX is the need for a Java Runtime Environment (JRE) to be installed on the client. The JRE has a lower installed base than for instance Flash Player. Another issue is that depending on the requirements and development time, you may need a different version of the JRE. Furthermore, in contrast to the Flash player, the JRE has a substantial download size of approximately 14Mb for offline installation on the Windows platform at the time of writing. Table 1-1 provides an overview of the market penetration and download size of some of the packages discussed in this section.

More information on Java applets and JavaFX can be found at `http://java.sun.com/javafx`.

Silverlight

Silverlight is Microsoft's recent attempt to provide a platform similar to Flash. It's restricted to a subset of the .NET framework and should therefore be more suitable for developing rich Internet applications. Although Silverlight is starting to get some attention, it has a long way to go before it can call itself a serious alternative to Flash. Currently the biggest hurdle for Silverlight is enlarging its installed base. At the time of this writing, Silverlight's market penetration is negligible. As it has taken Adobe many years to reach its current market share, it will probably be a long time before Silverlight can even begin to challenge it.

Another issue with developing rich Internet applications using Silverlight is that runtimes are currently available for the Windows platform only. For the foreseeable future, no Mac and Linux users will be able to use applications developed in Silverlight. Also, the download size of the Silverlight runtime is large compared to Flash.

For these reasons, we don't consider Silverlight to be a serious option for developing rich Internet applications at the time of this writing, at least not until it acquires a considerable installed base and Microsoft releases runtimes for Linux and Mac users.

More information on Silverlight can be found at `http://www.silverlight.net`.

Table 1-1. *Installation Solutions' Market Penetration and Download Size*

Product	Market Penetration (Rounded)	Download Size (in Mb)
Flex/Flash	99%	1.5
Java/JavaFX	85%	14
Silverlight	0%	10

OpenLaszlo

Another product that we want to highlight is OpenLaszlo, released by Laszlo Systems under the Common Public License. OpenLaszlo takes the approach to define your UI in Laszlo's own LZX programming language. LZX is basically XML with embedded JavaScript snippets describing application logic. OpenLaszlo then takes the UI definitions and generates a rich Internet application. Previous versions only allowed the application to be translated into a fully functional Flash application. This runs into the same problems as the Flex approach. But starting with version 4 of OpenLaszlo, it now supports translating the UI into a DHTML application. The latest version also supports cross-compilation to embedded platforms such as mobile phones and other devices.

The main problem with OpenLaszlo is that it requires all application logic to be written in JavaScript. This leads to the same problems we discussed in the section about handwritten JavaScript. However, OpenLaszlo claims to eliminate a number of cross-browser compatibility issues, because the compiler is aware of them (see Figure 1-5).

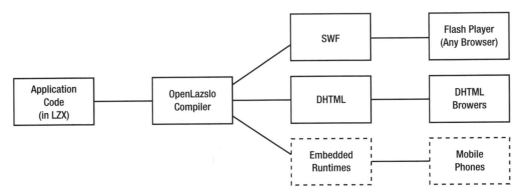

Figure 1-5. *OpenLaszlo application code compiled to different output formats*

More information about OpenLaszlo can be found at http://www.openlaszlo.org.

Echo2

The Echo Framework is yet another approach to developing rich Internet applications. The stable version at the time of writing is Echo2. Echo2 takes a nice approach to building these applications by allowing you to write them in Java. In Echo2, you write a servlet that handles all user requests and creates an application for each unique user. An application is created by extending the ApplicationInstance class. This application instance determines the UI of the application and handles user events. Because a new instance of the application is created for each user, it also holds all state. Internally, the application instance is stored in the user session.

The Echo framework takes a revolutionary approach to developing rich Internet applications. But in our opinion, there are two main problems with Echo2:

- **(Almost) every user action results in a call to the server**—because of the way Echo2 works internally, keeping state on the server in the user session, every action that the user performs needs to be communicated to the server. In our opinion, a rich Internet application should communicate with the server only when needed. In other words, the application should run entirely in the browser and only communicate to the server when it needs to retrieve data or perform a server-side action, or both.

- **Keeps all state on the server**—by nature, a rich Internet application maintains most, if not all, state on the client. This makes it possible to offload the server and scale better. One thing we've learned over the years in developing Java applications that handle large number of users is that you should keep as little state on the server as possible. Building rich client-side applications makes that possible to a great extent; but we feel that Echo2 hinders that by keeping most state on the server.

More information about Echo2 can be found at http://echo.nextapp.com/site/echo2.

GWT

As GWT is the subject of this book and is introduced in detail in the next chapter, we won't go into much detail here. But looking at GWT in contrast to the previously discussed solutions, there are two main things to note. First of all, GWT looks a lot like OpenLaszlo in the sense that the application you develop in GWT will eventually be compiled into a DHTML application and run entirely in the browser using XHTML and JavaScript.

But the main advantage of GWT over, for instance, OpenLaszlo is that instead of defining your UI in XML and JavaScript, applications are developed in Java. So for Java developers, this is a natural fit. You can reuse your existing expertise and best practices, favorite IDE, and development tools. The benefit of using GWT over other tools such as Echo2 is that GWT code compiles to a fully client-side JavaScript application and not just a proxy to the server-side Java application.

The most serious competitor GWT is Flex. But in our opinion, GWT has two advantages: first it's completely open source, whereas Flex is just partly open source; and second, a compiled GWT application runs inside any modern browser (assuming JavaScript is turned on) while Flex applications run only on systems where the Flash player is installed.

Summary

In this chapter, we introduced the concept of a rich Internet application (RIA) and illustrated where it came from by giving some historic background. We went from the mainframe application with its terrible user experience and limited cost effectiveness to rich Internet applications that are superior in both respects.

Next, we introduced Ajax, discussing every letter in the original acronym and showing why it's no longer an acronym. Most importantly, we discussed the advantages and disadvantages of using Ajax for developing RIAs, and laid down some guidelines on which applications are best suited to Ajax.

Last, we gave our take on several approaches to building Ajax applications, introducing some different strategies together with their strengths and weaknesses. This revealed why we believe GWT is the best solution currently available for developing RIAs, and why the rest of this book deals with GWT and not one of the other technologies.

The next chapter will introduce GWT in more detail, showing a typical GWT application layout. It will also introduce the sample application that we're going to gradually build in the course of this book.

## CHAPTER 2

Introducing Google Web Toolkit (GWT)

As we saw in the previous chapter, there's a real need to build more interactive, user-friendly web-based applications. We've introduced these rich Internet applications (RIA) and have shown you different approaches to developing them. From the available alternatives, we've concluded that GWT fits our needs best.

This chapter will introduce GWT and explain why we think GWT is the best choice, detail the basics of GWT, and show you the typical way you'll work with it. The chapter will also introduce the sample application that we'll build throughout the remainder of this book. Last, the chapter will introduce development tools that will come in handy when you start developing applications using GWT.

Why GWT?

When comparing GWT to the alternative approaches in the previous chapter, we briefly pointed out how GWT compares to those alternatives. But let's take a closer look at why GWT is the framework we prefer to use to write RIAs.

From JavaScript to Java

As we discussed in the previous chapter, writing Ajax applications in the traditional manner is difficult and error-prone. Although many frameworks try to provide a great deal of abstraction, with most (if not all) of them you still end up having to write custom JavaScript. And as we discussed, writing and maintaining JavaScript applications is an entirely different discipline than working with Java. This is worsened by the fact that JavaScript tends to behave differently on different browsers. So in the end, you still end up spending a lot of valuable time having to code for browser differences instead of focusing on real application logic.

This is where GWT comes in, providing a real abstraction layer that hides the details of JavaScript and even the differences between specific browser environments. As we'll see in the remainder of this book, as a developer using GWT, you don't have to deal with JavaScript or browser differences. If you really want to (and we actually recommend avoiding it if possible) you can include "native" JavaScript as part of your application. This is only useful when you want to wrap existing JavaScript libraries. But again, these cases tend to be rare and should be avoided in our opinion.

Using GWT, you can continue to write your application in Java, leveraging existing best practices such as your favorite IDE, compile-time checking, unit testing, and even continuous integration. GWT will basically translate all your Java UI code to JavaScript, providing a strongly typed language to work with. GWT will also handle all browser-specific quirks for you, so you can focus on writing the code that actually does something.

Considerations for Using GWT

Before we dive into the basics of GWT and explain how GWT allows you to focus on the important stuff, we first want to point out a couple considerations that you should be aware of before you start writing your first GWT application:

- **Not indexable by search engines**—as discussed in the previous chapter, Ajax applications (and therefore also GWT applications) aren't indexed well by search engines. This is because search engine crawlers don't handle JavaScript (yet) and therefore just see the basic page that hosts the Ajax application; they're unable to "view" the dynamic elements that depend on JavaScript.

- **Not nicely degradable**—closely related to the previous consideration is the fact that applications developed using GWT don't degrade well. This means that when users of the applications have disabled JavaScript, they'll just see the basic page and nothing more. This means that all we can do is tell the user that he should enable JavaScript in order to use the application. If that's acceptable, there's no problem, but if a requirement for the application is to support users who have JavaScript turned off, then GWT isn't the right choice. Using GWT when you have a requirement to support non-JavaScript users effectively means that you have to create and maintain a separate version of your application for those users. This is unlike some alternative frameworks for building Ajax applications that probably degrade much more gracefully, but are less user-friendly.

- **No clear separation between code and styling/layout**—many frameworks provide good separation between the actual code written by developers and the HTML and styling that designers might deliver. GWT (as we'll see in the remainder of this book) doesn't provide this separation. Although the host page is plain HTML and can therefore be created by a designer, and GWT provides good support for styling using Cascading Style Sheets (CSS) as we'll see later, the rest of your GWT application is controlled by Java code. This effectively means that things such as layout and specific appearance are usually captured in the Java code. Therefore, GWT isn't suitable for designers, as they prefer using plain HTML with placeholders for inserting dynamic content (for example, Wicket). Of course, designers can come up with designs that developers then translate into Java.

Luckily for us, these considerations tend not to be a big problem for the type of application that we'll use GWT for. However, it's important to make sure they aren't going to be a problem before actually making the choice to use GWT.

The Basics

Now that we've given you some more insight into why we think GWT is the best choice and also some considerations to keep in mind, let's look at the basics of GWT.

GWT can roughly be divided into three main parts, although the last one especially has many separate subdivisions:

- **Java to JavaScript compiler**—basically, this is the heart of GWT, and its most impressive part. This is what makes GWT such a powerful tool for building RIAs. The compiler will make sure that all code that you write is eventually translated into JavaScript (even browser-specific versions, as we'll see later).

- **JRE Emulation library**—as mentioned in the previous chapter, JavaScript is a very different language from Java. But GWT needs to compile the code you write in Java into JavaScript. In order for this to work, GWT has to provide an emulation of the core Java constructs and classes so they can be translated to code that works in JavaScript.

- **UI building library**—this part of GWT consists of many subparts. This makes up almost the entire code base provided by GWT, including the actual UI components, RPC support, history management, and much more.

We'll go into more detail on each part in the next few sections.

Java to JavaScript Compiler

The heart of GWT is the Java to JavaScript compiler. The story behind this is that Google started developing RIA applications themselves and ended up facing the issues we illustrated in the first chapter. Coming from a Java background, they asked themselves how to best develop these RIAs and came up with GWT, the main idea being to write their applications in Java. Obviously for this to work, they needed something that could turn their Java code into sensible JavaScript. And if that wasn't challenging enough, they also wanted to make sure that developers didn't need to worry about different browser quirks. So the compiler also had to somehow facilitate compiling different versions for different browsers. And that's exactly what they came up with.

The nice thing about the compiler is that it's just a Java program that you can start by running the class `com.google.gwt.dev.GWTCompiler`. Although this is a nice feature, you'll probably be running one of the command-line tools or run it from your favorite IDE or build tool. However, the important thing to note is that in contrast to the normal Java compiler, the GWT compiler will compile only the code that's actually used within your module. This is a good thing, as it avoids having to transfer to the client JavaScript code (or even entire libraries) that's never used. However, this principle doesn't allow for runtime loading of classes, as they aren't compiled to JavaScript. Therefore, all code must somehow be referenced so it can be included at compile time. This fits in with the fact that normal Java reflection is unavailable, as we'll see in the next section.

■**Note** Because the GWT compiler has to walk through your code in order to see what's used and therefore compiled to JavaScript, GWT compilation typically tends to take longer than normal Java compilation. Just keep in mind that this is necessary in order to create highly optimized JavaScript to send to the client.

One last thing we need to look at is the actual output of the compiler. The output of the GWT compiler (in this case, for the "Hello World" sample application we'll introduce later) will typically resemble the following structure for the resulting output:

```
065830997FFBD2DC13A986D8939F5704.cache.html
065830997FFBD2DC13A986D8939F5704.cache.js
065830997FFBD2DC13A986D8939F5704.cache.xml
0791B818FB6E04B9F03E69AE31715E7D.cache.html
0791B818FB6E04B9F03E69AE31715E7D.cache.js
0791B818FB6E04B9F03E69AE31715E7D.cache.xml
10B80E29ACBFA1FBEF8A475830840009.cache.html
10B80E29ACBFA1FBEF8A475830840009.cache.js
10B80E29ACBFA1FBEF8A475830840009.cache.xml
439FF78FFF7914AF6A60AD1111599BC0.cache.html
439FF78FFF7914AF6A60AD1111599BC0.cache.js
439FF78FFF7914AF6A60AD1111599BC0.cache.xml
B7B701C677F4C1BBA4B386753292D960.cache.html
B7B701C677F4C1BBA4B386753292D960.cache.js
B7B701C677F4C1BBA4B386753292D960.cache.xml
index.html
clear.cache.gif
com.apress.beginninggwt.HelloWorld-xs.nocache.js
com.apress.beginninggwt.HelloWorld.nocache.js
gwt.js
history.html
hosted.html
```

The main thing to note from this output is that the result of the compilation isn't just one JavaScript file, but several: one for each supported platform. The class com.apress. beginninggwt.HelloWorld.nocache.js takes care of loading the correct file for any specific platform. Because the compiler only generates one file per platform, the client (and any intermediate proxy servers) can cache the entire application optimally. Since the application code doesn't change between releases, the application can be cached for eternity. This will greatly reduce the load and bandwidth for the server.

In order to start and load the application, you just need to open the index.html file in a browser. This HTML file contains a reference to the nocache.js file.

JRE Emulation Library

So the GWT compiler allows us to write Java code and then have that translated into JavaScript. But for this to work, GWT has to provide a mapping of the Java Runtime Environment (JRE) onto JavaScript. This is exactly what the JRE Emulation library does. It has two parts. The first part deals with Java language support and the (mostly minor but important) differences between the GWT emulation and the real Java version. The second part deals with what classes are emulated by GWT and can therefore be used by you as a developer.

Language Support

You can use the full extent of the Java language when developing applications that will be compiled to JavaScript by the GWT compiler. But there are some differences that you should be aware of in order to avoid problems at a later stage. The following list below isn't exhaustive, but just lists the snags you're most likely to run into at some point:

- **Long support**—as JavaScript doesn't have a `long` representation as part of its language specification, you can't pass a `long` from your Java code to JavaScript Native Interface (JSNI) methods. JSNI is discussed in detail in Chapter 8; meanwhile just remember that you can't pass `long` to your native JavaScript methods. However, you can safely use `long` types if they remain in the context of your Java code. GWT will make sure that they're translated into something that works in JavaScript.

- **Exception handling**—exceptions generally work the same as in normal Java code, apart from two special cases. First, the `getStackTrace()` method doesn't return anything useful when running as JavaScript. Second, default exceptions such as `Null-PointerException` and `OutOfMemoryError` are never thrown in your code. You should therefore perform explicit `null` checks yourself.

- **Single-threaded**—as the JavaScript interpreters are single-threaded, your application becomes single-threaded as well. So all threading-related methods and keywords (such as `synchronized`) have no effect and will be ignored by the GWT compiler.

- **No reflection**—as mentioned earlier, you can't use reflection to load classes dynamically. This is directly related to the fact that the GWT compiler needs to know about each class and method you use, in order to generate one optimized JavaScript file per platform. This would be impossible if you were allowed to load classes dynamically.

■**Caution** Before GWT version 1.5, the language support for JRE emulation worked only with pre–Java 1.5 syntax. That meant that things such as annotations, enumerations, and generics weren't supported. That's why older GWT code and projects might appear strange in terms of setup and language support.

Emulated Classes

As we've seen, you can use most of the Java language when developing GWT applications. But not everything is possible when developing code that needs to be translated to JavaScript and then run in a browser environment. You probably know that writing a file isn't really an option within a browser. Also, issuing a query to an SQL database isn't an option. So how do you know what you can and can't do? The answer is fairly simple: you can only use the classes that GWT provides an emulation for. And even for emulated classes, you can only use the methods that are actually emulated. The classes you can use are those in the `java.lang` and the `java.util` packages, along with a limited subset of the `java.io` and `java.sql` packages. Table 2-1 lists all classes that are emulated by GWT at the time of writing. Please note that for some of them, only a subset of methods is emulated.

■Tip In order to make sure that the code you write adheres to the requirements in terms of using emulated classes, make sure to compile your code often. Compiling and running your code in hosted mode (discussed later) gives warnings or errors if your code doesn't adhere to the requirements.

Differences in Classes

There are also two minor differences in the emulated classes that you should keep in mind when writing GWT application code:

- **Regular expressions**—Java and JavaScript have different syntax for regular expressions. Although these differences are subtle, they tend to have dramatic results, so be careful when using regular expressions.

- **Serialization**—Java serialization depends heavily on reflection, and is therefore unavailable in GWT. However, GWT provides its own mechanism for doing serialization as part of its RPC support, as explained in Chapter 6.

Convenient Classes

As you might have already noticed, some basic classes that developers tend to use a lot aren't available as part of the GWT emulated classes. However, GWT provides its own convenient classes to make up for this. The following classes come in handy when building real-world applications in GWT:

- `com.google.gwt.i18n.client.DateTimeFormat`—replacement for the `java.util.DateTime-Format` class in normal Java. Note that this replacement only supports a subset of the normal Java version.

- `com.google.gwt.i18n.client.NumberFormat`—the same kind of replacement, but then for the `java.util.NumberFormat`, again providing only a subset of its features.

- `com.google.gwt.user.client.Timer`—a simplified, browser-safe timer class that can be used to mimic a threaded environment, and which allows you to schedule tasks and actions. It's a simplified version of the `java.util.Timer` class.

Table 2-1. *The Emulated JRE Classes That Are Part of GWT*

Package	Class
java.lang	ArithmeticException
	ArrayIndexOutOfBoundsException
	ArrayStoreException
	AssertionError
	Boolean
	Byte
	CharSequence
	Character
	Class
	ClassCastException
	Cloneable
	Comparable
	Deprecated
	Double
	Enum
	Error
	Exception
	Float
	IllegalArgumentException
	IllegalStateException
	IndexOutOfBoundsException
	Integer
	Iterable
	Long
	Math
	NegativeArraySizeException
	NullPointerException
	Number
	NumberFormatException
	Object
	Override
	Runnable
	RuntimeException
	Short
	StackTraceElement
	String
	StringBuffer
	StringBuilder
	StringIndexOutOfBoundsException
	SuppressWarnings
	System
	Throwable
	UnsupportedOperationException
	Void
java.lang.annotation	Annotation
	AnnotationFormatError
	AnnotationTypeMismatchException
	Documented
	ElementType
	IncompleteAnnotationException
	Inherited
	Retention
	RetentionPolicy
	Target

Continued

Table 2-1. *Continued*

Package	Class
java.util	AbstractCollection
	AbstractList
	AbstractMap
	AbstractQueue
	AbstractSequentialList
	AbstractSet
	ArrayList
	Arrays
	Collection
	Collections
	Comparator
	ConcurrentModificationException
	Date
	EmptyStackException
	EnumMap
	EnumSet
	Enumeration
	EventListener
	EventObject
	HashMap
	HashSet
	IdentityHashMap
	Iterator
	LinkedHashMap
	LinkedHashSet
	LinkedList
	List
	ListIterator
	Map
	Map.Entry
	MissingResourceException
	NoSuchElementException
	PriorityQueue
	Queue
	RandomAccess
	Set
	SortedMap
	SortedSet
	Stack
	TooManyListenersException
	TreeMap
	TreeSet
	Vector
java.io	FilterOutputStream
	OutputStream
	PrintStream
	Serializable
java.sql	Date
	Time
	Timestamp

Library Usage

Typically, if what you want is outside the listed classes, you probably can't use it. This also means that using external libraries such as log4j isn't permitted. The only libraries that you can use are the ones that are tailor-made for GWT. This is because those libraries only use classes that are allowed and emulated by GWT, and more importantly because they typically include the source code as part of the library. This is important because, as we've already seen, the GWT compiler needs to traverse the entire path through the source code in order to see what code is actually used. That also holds true for any library code that you include in your application.

UI Library

So far we've looked at the language support provided by GWT and the emulation classes that you can use. It may seem that this is a very limited subset of the "real" Java and that you have to be well aware of this. But in reality, you will get used to it quickly and just take it for granted. In practice, you'll just start writing Java code and accept that it's going to run as JavaScript later.

So far we've looked at constraints on you as a developer when creating GWT applications. But now let's look at what GWT gives you to make your life easier. Please note that most if not all of the things we discuss in this chapter are discussed in more detail in the remainder of this book.

Basic Concepts

Before we can take a detailed look at the different features provided by GWT's UI library, we must first introduce some of GWT's basic concepts.

Modules

Modules are a basic concept in GWT. The configuration of each individual application is called a module. Typically this module configuration is provided in XML format. This module XML is described in more detail in a later section. For now, it's important to know that it details the configuration for an application and that it defines (among other things) the application startup class.

Host Page

As the GWT application has to be loaded and bootstrapped by a browser, it needs to be embedded in a normal HTML page. This page is the GWT application's host page. Note that this can be a static HTML page specifically created for your GWT application, but it can also be a dynamically generated page of an ordinary web application that happens to load a GWT application.

Cross-Browser Support

As mentioned earlier, a major problem when developing RIAs is that a lot of effort goes into working around browser quirks. This isn't something you want to do as a developer, but it's also a waste of time from a management perspective. You want developers to focus on the actual logic, not on environment specifics. Luckily, GWT takes this out of our hands. Code written for GWT will work on all major browsers. At the time of writing, applications developed with GWT will work similarly on the most recent versions of Internet Explorer, Firefox, Safari, and Opera.

However, you must be aware that the application you develop will eventually be turned into an HTML interface that is rendered by a browser. Unfortunately, these HTML interfaces tend not to work exactly the same on different browsers. In particular, layout and styling might turn out quite different. Therefore it remains important to test your applications on all the browsers they need to support. In Chapter 7, we'll show you how to test your application on different browsers and even different operating systems.

A special note in this respect is that GWT depends on and promotes the use of CSS for styling purposes. Styling with CSS is discussed in more detail in Chapter 3.

Different Modes for Running GWT Applications

One of GWT's major advantages is that you can reuse your existing Java best practices when writing applications for GWT. In order to do this, we need a way to run the code in both a Java environment and a JavaScript environment. In other modes, there are two different modes in which you can run a GWT application: hosted and web mode.

Hosted Mode *Hosted mode* is where your Java code actually runs as Java inside a browser environment. GWT hosted mode is where you can set breakpoints in your Java code and then just debug it as if it were normal Java code, except that you can view the result in a browser. (Actually it isn't really a browser, but a sort of emulated version of your default browser.)

■**Caution** The term *hosted mode* is used for two things in the context of GWT. First, it refers to running GWT code as Java code, as just described. But it also refers to the environment in which the code is run—the emulated browser environment.

Web Mode In contrast to hosted mode, web mode is the mode in which the Java code is translated to JavaScript and runs inside a browser. So web mode can be considered equivalent to running in the browser.

GWT Features

This section introduces a number of the features provided by GWT. Again, note that most of these features are discussed in more detail in the remainder of this book.

Widgets and Layout

A large part of the work of building a RIA is actually creating the user interface. At its most basic, this consists of creating and adding widgets and laying them out relative to each other. Therefore, a large part of the library provided by GWT consists of widgets and layout classes. Basically, the widgets consist of real widgets such as buttons and text fields, as well as panels that provide basic layouts. But there are also more advanced features such as styling using CSS and an event mechanism. Chapters 4 and 5 deal with widgets and layout.

Server Communication

Most GWT applications need some kind of server back end to retrieve and store data and perform other actions. Luckily, GWT provides an easy-to-use RPC mechanism for communicating with a Java server.

If your application needs to connect to an existing back end or you want finer-grained control over communication with the back end, GWT offers the right tools, including support for XML and JSON back ends. Chapter 6 deals with server communication.

Testing Support

One advantage of GWT code over normal Ajax applications is that you can easily test the code you write. You can reuse your best practices in terms of unit testing, and for some corner cases GWT provides its own testing support on top of the de facto testing framework JUnit.

In addition to testing support, GWT also provides powerful ways to benchmark your code. This will also be discussed in Chapter 7.

Advanced Features

The more advanced features such as JavaScript Native Interface (JSNI), deferred binding, image bundles, localization, and history support are all discussed in the last chapter of this book.

GWT Application Layout

So far we've seen the features GWT provides to help you as a developer. Before we start using them, we have to take a closer look at the typical way a GWT application is laid out. This might seem trivial, but it's important when working with GWT. As a rigorous rule of thumb: if you get the application layout wrong when working with GWT, you're bound to run into weird problems. As we'll detail in the next sections, in particular the client, server, and module locations are important, especially how they're laid out relative to each other.

But first let's look at the project structure. GWT doesn't really care how you lay out the directories in your application. But it's of the utmost importance to lay out the package structure correctly within your source directory (or potentially more directories). GWT relies heavily upon this package structure to infer many things about your application.

■**Tip** GWT ships with several convenient scripts or command-line tools that help you set up your project structure correctly. It's wise to use these scripts, as they save you from making typos and ending up with strange errors. The details of the creator scripts (and other convenient scripts) are discussed in Chapter 3.

A typical GWT application consists of three mandatory parts and one optional part. These four parts are

- **Module descriptor**—*module* is the name GWT uses for an individual application configuration. Therefore, a module descriptor is the configuration file that describes that configuration.

- **Public resources**—these are all files that will be served publicly. They include the host HTML page (discussed later) and all other resources such as style sheets and images. These resources are packaged as part of your application.

- **Client-side code**—this is the Java code that the GWT compiler translates into JavaScript, which will eventually run inside the browser. Note that this code needs to adhere to the restrictions outlined earlier in this chapter as to what classes can and can't be used.

- **Server-side code (optional)**—this is the server part of your GWT application, the remote back end to your client-side application. Obviously, if your application doesn't require back-end services (in Java), then you don't need this part. Server-side code, as well as how you can write and use it, is discussed in more detail in Chapter 6.

The following sections describe the first two of these parts in more detail. But first, let's have a look at how these separate parts are laid out within the package structure. Note that this doesn't necessarily mean that the parts have to reside in the same source directory. For instance, if you're using Maven as a build tool, you might want to separate the Java source code and the resources into different directories. The layout in Table 2-2 only describes the different parts within the package structure.

Table 2-2. *Sample Locations of Different Parts of a Typical GWT Application Layout*

Name	Location
Project root	com/apress/beginninggwt/
Module descriptor	com/apress/beginninggwt/HelloWorld.gwt.xml
Public resources	com/apress/beginninggwt/public/
Client-side code	com/apress/beginninggwt/client/
Server-side code	com/apress/beginninggwt/server/

Module Descriptor

As discussed previously, the module descriptor is the file that describes the configuration of an individual GWT application or module. This so-called *module descriptor* comes in the form of an XML file. The configuration defined in the descriptor contains the following entries:

- **Inherited modules**—these entries are comparable to import statements in normal Java classes, but for GWT applications.

- **Entry point class**—this entry details which classes serve as the entry points, like the classes containing the main(String[]) method in normal Java classes. Only, GWT entry point classes have to implement the EntryPoint interface provided by GWT. Note that these entry point classes are optional and there can be more than one.

- **Source path entries**—the module descriptor allows you to customize the location of the client-side code (defaults to the client package relative to the module descriptor location, as you can see in Table 2-2).

- **Public path entries**—these allow you to handle public path items such as source path entries (this also defaults to the public folder relative to the module descriptor location).

- **Deferred binding rules**—these are more advanced settings that you can use to customize all kinds of aspects of your GWT application. These settings usually aren't used by the developer directly, and are therefore not discussed in this chapter. However, deferred binding is discussed in some detail in Chapter 8, when we discuss localization.

So let's look at an example of a module descriptor file. We have to create a module descriptor with the name of the module (in this case HelloWorld) and with the extension .gwt.xml, resulting in HelloWorld.gwt.xml. Leaving out the advanced features and keeping the defaults, we're left with only the inherited modules and entry point class entries, as shown in Listing 2-1.

Listing 2-1. *A Sample HelloWorld Module Descriptor File*

```
<module>

    <inherits name='com.google.gwt.user.User'/>
    <entry-point class='com.apress.beginninggwt.client.HelloWorld'/>
</module>
```

The module descriptor in Listing 2-1 is typical of simple GWT applications. In this case, we tell GWT to create an application that inherits from the base GWT module for users. The GWT user module contains most of the code you typically need to run a GWT application. It contains all the default classes such as the EntryPoint interface we're going to use next.

As mentioned earlier, the entry point class is rather like the class containing the main(String[]) method in normal Java classes. As the name suggests, it's the entry point for the application to start. In the case of our sample module descriptor, we define an entry point class GWTasks that starts the application. In Listing 2-2, we've specified a class named HelloWorld, located in the default source path directory, as the entry point.

Listing 2-2. *A Sample HelloWorld Entry Point Class*

```
public class HelloWorld implements EntryPoint {
    public void onModuleLoad() {
        // initialize the application
    }
}
```

Each class defined as an entry point should inherit from the EntryPoint interface provided by GWT. This interface defines one method that the GWTasks class has to implement. This method, onModuleLoad(), is the method that serves as the real entry point to the application. The GWT compiler will start analyzing and eventually translating your application starting at this point. This is where, in the following sections and chapters, we'll start adding code to make the application do some real work. But for now, adding the additional line in Listing 2-3, we just tell the user that the code is working.

Listing 2-3. *A Simple Hello World Implementation of the onModuleLoad Method*

```
public void onModuleLoad() {
    Window.alert("Hello World!");
}
```

Note that the Window class is a utility class provided by GWT. In this case, we use it to show a JavaScript alert to the user.

Public Resources

In order to be able to run our Hello World code, we need one last thing: the host HTML page that contains the GWT application. We already discussed this host page in a previous section, but now let's create one for this sample application (see Listing 2-4).

Listing 2-4. *The Host Page That Contains the Hello World Sample Application*

```html
<html>
    <head>
        <title>Sample application: Hello World</title>
        <link rel="stylesheet" href="styles/main.css">
    </head>
    <body>
        <img src="images/logo.gif" alt="Apress Logo"/>
        <h1>Hello World</h1>
        <p>
            Welcome to the 'Hello World' sample application. This sample will do
            nothing more than show this HTML snippet and an alert to the user.
        </p>
        <script src="com.apress.beginninggwt.HelloWorld.nocache.js"
                type="text/javascript"></script>
    </body>
</html>
```

In Listing 2-4, note that there are two resources: a logo image and a style sheet. Also note the script that actually loads the sample application. This host page and all resources it references need to be placed in the public resources directory. As mentioned previously, the default location is in a directory named public relative to the directory where the module descriptor is located. But you can customize this by adding an entry to the module descriptor. The logo image and style sheet that are referenced in the host page need to be placed in that directory as well. Make sure that you put them in the appropriate subdirectory. For completeness, Listing 2-5 shows the content of our style sheet.

Listing 2-5. *The Sample Style Sheet That's Included in the Host Page*

```
body {
    text-align: center;
}
img {
    border: 1px solid black;
}
h1, p {
    font-family: verdana, sans-serif;
}
```

Now run this sample in order to see it in action, using your favorite tool. If you run the sample application in hosted mode, you should see something resembling Figure 2-1.

■**Note** A detailed how-to guide on how to set up a GWT project correctly in your favorite IDE is provided in the appendix of this book. In order to run this sample application and all following code samples, read the appendix on how to set it up in your IDE.

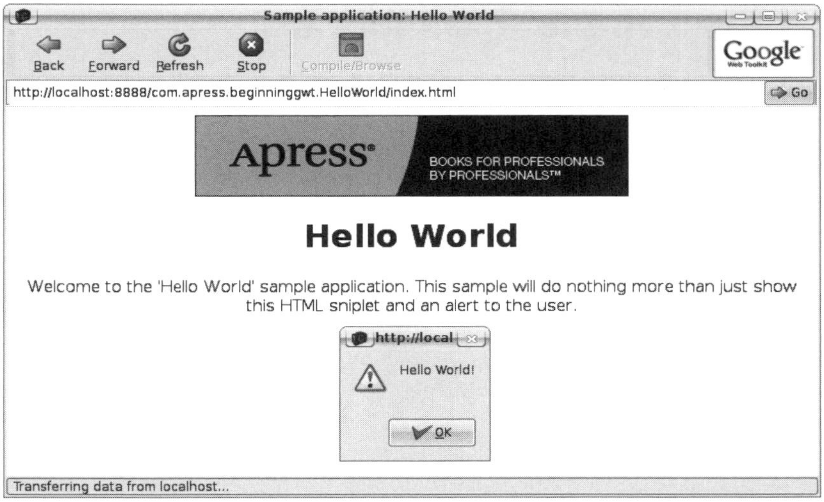

Figure 2-1. *The result of running the HelloWorld sample application in hosted mode*

If you now click the OK button on the JavaScript alert box and then click on the Compile/ Browse button, the GWT compiler will compile the application to JavaScript and start your default browser. The browser will run the full JavaScript version of your application. That's the web mode that we discussed in an earlier section. The result should look like Figure 2-2.

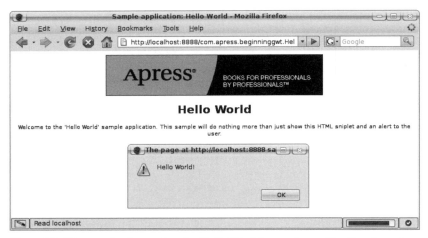

Figure 2-2. *The result of running the HelloWorld sample application in web mode*

That's it for the basics of GWT. We've now built our first real GWT application that adheres to the default GWT application layout. Next, we'll introduce the sample application that we'll use as a reference for the rest of the book.

Introducing the Sample Application

We've decided, whenever possible, to use one sample application throughout this book. This sample application will gradually evolve over the course of book, adding functionality as we go. We feel that reusing the same sample application decreases the effort needed to understand the individual code samples. But maybe even more important, we feel that building something real (and even usable) over the course of the book is a much more pleasurable experience.

The sample application for this book is GWTasks, an application that allows users to efficiently manage their tasks. Obviously, this sample application will be in the form of an RIA developed using GWT. The application will provide basic functionality such as logging in, registering a user, and managing categories and tasks using a web-based UI. Note that the application is kept fairly simple to make sure the code base remains easy to grasp.

Note that in addition to the GWTasks application, which is used to illustrate most GWT features as we progress through the book, some chapters also have individual code samples (like the previous samples in this chapter). All of these samples (as well as the final GWTasks application) are part of the code base that you can download from the Apress web site.

So here's how you can see the GWTasks application in action to get a feel for what you'll be building. To get started with the sample application, you must first download the source code from the Apress web site. The next thing to do is set up the project in your favorite IDE. You can either use the command-line tools (discussed in Chapter 3) or follow the instructions in Appendix A on how to set up a GWT project in your favorite IDE (only Eclipse or IntelliJ IDEA are discussed in the appendix).

Once you have the project set up correctly, you should be able to run the sample application (again using the command-line tools or using your IDE specific launch functionality). Once successfully started, you should see a screen similar to the one in Figure 2-3.

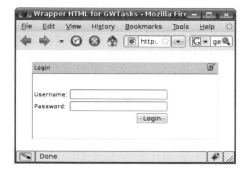

Figure 2-3. *The login screen of the GWTasks sample application*

Clicking on the icon in the right corner of the Login dialog opens the Register pop-up dialog (see Figure 2-4), which you can use to register a new user. Either submit the form or click the Cancel button to go back to the Login dialog.

Figure 2-4. *The register screen of the GWTasks sample application*

Submitting the Login form will bring you to the main screen of the GWTasks application, as shown in Figure 2-5. This screen allows you to manage your categories and tasks. Just create some categories and tasks and see how you can interact with the application.

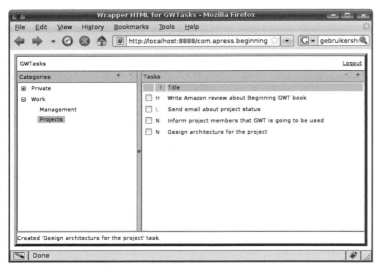

Figure 2-5. *The main screen of the GWTasks sample application*

Now before we go to the next chapter to start building the GWTasks sample application, let's first take a look at some development tools that we think will come in handy during development.

Handy Development Tools

As discussed earlier, developing rich Internet applications using GWT allows you to use your Java development tools. So you can reuse your favorite IDE, your existing build tool, and even your entire continuous integration setup. However, as you eventually develop a web application, you'll need some additional tools to help you. Note that these tools are not GWT-specific; they can be used to help you with any web development.

Most of the tools listed in this section are add-ons to Firefox. We realize that not everyone uses Firefox, but there are two reasons why we recommend these (and therefore Firefox). First, unlike most browsers, Firefox is full-featured, as well as available on most platforms. Second, many of the most powerful tools are available only as Firefox add-ons.

All the tools Firefox add-ons can be downloaded and installed from their web sites, or can be installed directly from the Firefox Add-ons site at http://addons.mozilla.org/firefox/. Just go to the site, search for the tool you want, and click the Add to Firefox button. The first time you do this, you may have to add the Firefox Add-ons site to the list of sites that are trusted to installing software inside Firefox.

If you don't have Firefox installed already, we strongly recommend doing so. Go to the Firefox download site to download the latest version: http://getfirefox.com.

Web Developer Add-on

The web developer plug-in is a Firefox extension developed by Chris Pederick. It adds to the browser a menu and toolbar that provide several web developer tools (see Figure 2-6). The web developer plug-in provides a great many tools, but we only list the ones we use most and consider the most valuable.

⊖ Disable ▾   ⚹ Cookies ▾   ▢ CSS ▾   ▤ Forms ▾   ▥ Images ▾   ① Information ▾   ⊚ Miscellaneous ▾   ✎ Outline ▾   ⁝⁝ Resize ▾

Figure 2-6. *The web developer add-on toolbar (only part of the toolbar is shown)*

View Source ➤ View Generated Source

This is a useful feature, especially when developing Ajax and JavaScript applications. Typically, these applications start off with a relatively simple HTML page and then dynamically build up, or replace, part of the page. Therefore, the View Source feature no longer works very well, as it only shows a limited subset of what appears on the screen. But the View Generated Source functionality is quite useful, as it shows the source of the content that's displayed on the screen. It prints out the entire DOM tree as it is at the moment you request it. Therefore, you can inspect it as you normally would. An added feature is that you can actually copy and paste the source and save it as static HTML for debugging or testing purposes.

Resize ➤ 800×600 (and Others)

The resize feature is also really handy. It allows you to resize your browser window to predefined dimensions at the click of a mouse. In the Preferences menu of the add-on, you can set your own predefined dimensions. It's convenient to predefine the screen resolutions that your application needs to support (and some intermediate ones). This allows you to make sure that your application resizes correctly in all of these resolutions.

There are two important things to keep in mind when using this add-on. First of all, remember that a certain screen resolution doesn't necessarily correspond to the actual browser window size. The user can obviously have a nonmaximized browser window. Second, the rendering and browser's actual view port size depend on a number of factors, such as operating system, window decoration, and enabled toolbars. So although we feel that this feature is useful to test on different resolutions easily, we do want to stress that you can never be sure what the user will actually see.

Miscellaneous ➤ Clear Private Data ➤ Cache (and Others)

Another useful feature is the ability to clear all kinds of private data, such as the cache, history, and HTTP authentication. Especially when working with caching headers, for example to improve performance, you need an easy way to clear these kinds of data in the browser.

Tools ➤ Validate HTML (and Others)

One last, very important feature of the web developer add-on is that it allows you to easily validate different parts of your web application, such as the HTML itself, but also the CSS style sheet, and so on. There are useful icons on the right side of the toolbar (see Figure 2-7) that indicate for the current page whether the HTML, CSS, and JavaScript contain errors.

Figure 2-7. *The quick icons on the web developer add-on toolbar*

The project page for this tool is `http://chrispederick.com/work/web-developer/`.

Firebug

Firebug is another Firefox add-on that provides a lot of the same functionality as the web developer add-on for inspecting the current DOM and HTML. Firebug is actually the most powerful tool discussed in this section, and an absolute necessity when working with HTML interfaces, especially those containing JavaScript. So when functionalities overlap between Firebug and the web developer add-on, we usually prefer Firebug.

The great thing about Firebug is that it not only allows you to inspect almost all of the aspects of an HTML page and its resources, but also to "live edit" them. So for instance, Firebug allows you to add, modify, and remove style properties on certain elements on the fly. But let's start at the beginning.

Usually, once Firebug is installed, it's represented by a green, round icon, or a bug-like icon depending on the version, in the right bottom corner of your Firefox browser window. You have two options: based on your preference, you can either expand the add-on into the current window by clicking on the icon or right-click the icon and choose to open Firebug in a separate window. See Figure 2-8 for an example.

Figure 2-8. *The expanded Firebug toolbar for the Hello World sample application*

Firebug provides a lot of valuable functionality that you need. The following sections detail some of the most important and relevant ones.

Inspecting and Editing HTML

Firebug has a feature similar to the View Generated Source function in the web developer add-on, but even more powerful. This allows you to browse the source code "live." You can expand, collapse, and navigate the source tree of the code at any given moment. The nice thing is that you can actually click an HTML element, and that element is then highlighted in the normal browser view. This makes it easy to see how your HTML page is built.

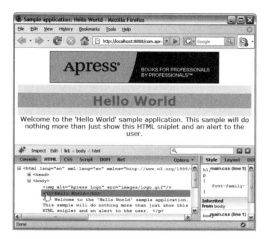

Figure 2-9. *The live source view of Firebug's HTML tab*

In addition to highlighting the element in the normal browser view when you select an item in the source view, you can also do it the other way around. You can (after telling Firebug to inspect the page) simply hover and click elements in your HTML page to have the source view jump to that element in the source. You can even search for elements in the source.

An even more powerful feature is that you can modify the HTML on the fly. You can change, add, and remove elements as you wish. The browser is immediately updated in response to your changes. This is a powerful feature that lets you, for instance, try out a fix before implementing it and having to reload or even recompile the whole application.

Inspecting and Editing CSS

Firebug also provides the features we just described for CSS as well as for HTML and source elements. You can inspect the specific styling that is applied to each element. This includes not only styles that are directly applied to an element, but also styles that are inherited from other styling rules.

As with HTML, the CSS functionality allows you to modify styles on the fly. You can add, remove, and even temporarily disable styling rules. When modifying and creating styling rules, you can also enjoy autocomplete functionality, as well as previews for colors and images.

Figure 2-10. *The live source view of the CSS tab of Firebug*

Debugging and Profiling JavaScript

This is the most powerful feature of Firebug: a full JavaScript debugging tool. In Firebug, you can easily inspect all the JavaScript files and snippets that are part of the current page. You can set breakpoints and even add conditions to them, as with any good debugger. You can also step through the JavaScript code and put watch expressions on elements in the DOM tree.

■**Caution** As discussed earlier, GWT allows a number of different output styles for the compiler (obfuscated, pretty, and detailed). Make sure you use the detailed style if you plan to use the Firebug debugger (or any other debugger for that matter). The obfuscated output style puts all output on one line, and is therefore not very handy for inserting breakpoints.

In addition to providing a powerful debugger for JavaScript, Firebug also allows you to profile your JavaScript code. You can easily find bottlenecks in the code.

Monitoring Network Activity

Another powerful tool provided by Firebug is the ability to monitor network activity for a certain web page. This allows you to get a detailed overview of what's loaded as part of your web page, and more important, how long each of these resources takes to fully load.

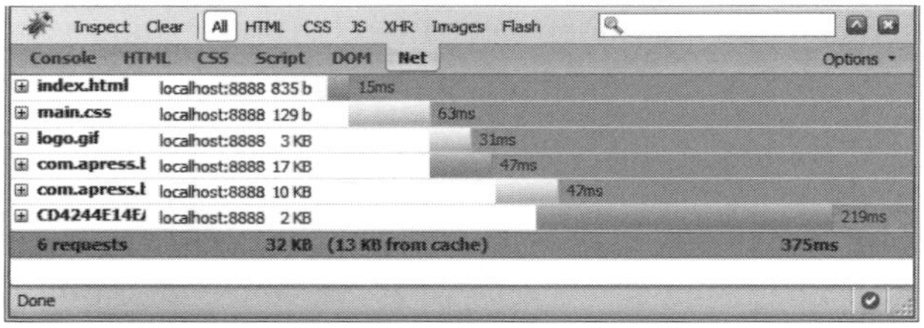

Figure 2-11. *A detailed view of Firebug's Net tab*

This allows you to tweak your page to the fullest extent. It shows whether images, style sheets, and scripts are compressed and cached correctly. Firebug also lists the HTTP headers that are sent and received, as well as the amount of caching that's applied.

The project page for this tool is http://www.getfirebug.com/.

LiveHTTPHeaders

Another valuable add-on to Firefox is LiveHTTPHeaders, which lets you look inside the HTTP headers that the browser sends and receives for loading a page. This is handy, especially for making sure that not too many requests are issued to different servers. As you may know, browsers can typically issue only around three simultaneous requests to the server. Because many web pages include more than three resources, page loading can be stalled by the browser waiting for requests to become available again to use for retrieving other resources. This is especially true of slow connections to sites such as advertisement servers.

LiveHTTPHeaders allows you to easily monitor the headers and the number of requests that the browser sends and receives. Although Firebug provides similar functionality, we list LiveHTTPHeaders for three reasons. First, it's quicker and easier to use. Second, similar add-ons are also available for Internet Explorer and many other browsers. And last, it allows the replay of packets, which is useful for testing what type of input a web application will accept.

The project page for this tool as an add-on for Firefox is `http://livehttpheaders.mozdev.org/` and a similar add-on for Internet Explorer is a project called ieHttpHeaders: `http://www.blunck.se/iehttpheaders/iehttpheaders.html`.

Cacheability Engine

The last development tool that we want to point out is a cacheability engine. Basically, this is a web site where you can type in a URL, and then the engine determines the cacheability of the page the URL points to. This means that the engine examines the specified page and all referenced resources and checks to what extent they can be cached by client browsers and intermediate proxy servers.

The cacheability of a page and its resources is useful information, not only because it can greatly reduce server load and save bandwidth, but more importantly to enhance the user experience. As stated in the previous section, for most web pages, the browser actually waits to retrieve resources. If you get the caching of these resources right, then the browser no longer has to issue a request to the server, because the resource can just be retrieved from the local cache. This greatly enhances the user experience, because page loading feels much more responsive.

There are many cacheability engines available on the Web. The end of this section lists some of them, but if you type "cacheability engine" into Google, then you'll find several others. These engines also provide a lot of information on how to improve the cacheability of your application.

■**Note** In order for these cacheability engines to test your application, it needs to be accessible from the Internet. So you either need to install your application on a public server or make sure that you route a combination of an outside IP address and port number to the server hosting your application.

Three cacheability engines that are available at the time of writing are available at `http://www.mnot.net/cacheability/`, `http://www.ircache.net/cgi-bin/cacheability.py`, and `http://www.web-caching.com/cacheability.html`.

Summary

This chapter has shown you why we think GWT is the best choice for writing the kind of rich Internet applications introduced in Chapter 1. We explained the basic rationale behind GWT and its inner workings. This included a high-level overview of the features provided by GWT that allow you as a developer to build interactive, user-friendly web applications.

You saw the typical GWT project structure when you built your first GWT application. Several concepts and typical parts of a GWT application were introduced as we built that application.

Next, this chapter introduced the sample application that we'll build in the course of the book. This GWTasks application will serve as a way of introducing and illustrating all interesting aspects of GWT.

Last, this chapter introduced some tools that we find to be essential when developing web applications in general, and especially GWT applications.

■ ■ ■

## CHAPTER 3

Getting Started

In this chapter, we'll start using the Google Web Toolkit (GWT). We'll show you what's in the package and what you need to know to start developing applications using GWT. We'll do this by showing you how to set up the development environment and start running the sample application that accompanies this book. In the remaining chapters, we'll use the sample application to illustrate different aspects of developing applications in GWT. Eventually, the sample application will become a full task-management application as described in Chapter 1.

Installing GWT

In order to run the sample application, you need to install GWT on your developer machine. If you already have GWT installed, you can skip this section; just make sure that you have the correct version installed. This book is targeted at GWT version 1.5, so make sure you have at least this version. Furthermore, you'll need a Java SDK of at least version 1.5. You can download the Java SDK from http://java.sun.com.

The first thing you have to do is download the binary distribution from Google. Google has put the toolkit distribution on their developer community site at http://code.google.com. Google uses this site to host their APIs and libraries, but you can host your project there as well. The project site for the toolkit can be found at http://code.google.com/webtoolkit. Besides the distribution, you'll find the reference API, sample applications, blogs, articles, and a lot of third-party libraries that provide additional functionality for GWT. When you click the download link, the site suggests the latest GWT release for your operating system. Fortunately, there's little difference in developing GWT applications on the different platforms. We'll use the Windows platform as an example, as it's still the most commonly used platform. However, developing on other platforms should be quite similar.

It has proved necessary to maintain separate distribution kits for the three major platforms (Windows, Mac, and Linux), because the hosted mode environment uses a different browser depending on the platform to visualize the application. On the Windows platform, GWT uses Internet Explorer, whereas on Linux it comes with a packaged version of Mozilla Firefox. It's important to know that the compiled and deployable application, which consists of JavaScript and HTML, will work on all platforms and browsers. And more important, this is done without you having to worry about the differences during development.

After downloading the distribution pack, you should unpack the archive into a convenient place. For easy reference, you can add an environment variable (GWT_HOME) pointing to this place. Because GWT comes with a set of command-line scripts, we also advise you to add the installation directory to your PATH environment variable so the scripts can be called from any location without an explicit reference to the installation directory.

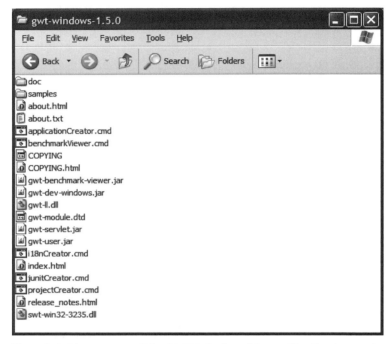

Figure 3-1. *The content of the GWT Windows binary distribution package*

Figure 3-1 shows the content of the binary distribution for the Windows platform. The package consists of the following sets of files:

- gwt-servlet.jar and gwt-user.jar are the libraries that contain the GWT API. These files are used during development, but are also required at runtime.

- gwt-dev-windows.jar is the platform-specific library. It contains the GWT compiler, and along with the DLL files is responsible for hosted-mode emulation. In the Linux and Mac distributions, this file is called gwt-dev-linux.jar and gwt-dev-mac.jar, respectively.

- applicationCreator.cmd, benchmarkViewer.cmd, i18nCreator.cmd, junitCreator.cmd, and projectCreator.cmd are command-line scripts that facilitate the development of your GWT application. We'll discuss a couple of these scripts in this chapter. The more advanced scripts will be covered in their corresponding chapters.

- The doc and samples directories and the HTML and text files contain the Javadocs of the GWT libraries, as well as sample applications to show the usage of the most commonly used components.

Project Structure

Now that you have GWT installed on your system and have a basic understanding of what's inside, you're ready to start your first project. The guys at Google created a convention for the structure of GWT projects. It remains popular for authors of toolkits such as GWT to use the principle of convention over configuration, eliminating large and complex configuration files but without losing the flexibility to configure the toolkit any way you like. Before we tell you how to configure GWT to fit any structure, let's look at the structure Google proposes. We'll show what their convention looks like by creating the first part of our sample application.

You start with a directory for the project (`gwtasks`). Inside this directory, only one subdirectory is needed. That's where the sources are placed, so it should be no surprise that it's called `src`. Here you can create a package structure just as with any other Java application. Figure 3-2 shows the directory structure for your project. In the package structure, you can see three files with the same name, but different extensions. Each of these files is essential to GWT. Together they define the GWT module for the application.

As you can see, the Java file is placed inside a `client` folder. Every class in the client package will be compiled into JavaScript by the GWT compiler. The class inside `GWTasks.java` extends the GWT class `EntryPoint` and represents the start of our application. In this respect, it's just like the main method for a Java application.

Figure 3-2. *Directory structure of a basic GWT application*

The HTML file is placed inside a folder called `public`. This is where all resources that should be made available to the client, such as images and style sheets, will go. The HTML file is our visual starting point. It contains a basic HTML structure in which we'll place our user interface and a JavaScript include tag pointing to our GWT module.

The third file contains the configuration of our GWT module. Here, we can enable and configure specific GWT features we want to use. For now, two things get configured here: we specify that we want the GWT user interface components and we specify which class will be our entry point.

Utility Scripts

Fortunately, we won't have to create this directory structure ourselves. GWT comes with a set of easy-to-use scripts. Two of these scripts are particularly convenient for starting a new GWT module.

Application Creator Script

The application creator script creates a project structure as described in the previous section. Calling it without any arguments will display the argument options. Note that because we added the GWT installation directory to our PATH environment variable, we don't have to refer to the installation directory. Instead, we can call the script directly.

```
>applicationCreator
Missing required argument 'className'
Google Web Toolkit 1.5.0
ApplicationCreator [-eclipse projectName] [-out dir] [-overwrite] [-ignore] ➡
 [-addToClassPath classPathEntry] [-addModule module] className

where
  -eclipse       Creates a debug launch config for the named eclipse project
  -out           The directory to write output files into (defaults to current)
  -overwrite     Overwrite any existing files
  -ignore        Ignore any existing files; do not overwrite
  -addToClassPath Adds extra elements to the class path.
  -addModule     Adds extra GWT modules to be inherited.
and
  className      The fully-qualified name of the application class to create
```

Only one argument is mandatory: the fully qualified class name of the GWT application. As we've seen in Figure 3-2 the package name of the class should end with client. This is part of the GWT convention, and is enforced by the applicationCreator script. The optional argument eclipse allows you to specify an Eclipse launcher configuration to start the application in hosted mode from within Eclipse. This is particularly useful when debugging the GWT module. With the optional out argument, you can specify the folder in which the application should be created. If this is omitted, the application gets created in the current folder. The options ignore and overwrite allow you to specify whether existing files can be overwritten or should be ignored—that is, not re-created. These options are used when you want to regenerate some of the files. For example, you would use the ignore option if you messed up the .gwt.xml file and want the original file back. Just delete the .gwt.xml file and call applicationCreator again. If you just want to start again, you can use the overwrite option. The files you've created will remain untouched, but the script will overwrite any of the files it generates. In particular, this means it will overwrite the .java, .gwt.xml, and .html files. Finally, the options addToClassPath and addModule enable you to configure your project environment. The first allows you to extend your classpath by passing an additional library. The latter is used to enable the use of other GWT modules. More on this feature can be found in Chapter 6.

Besides creating the project structure and the three basic GWT-files, the application creator script creates two convenient scripts in the root of the project: one to compile the project and another to run the project in hosted mode. Both scripts call a Java application with the required GWT libraries on the classpath.

Let's start creating the sample application by making a call to this script. We want it to create an Eclipse launcher called gwtasks and put everything in a folder with the same name. Our module name should be GWTasks, and it should be in package com.apress.gwt.client.

```
> applicationCreator -eclipse gwtasks -out gwtasks com.apress.gwt.client.GWTasks
Created directory gwtasks/src
Created directory gwtasks/src/com/apress/gwt
Created directory gwtasks/src/com/apress/gwt/client
Created directory gwtasks/src/com/apress/gwt/public
Created file gwtasks/src/com/apress/gwt/GWTasks.gwt.xml
Created file gwtasks/src/com/apress/gwt/public/GWTasks.html
Created file gwtasks/src/com/apress/gwt/public/GWTasks.css
Created file gwtasks/src/com/apress/gwt/client/GWTasks.java
Created file gwtasks/GWTasks.launch
Created file gwtasks/GWTasks-shell
Created file gwtasks/GWTasks-compile
```

Now that we have our application, we can start it. Step inside the newly created project folder and make a call to the GWTasks-shell script. This will launch the hosted mode browser and point it at our freshly created application, which should look like Figure 3-3. Go ahead and have a look around the web site. As you can see, it already contains some sample functionality.

Figure 3-3. *Running the sample application in hosted mode*

Project Creator Script

Now that we have a basic project structure, we want to start programming. Google has added a script to generate the Eclipse project files. Fortunately for IntelliJ Idea 7 users, these files can also be used to start your Idea project. The projectCreator script can also be used to generate an Ant script. However, this script is only useful if you want to package the GWT module in a Java archive to be used inside another project. To be able to use an archive, it must contain both the .class files and the .java files. The .class files are needed so the archive can be used just like any other archive. The .java files are needed so the GWT compiler can generate the JavaScript for the components.

```
>projectCreator
Please specify either -ant or -eclipse.
Google Web Toolkit 1.5.0
ProjectCreator [-ant projectName] [-eclipse projectName] [-out dir] ➡
[-overwrite] [-ignore] [-addToClassPath classPathEntry]
where
  -ant            Generate an Ant buildfile to compile source (.ant.xml will be ➡
appended)
  -eclipse        Generate an eclipse project
  -out            The directory to write output files into (defaults to current)
  -overwrite      Overwrite any existing files
  -ignore         Ignore any existing files; do not overwrite
  -addToClassPath Adds extra elements to the class path.
```

Calling the script from our project folder, we only have to specify the argument for Ant and/or Eclipse, depending on the purpose of the project. We can specify gwtasks as a project name for both options.

```
gwtasks> projectCreator -ant gwtasks -eclipse gwtasks
Created directory test
Created file gwtasks.ant.xml
Created file .project
Created file .classpath
```

The Ant script contains four tasks. The default target compiles the sources into a bin folder using the Java compiler from your JDK. This implies that it doesn't generate any JavaScript. It's a normal Java compilation. Both target package and all will compile the code into class files and bundle the project into a Java archive (JAR) containing both the source and the binary files. Finally, the target clear will remove all compiled output from the project structure.

Writing Code

Now that we have our project set up, we can open it inside our IDE. In Appendix A, you can read more detailed information on how to use either Eclipse or IntelliJ Idea for GWT development. Let's start building our sample application with a simple component. You need a logon screen to register for the application. It will be quite simple, showing two input fields with a description and a button to perform the login action.

Cleaning Up Generated Code

First we have to clean up the generated sample application. Open gwtasks.html from the public folder in your favorite editor. As you can see, the head element contains the title of the page, a section defining some styles for the page, and an important JavaScript include. This JavaScript include is the only thing linking the application to the HTML page. The file that gets included will be generated by the GWT compiler and contains the code to start the application.

The body section contains an iframe for history support. The iframe tag is a special HTML that allows you to include another document inside your HTML page. The iframe is needed to support the browser's Back and Forward buttons inside your dynamic RIA. To make the support fully functional, some code is needed in the application as well, to specify how the application should react to these buttons. This will be covered in more detail in a later chapter.

All we really need to get started with our sample application is a clean HTML page containing the JavaScript include and a point of reference where we can put our GWT components. Listing 3-1 shows the file after we're done cleaning it up; as you can see, it already contains some elements to conveniently put our component in the center of the screen.

Listing 3-1. *A Clean HTML File*

```html
<html>
    <head>
        <script language='javascript' src='com.apress.gwt.GWTasks.nocache.js'>
        </script>
    </head>
    <body>
        <table align=center>
            <tr>
                <td id="slot1"></td>
            </tr>
        </table>
    </body>
</html>
```

Now we can start coding some Java. After opening the file GWTask.java in your favorite editor, you can see that the class is inherited from the GWT class com.google.gwt.core.client. EntryPoint and implements only one method, onModuleLoad. This method is called as soon as the application is started, just like the main method in a Java application. From this point, we're going to build our application. You can clean up the existing code by removing all lines inside the onModuleLoad method.

Start Coding

Now we can really start coding. If the logon page were created in HTML, it would contain two input tags: one of type text and one of type password. GWT provides two classes which do exactly that. Create a TextBox for the username, and a PasswordTextBox for the password. Furthermore, we need a button to submit the values of these text boxes to the server for authentication. Create a Button with value "Logon" for this purpose. Now that we have our basic components, we want to arrange them vertically and add labels for the two text boxes. We use a VerticalPanel and Labels to do that. Finally, we need to put the components into our HTML page. Inside the HTML page, we've defined a table cell with the ID slot1. Using the class RootPanel, we can retrieve a reference to that cell and add the panel to it. Listing 3-2 shows the resulting code.

Listing 3-2. *Creating a Logon Screen*

```
public void onModuleLoad() {
    final TextBox username = new TextBox();
    final PasswordTextBox password = new PasswordTextBox();
    final Button button = new Button("Logon");
    final VerticalPanel panel = new VerticalPanel();
    panel.add(new Label("username"));
    panel.add(username);
    panel.add(new Label("password"));
    panel.add(password);
    panel.add(button);
    RootPanel.get("slot1").add(panel);
}
```

As you can see in this small piece of code, creating an HTML page is relatively easy and shows remarkable similarities to programming a Swing application. In principle, you only have to create the components you want to display and arrange them using the different panels GWT provides. More on GWT's different panels is covered in Chapter 4.

Running Code

We have now written enough code to compile and run. Although it contains no functionality whatsoever, it does include some visual components. You can see the resulting output by starting the application in hosted mode, either by calling the GWTasks-hosted script in the root of our project or, if you're using Eclipse, by using the Eclipse launcher. The result should look something like Figure 3-4.

Figure 3-4. *The logon screen in hosted mode*

Another way to check the result is to compile the code into JavaScript by calling the GWTasks-compile script and open the result in your favorite web browser. The script creates a folder called www containing the web site. As the application doesn't contain any server-side code yet, the generated files can be hosted by any web server. It's completely platform-independent and contains only HTML and JavaScript.

Of course, there's no point in leaving the application like this. We want to introduce some functionality as well. Let's extend our panel by creating a welcome message when the user logs on with a known password. For this, we need to create an action that will be triggered when the button is clicked. We can add an EventListener to the Button and program the actions that need to be performed when the Button is clicked. Add the code from Listing 3-3 to the onModuleLoad method underneath the line that creates the Button. This code adds behavior to the click event. The onClick method is called whenever the Button gets clicked. We're using an anonymous inner class to define the logic that needs to be executed. Note that we can reference both the username and the password variable because we declared them as final in Listing 3-2.

Listing 3-3. *The Click Listener for the Submit Button*

```
...
button.addClickListener(new ClickListener() {
    public void onClick(Widget sender) {
        if("secret".equals(password.getText())) {
            Window.alert("Welcome " + username.getText());
        } else {
            Window.alert("Invalid authentication");
        }
    }
});
...
```

The call to the Window.alert method gets translated to the JavaScript alert method. It triggers a pop-up dialog box containing the text as a warning. You normally don't want to use this in your application except for debugging, but for the application in its current state, it will suffice.

If you still have the hosted mode running, all you need do to see and test the result is click the Refresh button in your browser window. This is one of the great advantages of GWT: it enables you to develop the front end without needing to recompile the entire application continuously. This results in a short development cycle. Depending on the input in the text boxes, the application now shows us either Figure 3-5 or Figure 3-6.

Figure 3-5. *Using the logon screen with valid credentials*

Figure 3-6. *Using the logon screen with invalid credentials*

Styling Code with CSS

If you would style every element inside your HTML page separately, you would have a hard time achieving a consistent style throughout your application. Fortunately, you can define your styles in a central place and bind these styles to the HTML elements. Each style can be bound either by creating a style for a specific tag or by defining a style and binding it to tags using the class attribute. These style definitions can either be defined in the head section of your HTML page or be included from a Cascading Style Sheet (CSS) file.

Every GWT component has its own style classifications associated with it. That way you can easily create a stylesheet for your GWT application without needing to assign style names to every component you create. This helps to make sure that your code remains clean. Of course, you may add or replace the style names with names of your choice. The GWT Javadoc contains a section about the CSS style rules that apply to each component by default. The GWT Javadoc is included in the binary package and available online at http://google-web-toolkit-doc-1-5.googlecode.com/svn/javadoc/1.5/index.html. For example, the TextBox class by default has the style name .gwt-TextBox assigned to it. Furthermore, the style name .gwt-TextBox-readonly is defined to style the text box when the readonly flag is set.

Now that we know that every component already has a style name associated with it, we can start creating a stylesheet. There are two ways to link a stylesheet to the application. The most commonly known way is to link it inside the HTML file like this:

```
<html>
        <head>
                <link rel="stylesheet" href="gwtasks.css"/>
        </head>
        …
```

Of course, there's also the option of specifying the styles inside the HTML directly, but best practice is to put the styles in a separate file.

GWT also provides a way to link the stylesheet more tightly to the Java code. Inside the module descriptor, you can specify stylesheets that are specific for your module by adding the following code somewhere inside GWTasks.gwt.xml:

```
<module>

    ...
        <stylesheet src="GWTasks.css"/>
    ...
</module>
```

The results are the same, as GWT dynamically writes every stylesheet in the descriptor into the resulting HTML page. The major benefit of this procedure arises when you're going to use the GWT module inside another application. In that case, you don't want to be forced to find out which stylesheets need to be included into your application just because you're using another module.

Now that we're referring to a stylesheet, we had better create one. The GWTasks.css file is created in the same directory as the .html file, so we need to open the stylesheet from the public folder. Inside the stylesheet, we can define formats for HTML elements and style classes. For now, we only want to style the GWT components we've used so far. By defining the following style, all the labels will have a font size of 9 pixels:

```
.gwt-Label {
        font-size: 9px;
}
```

Both text boxes and the button can be styled with the same style definition. Here we also want the font size to be 9, but we also want to define a fixed width and height for the objects:

```
.gwt-Button, .gwt-TextBox, .gwt-PasswordTextBox {
        font-size: 9px;
        height: 19px;
        width: 75px;
}
```

Hitting the Refresh button in the hosted-mode browser immediately shows the result of our new style. Figure 3-7 shows our final logon screen.

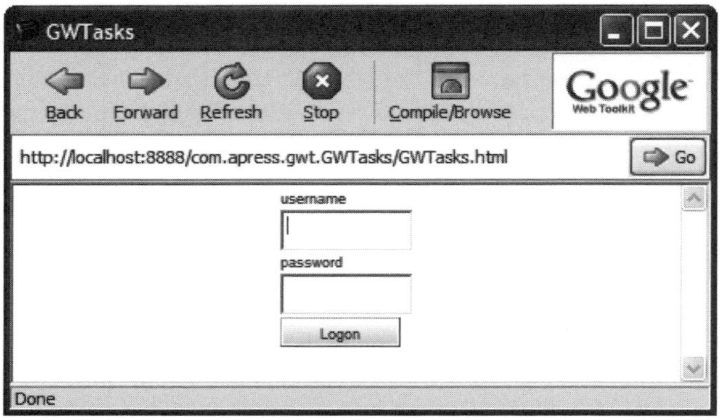

Figure 3-7. *The styled logon panel*

Debugging

While we have a relatively simple application, the code is easy to understand. But as soon as we start extending the application to a reasonable size, we want to be able to debug it. Fortunately, every GWT application can be debugged with the standard Java debug tools, because in hosted mode, the Java code is interpreted inside a normal Java Virtual Machine (JVM) instead of being compiled to JavaScript. If you're developing inside an IDE, starting the hosted mode in debug mode and connecting your debugger to the process is as easy as clicking a button. In Eclipse, you can use the launcher that was created by the application creator script. If you start the hosted mode through the GWT scripts, you need to manually change the script and add two parameters to the Java call. To enable the debugger, you have to add -Xdebug. This option enables the debug mode inside the JVM. Furthermore, you have to specify how you're going to connect to the JVM. Therefore, you have to add the option -Xrunjdwp as well. This is used to specify a number of options, including the port number on which the debugger can connect to the JVM. The complete script should look like Listing 3-4.

Listing 3-4. *Script for Starting Your GWT Application in Hosted Mode with Debugging Enabled*

```
java   -Xdebug ➥
-Xrunjdwp:transport=dt_socket,address=127.0.0.1:52996,suspend=y,server=n ➥
-cp "$APPDIR/src:$APPDIR/bin:$GWT_HOME/gwt-user.jar:$GWT_HOME/gwt-dev-linux.jar" ➥
com.google.gwt.dev.GWTShell -out "$APPDIR/www" "$@" ➥
 com.apress.gwt.GWTasks/GWTasks.html
```

After starting your application in hosted mode, the debugger can connect to the JVM on port 52996.

Summary

Now you've seen the fundamentals of GWT. We started this chapter by configuring our development environment. You've seen where to get the GWT distribution and should have an understanding of what it contains. Your development environment is set up and ready to start creating your GWT applications.

Using the command-line scripts from the distribution package, you can create a basic application, run it, and debug it. You've also seen how you can adjust the basic application and have begun creating the sample application. Using a limited set of GWT classes, you've created a basic logon screen and styled it using a stylesheet.

Chapter 4 will give a more thorough introduction on the widgets GWT provides. Using these widgets will enable you to build more enhanced and interactive interfaces.

CHAPTER 4

■■■

GWT UI Components

In every user interface design, there are three main aspects to consider: UI elements, layouts, and behavior. The UI elements are the core visual elements the user eventually sees and interacts with. The layouts define how these elements should be organized on the screen. And the behavior defines what happens when the user interacts with them.

There are many different ways of implementing these aspects within an application; it all boils down to what technologies are being used. Programming user interfaces in an object-oriented language such as Java differs quite a bit from programming them using languages like HTML and JavaScript. In Java, as in almost every pure OO language, each of these aspects needs to be represented as one or more classes. In Swing[1] applications, for example, component classes are used as building blocks of defining UI elements; containers and layout managers are responsible for laying out the components on the screen; and event and event listener classes are used to bind behavior to the components.

GWT defines its own object-oriented programming model for constructing user interfaces. In many ways, it's similar to Swing (in fact, a lot of the GWT API constructs were borrowed from Swing), yet there's still an essential difference between the two. While a Swing application is compiled to bytecode and runs natively within a JVM environment, a GWT application is compiled to JavaScript and runs within a web browser. In a sense, GWT attempts to provide the same programming and development experience as Swing does, only within a different world—the browser world, a world of HTML and JavaScript.

Bridging these worlds of Java, HTML, and JavaScript is a difficult and complex task, but GWT shines here, too. As you saw in the previous chapter, when building a GWT application, you typically don't need to bother with HTML or JavaScript. Instead, all focus goes to leveraging your Java language expertise and the well-defined GWT API in order to construct the desired web application. Consider for example Listing 4-1, where a simple Java class is used to print the inevitable "Hello World" message on the browser screen. For comparison purposes, Listing 4-2 shows the HTML code to achieve the exact same result.

---

1. Swing is the name of a set of APIs for building graphical user interfaces in Java. These APIs have been part of the standard Java Development Kit (JDK) since version 1.2.

Listing 4-1. *Example GWT Java Code That Prints "Hello World" on the Screen*

```
public class HelloWorldPage extends EntryPoint {
    public void onModuleLoad() {
        Label label = new Label("Hello World");
        RootPane.get().add(label);
    }
}
```

Listing 4-2. *HTML Code to Print "Hello World" on the Screen*

```
<html>
    <body>
        <div>Hello World</div>
    </body>
</html>
```

■**Note** As you saw in the previous chapter, the HelloWorldPage class is only one of three essential sources GWT needs to work with. The other two are the module definition file and the corresponding hosting HTML file. Nonetheless, as the application builds up, the Java code base grows while these extra two files typically remain unchanged.

GWT Component Model

The GWT API provides all the classes needed to create complex web-based user interfaces. It defines an extensible component model that already contains a set of widely used and common components. These components are part of a well-defined class hierarchy (see Figure 4-1) and therefore are naturally grouped based on their common functionality. You can use them directly or alternatively use them as base classes for more complex custom components.

All classes in this component hierarchy derive from the UIObject base class. Although the hierarchy defines multiple hierarchy trees and component groups, they can roughly be split into two main categories: widgets and panels. Widgets represent components the user can interact with, such as buttons or links. Panels represent all those components that serve as containers for other components. In terms of the aspects mentioned at the beginning of this chapter, widgets represent UI elements while panels are in charge of the layout.

The remainder of this chapter will focus on common widgets and panels. We'll see how to work with them and how they fit into our GWTasks sample application. Bear in mind that not all widgets and panels will be covered. We'll only focus on the most widely used ones, and more specifically on those required for our sample application. To learn more about other widgets and available functionality, we strongly recommend you check out the general documentation on the GWT web site at http://code.google.com/webtoolkit, as well as the GWT Class API reference.

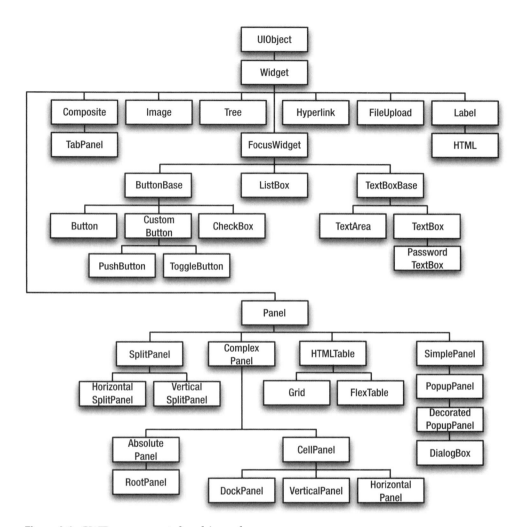

Figure 4-1. *GWT component class hierarchy*

The RootPanel

Before delving into the core widgets and panels, you first need to understand the function of the RootPanel. While panels in GWT are mainly used for layout, the appropriately named RootPanel serves as the top-level panel in the application. This panel provides the following three main methods:

- RootPanel get()—This method returns the panel that represents the body of the HTML page. Once fetched, the returned RootPanel can be used to add any number of widgets and/or panels to the body of the HTML.

- `RootPanel get(String id)`—A finer-grained version of the `get()` method that returns a `RootPanel` representing a specific element within the HTML page. In order for this method to work, the HTML host page needs to contain an element with a matching ID. A common practice is to define `<DIV>` elements in the HTML host page with specific IDs that will be accessible via this method. The GWT-compiled code takes care to put all components under the appropriate `<DIV>` elements.

- `Element getBodyElement()`—This method returns a Java object representing the body DOM element of the HTML host page.

The `RootPanel` is the only mechanism for binding components written in Java to the hosting HTML file, so in every application there must be at least one place where this panel is accessed. In the following sections, you'll see how this binding works in practice.

Basic Widgets

GWT ships with a large set of predefined widgets. In this section, we'll cover some of the basic ones that are essential building blocks for every GWT application. We'll use a few small sample applications to demonstrate these widgets. Consequently, it's important for you to be familiar with the `applicationCreator` tool we covered in the previous chapter. In the rest of this section, when asked to create a new application named "MyNewApplication", you're expected to follow these steps:

1. Run the `applicationCreator` tool with the following argument:
   `com.apress.beginninggwt.chap4.client.MyNewApplication`

2. Clean and edit the appropriate files (the generated entry point Java file and hosting HTML file containing sample code that needs to be removed).

3. Compile the application using the generated `MyNewApplication-compile` script.

4. Run the application using the generated `MyNewApplication-shell` script.

The Label Widget

The simplest widget to start with is the `Label` widget, as its sole purpose is to display plain text on the screen. The `StaticTextExample` (shown in Listing 4-3) is a small application that demonstrates how a label can be used to display a simple text on the screen:

Listing 4-3. *A Simple Label Example*

```
import com.google.gwt.core.client.EntryPoint;
import com.google.gwt.user.client.ui.RootPanel;
import com.google.gwt.user.client.ui.*;
public class StaticTextExample extends EntryPoint {
    public void onModuleLoad() {
        Label label = new Label("Some Text");
        RootPanel.get().add(label);
    }
}
```

Note Just like in any Java class, you must declare the appropriate import statements in order for this code to compile. For the sake of brevity, we've removed these declarations from future code listings. That said, as most of the GWT widgets are defined under the com.google.gwt.user.client.ui package, the import statements in Listing 4-3 should work in most cases. You can always use the GWT API documentation as a reference.

In the onModuleLoad method, we first create a new Label with the appropriate text. Here you can also see how the RootPanel is used to bind the label to the hosting HTML file. In this example, we use the simplest version of the RootPanel.get() method to bind the label directly to the body of the HTML page. Compiling and running this application will display the message "Some Text" onscreen (see Figure 4-2).

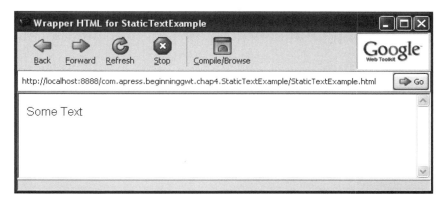

Figure 4-2. *SampleTextExample shell screenshot*

The HTML Widget

Sometimes you may want to give the Label widget HTML content instead of just plain text. Since Label only supports plain text, it will escape all HTML content and show it on screen. This can easily be fixed by replacing the Label with an HTML widget, which is a special label that supports HTML content. Listing 4-4 shows a modified version of the StaticTextExample application that displays the same message in bold text.

Listing 4-4. *Displaying HTML Content Onscreen*

```
public class StaticTextExample extends EntryPoint {
    public void onModuleLoad() {
        HTML html = new HTML("<B>Some Text</B>");
        RootPanel.get().add(html);
    }
}
```

As you can see, the Label has been replaced by an HTML widget, and the message text itself is wrapped within the HTML <B> element. Running this application will show the desired results.

The HTML widget is powerful, but you should be careful not to overuse it. Always ask yourself whether there's a more appropriate way to accomplish the same result. (In this case, a simple label with a customized style could do the trick.) It's advisable to use the HTML widget only for those cases where the GWT doesn't provide a better alternative.

To see the HTML widget in action, we'll use it to display an external link on the screen.[2] Note that this is strictly for demonstration purposes as the GWT Anchor widget already provides this functionality. Listing 4-5 shows how the example in Listing 4-4 can be modified to display a link to the GWT web site.

Listing 4-5. *Displaying an External Link Using the HTML Widget*

```
public class StaticTextExample extends EntryPoint {
    public void onModuleLoad() {
        String link = "http://code.google.com/webtoolkit";
        HTML html = new HTML("<a href=\"" + link + "\">GWT Website</a>");
        RootPanel.get().add(html);
    }
}
```

■**Note** Using the HTML widget extensively also makes it harder to unit test and debug your application. We've already covered debugging in the previous chapter and we'll cover testing in great detail in Chapter 7.

The Button Widget

The Button widget represents a simple button that the user can click. The button is normally used to let the user trigger an action of some kind. As such, Button enables registration of click listeners that will be called whenever it's clicked. The ButtonExample application (see Listing 4-6) shows how this widget can be used to display a button that the user can click to issue an alert message.

---

2. An external, as opposed to internal, link references content that is not part of the application itself—typically a web page from another web site.

Listing 4-6. *A Simple Alert Button Example*

```
public class ButtonExample implements EntryPoint {
    public void onModuleLoad() {
        Button alertButton = new Button("Alert");
        alertButton.addClickListener(new ClickListener() {
            public void onClick(Widget widget) {
                Window.alert("This is an alert!!! ");
            }
        });
        RootPanel.get().add(alertButton);
    }
}
```

The relevant code can be seen in the onModuleLoad() method in Listing 4-6. First a new Button is initialized and assigned to the alertButton variable. The constructor accepts as an argument a String to represent the button's caption (the text on top of the button). Next, we register a ClickListener on the button by calling its addClickListener() method. When clicked, the onClick(Widget) method will be called for all the button's registered click listeners. In our case, an alert will be shown to the user. Last but not least, the button is bound to the HTML host page using the RootPanel.

■Note The Window.alert(String) method is the GWT counterpart of the JavaScript window.alert(var) function used to display a browser native alert message.

As with many of the GWT widgets, it's also possible to further customize the button by setting some of its supported properties. For example, we could set its width and height and make it disabled by default (which means the user won't be able to click it). Listing 4-7 shows how this can be applied in our ButtonExample (highlighted in bold).

Listing 4-7. *Customizing the Look and Feel of the Button*

```
Button alertButton = new Button("Alert");
alertButton.setHeight("150px");
alertButton.setWidth("200px");
alertButton.setEnabled(false);
```

The ToggleButton Widget

The Button class is just one of several concrete implementations of the ButtonBase class (see Figure 4-1). Another interesting implementation is ToggleButton. A ToggleButton is a special button that at any time can be in one of two states: up or down. Clicking the button toggles its state (hence the name ToggleButton). While toggle buttons are widely used in desktop applications, supporting this type of button in a web application has always required quite a bit of JavaScript crafting. Fortunately, GWT abstracts this complexity away.

BROWSER NATIVE VS. EMULATED WIDGETS

When running the example in Listing 4-8, if you don't apply any of the GWT themes to the application, you might encounter a small surprise. The toggle button that was added to the root panel looked onscreen more like a label than a button (although it still functioned as a toggle button). Furthermore, if we hadn't used different captions for its different states, it would have been impossible to tell the current state of the button just by its appearance.

While normal buttons are compiled to a standard HTML <INPUT> element, there's no standard HTML element that can represent a toggle button. In fact, the widgets supported by the HTML standard are just a small subset of the widgets shipped with GWT. So how can the browser show all those widgets that aren't part of the HTML standard?

As it turns out, using some of the standard HTML elements (such as <DIV>, <SPAN>, and <UL>) along with JavaScript, it's possible to emulate almost any widget on screen. This is the approach GWT takes when it comes to nonstandard widgets. As an example, the ToggleButton can be emulated using a <DIV> element, where its content represents the caption of the button. Using JavaScript, it's possible to add state to the element at runtime and register an onclick callback function on it that will toggle that state. The consequence of this approach is that emulated widgets may end up being rendered by the browser differently than expected. The ToggleButton, for example, would end up being rendered like any standard <DIV> element in the page. This is of course not the case with standard HTML widgets, as the browser supports them natively.

While this might seem like a big problem, there are actually advantages in using emulated widgets instead of native ones. The main advantage is that the look and feel of the widget aren't dependent on the specific browser used (whereas an HTML button is rendered on Internet Explorer differently than on Firefox) and can be customized using standard CSS configuration. Applying one of the GWT themes to the application does exactly that.

Listing 4-8 shows an enhanced version of the ButtonExample that demonstrates how the ToggleButton can be used. In this example, another toggle button is added to the application to control which message the alert shows.

Listing 4-8. *Using a ToggleButton*

```java
public class ButtonExample implements EntryPoint {
    public void onModuleLoad() {
        final ToggleButton messageToggleButton = new ToggleButton("UP", "DOWN");
        RootPanel.get().add(messageToggleButton);
        final Button alertButton = new Button("Alert");
        alertButton.addClickListener(new ClickListener() {
            public void onClick(Widget widget) {
                if (messageToggleButton.isDown()) {
                    Window.alert("HELLLLP!!!!");
                } else {
                    Window.alert("Take it easy and relax");
                }
            }
        });
        RootPanel.get().add(alertButton);
    }
}
```

In this example, the messageToggleButton state determines which message will be displayed in the alert. When the toggle button is up, a "calm" message is displayed; when it's down, a "stress" message is shown. Note how the ToggleButton is initialized with two constructor arguments. As with the Button widget, these arguments determine the captions of the button, one for each state. In our example, we use these captions to indicate its state on the screen (there's no such indication by default—see the sidebar for further details).

The Hyperlink Widget

You already saw how you can embed an external link using the HTML widget. Internal links, on the other hand, can be embedded using the Hyperlink class. Let's change our ButtonExample once more; this time we'll use a Hyperlink instead of a normal Button (see Listing 4-9).

Listing 4-9. *Using a Hyperlink*

```
public class ButtonExample implements EntryPoint {
    public void onModuleLoad() {
        final ToggleButton messageToggleButton = new ToggleButton("UP", "DOWN");
        RootPanel.get().add(messageToggleButton);
        Hyperlink alertLink = new Hyperlink("Alert", "alert");
        alertLink.addClickListener(new ClickListener() {
            public void onClick(Widget widget) {
                if (messageToggleButton.isDown()) {
                    Window.alert("HELLLLP!!!!");
                } else {
                    Window.alert("Take it easy and relax");
                }
            }
        });
        RootPanel.get().add(alertLink);
    }
}
```

The Hyperlink acts in many ways like a button. All you needed to do in the listing was replace the Button with a Hyperlink, and as the latter also supports click listeners, the rest of the code just works without any additional modifications.

It might seem that the only real change in our application is visual; that is, instead of clicking a button, the user now clicks a link. But there's more to Hyperlink than meets the eye. When clicked, the Hyperlink not only notifies all its click listeners about the event, it also adds an entry to the browser's history. Note in Listing 4-9 the extra argument that's passed to the Hyperlink constructor. This argument is the token that the Hyperlink will add to the history. We'll discuss browser history support in great detail in Chapter 8, but for now, suffice it to say that this integration enables the browser's Back and Forward buttons to be aware of the actions the user performs in the GWT application.

Form Widgets

Now that we've covered some of the basic widgets and seen how we can work with them, we'll turn to a more practical approach and use our sample application to introduce form widgets.

Form widgets are a group of widgets that correspond to elements in a typical web form. Some of the more popular form widgets include text fields, password fields, multiline text areas, radio buttons, check boxes, and lists.

GWT supports all the standard HTML form widgets, and more, out of the box. As opposed to their usage in HTML, you can use them in more flexible ways, and they don't need to be bound to an HTML form. In this section, we'll introduce these widgets as we implement two important forms in the sample application: the user registration form and the task form.

The User Registration Form

Before we go over the implementation of this form, we first need to understand its purpose and requirements.

As in most multi-user applications, our task management application should enable users to create new accounts. An account holds the following information:

- Full Name—the user's full name.

- Email—the user's e-mail address.

- Username—the username the user will use to log in to the application.

- Password—the password that will authenticate the user when logging in to the application.

We represent this account data in code using the AccountInfo class shown in Listing 4-10. This class will be part of the code base of a new UserRegistrationForm application.

Listing 4-10. *The AccountInfo Class*

```
public class AccountInfo {
    private String fullName;
    private String email;
    private String username;
    private String password;
    public AccountInfo() {
    }
    // setters and getters
    ...
}
```

As for the form implementation itself, we'll have to write two main files:

- UserRegistrationForm.html—This hosting HTML file contains a simple HTML table for the form layout. Each table cell contains a descriptive and unique ID attribute used when binding specific widgets with the RootPanel.get(String) method. Listing 4-11 shows the main content of this file.

- `UserRegistrationForm.java`—Shown in Listing 4-12, this entry point class contains the actual code that defines the form widgets and the form submission logic.

Listing 4-11. *UserRegistrationForm.html*

```html
<html>
    ...
    <body>
        <h1>UserRegistrationForm</h1>
        <table>
            <tr>
                <td id="usernameLabel"></td>
                <td id="usernameField"></td>
            </tr>
            <tr>
                <td id="passwordLabel"></td>
                <td id="passwordField"></td>
            </tr>
        </table>
        <p/>
        <div id="submitButton"></div>
    </body>
</html>
```

Listing 4-12. *UserRegistrationForm.java*

```java
public class UserRegistrationForm implements EntryPoint {
    public void onModuleLoad() {
        // username field
        Label usernameLabel = new Label("Username:");
        final TextBox usernameField = new TextBox();
        RootPanel.get("usernameLabel").add(usernameLabel);
        RootPanel.get("usernameField").add(usernameField);
        // password field
        Label passwordLabel = new Label("Password:");
        final PasswordTextBox passwordField = new PasswordTextBox();
        RootPanel.get("passwordLabel").add(passwordLabel);
        RootPanel.get("passwordField").add(passwordField);
        // retype password field
        Label retypePasswordLabel = new Label("Retype Password:");
        final PasswordTextBox retypePasswordField = new PasswordTextBox();
        RootPanel.get("retypePasswordLabel").add(retypePasswordLabel);
        RootPanel.get("retypePasswordField").add(retypePasswordField);
        // the button that will submit the form
        Button submitButton = new Button("Register");
        RootPanel.get("submitButton").add(submitButton);
```

```
            submitButton.addClickListener(new ClickListener() {
                public void onClick(Widget widget) {
                    AddressInfo addressInfo = new AddressInfo();
                    addressInfo.setUsername(usernameField.getText());
                    addressInfo.setPassword(passwordField.getText());
                    register(addressInfo);
                }
            });
        }

        /**
         * Registers the user in the system.
         */
        protected void register(AddressInfo addressInfo) {
            Window.alert(addressInfo.toString());
        }
    }
```

■**Note** For brevity, the form shown in Listing 4-12 only enables you to enter the user's username and pass-word information. A complete implementation of this form (which can be found in the source code accompanying the book) enables you to enter all properties defined by the AddressInfo class.

Listing 4-12 shows the basic usage of the TextBox and PasswordTextBox widgets. These widgets represent simple input fields where short text-based information can be entered. The main difference between them is in their onscreen appearance (text entered in a PasswordTextBox is masked and hidden from the user). In our example, the TextBox is used to collect the username while the PasswordTextBox accepts the password.

The submitButton is responsible for submitting the form. When clicked, the registered ClickListener collects all the data from the TextBox and PasswordTextBox widgets by calling their getText() methods. It then uses this data to create a new AddressInfo, which is passed to the register() method where the actual registration is performed.

■**Note** For now, all the register(AddressInfo) method does is display the address information in an alert dialog. We'll see how this can be replaced with a real registration procedure when discussing managers in Chapter 5.

Note how each field is bound to its appropriate position on the screen using the RootPanel.get(String) methods. In addition, a Label widget is used to indicate what type of information should be entered in the field. We could have hard-coded these labels in the

HTML host page instead, but we recommend keeping as much functionality as possible in Java code and minimizing the amount of raw HTML code in the application (mainly for maintenance and debugging reasons).

Adding Validation

While the current implementation of our registration form works, it isn't yet complete. In its current state, it's possible for the user to add invalid information that will then be saved in our system. To prevent this from happening, we want to perform extra checks and validate the data prior to its submission. In our example, we'll validate that the user submits a nonblank password and also verify that the retyped password is correct. Listings 4-13 and 4-14 show snippets of HTML and Java code modified to support this new functionality.

Listing 4-13. *Defining the Location of the Error Messages in UserRegistrationForm.html*

```
<html>
    ...
    <tr>
        <td id="passwordLabel"></td>
        <td id="passwordField"></td>
        <td id="passwordErrorLabel"></td>
    </tr>
    <tr>
        <td id="retypePasswordLabel"></td>
        <td id="retypePasswordField"></td>
        <td id="retypePasswordErrorLabel"></td>
    </tr>
    ...
</html>
```

Listing 4-14. *Validating the Retyped Password in UserRegistrationForm.java*

```
public class UserRegistrationForm implements EntryPoint {
    private PasswordTextBox passwordField;
    private Label passwordErrorLabel;
    private PasswordTextBox retypePasswordField;
    private Label retypePasswordErrorLabel;
    public void onModuleLoad() {
        ...
        passwordErrorLabel = new Label();
        RootPanel.get("passwordErrorLabel").add(passwordErrorLabel);
        retypePasswordErrorLabel = new Label();
        RootPanel.get("retypePasswordErrorLabel").add(retypePasswordErrorLabel);
        ...
        submitButton.addClickListener(new ClickListener() {
            public void onClick(Widget widget) {
                if (validateFormInput()) {
                    AddressInfo addressInfo = new AddressInfo();
                    addressInfo.setUsername(usernameField.getText());
```

```
                    addressInfo.setPassword(passwordField.getText());
                    register(addressInfo);
                }
            }
        });
    }

    /**
     * Validates the form input and returns whether the input is valid or not.
     */
    protected boolean validateFormInput() {
        // validating the password is not empty
        String password = passwordField.getText();
        boolean passwordIsValid = password.length() > 0;
        passwordErrorLabel.setText(passwordIsValid ? "" : "Required");
        // validating that the retyped password matches the password
        String retypedPassword = retypePasswordField.getText();
        boolean retypeIsValid = retypedPassword.equals(password);
        retypePasswordErrorLabel.setText(retypeIsValid ? "" : "Incorrect");
        return usernameIsValid && passwordIsValid && retypedIsValid;
    }
    …
}
```

As shown in Listing 4-14, a new Label has been added next to every input field; this will be used to show validation error messages to the user. In addition, the validateFormInput() method was added to the class. This method validates the data entered in the password fields and shows appropriate error messages to the user if invalid input is encountered. The method returns true only when all validation checks are passed. The click listener that handles form submission can now call the validateFormInput() method and continue to submit the data only if it returns true. Note that we also extracted the password widgets (along with the new error labels) and stored them as class fields instead of local variables. This gives validateFormInput() easy and clean access to the text entered in these widgets and, when necessary, lets it write appropriate error messages in the appropriate labels.

Although this example is quite narrow in its validation requirement, extra validation checks can be added in the same manner for all other fields as well.

Styling Validation Error Messages

When displaying validation error messages to the user, a common practice is to highlight these messages onscreen to grab the user's attention.

As we already introduced new labels for the error messages, highlighting the error messages is as easy as adding extra styles to these labels. This can be done by calling the addStyleName(String) method of the Label. The name of the style must correspond to a CSS class defined in the application (either by embedding/linking it within the hosting HTML file or by configuring the <stylesheet> element in the application module descriptor). This CSS class determines the actual styling of the text. Listings 4-15 and 4-16 show the changes in the code required for this to work.

Listing 4-15. *Defining Error Label CSS Class in UserRegistrationForm.html*

```
<html>
    <head>
        ...
        <style>
            ...
            .errorLabel {
                color: red;
            }
        </style>
    <head>
    ...
</html>
```

Listing 4-16. *Adding a New Style to the Error Label in UserRegistrationForm.java*

```
...
passwordErrorLabel = new Label();
passwordErrorLabel.addStyleName("errorLabel");
RootPanel.get("passwordErrorLabel").add(passwordErrorLabel);
retypePasswordErrorLabel = new Label();
retypePasswordErrorLabel.addStyleName("errorLabel");
RootPanel.get("retypePasswordErrorLabel").add(retypePasswordErrorLabel);
...
```

With this custom styling in place, whenever the user enters invalid data, a red error message will appear onscreen next to the appropriate widget.

Figure 4-3 shows how the final version of the UserRegistrationForm application looks when run within the GWT shell.

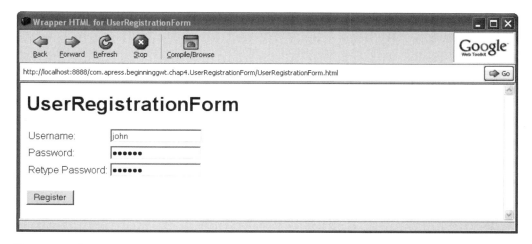

Figure 4-3. *The UserRegistrationForm application screenshot*

Now that we've seen how to work with the TextBox and PasswordTextBox widgets in a simple registration form, let's see how we can leverage other available form widgets to create the richer task form.

The Task Form

As with the user registration form, before we start implementing the task form, we first need to understand what it's used for and what kind of data it will collect from the user.

As the main goal of GWTasks is to manage user tasks, this application must give the user a mechanism for adding new tasks to the system. This is the main goal of the task form. Tasks are represented by the TaskInfo class (shown in Listing 4-17), which will be placed in the client package of a newly created TaskForm application.

Listing 4-17. *The TaskInfo Class*

```
public class TaskInfo {
    public enum Priority { LOW, NORMAL, HIGH }
    // a required short descriptive title
    private String title;
    // option (may be null) extra text describing the task in details
    private String description;
    // defines the priority of the task
    private Priority priority = Priority.NORMAL;
    public TaskInfo() {
    }
    // getters and setters
    ...
}
```

As can be seen in Listing 4-17, the TaskInfo defines three properties: title, description, and priority. The title property is mandatory; the others are optional. This requirement already tells us something about the kind of validation checks the task form should have. Another thing to note is that each property carries a different type of information, which implicitly hints how it should be presented to the user. For example, while the title property should be short and concise, the description property can hold long and detailed text. This difference implies that while the user can enter the title using a simple TextBox, a different kind of widget should be used for the description field, namely the TextArea widget.

Assuming the structure of the HTML host page of the form is clear by now (as it doesn't differ much from the one used in the UserRegistrationForm), let's focus on the TaskForm class.

Implementing the Form

We'll build this form a step at a time, starting with an initial implementation that enables the user to enter the task title and description. Listing 4-18 shows the initial TaskForm class implementation.

Listing 4-18. *TaskForm.java*

```java
public class TaskForm implements EntryPoint {
    private TextBox titleField;
    private Label titleErrorLabel;
    private TextArea descriptionField;
    private Label descriptionErrorLabel;
    public void onModuleLoad() {
        titleField = new TextBox();
        titleErrorLabel = createErrorLabel();
        RootPanel.get("titleLabel").add(new Label("Title"));
        RootPanel.get("titleField").add(titleField);
        RootPanel.get("titleErrorLabel").add(titleErrorLabel);
        descriptionField = new TextArea();
        descriptionErrorLabel = createErrorLabel();
        RootPanel.get("descriptionLabel").add(new Label("Description"));
        RootPanel.get("descriptionField").add(descriptionField);
        RootPanel.get("descriptionErrorLabel").add(descriptionErrorLabel);
        Button submitButton = new Button("Add Task");
        submitButton.addClickListener(new ClickListener() {
            public void onClick(Widget widget) {
                if (validateForm()) {
                    TaskInfo task = new TaskInfo();
                    task.setTitle(titleField.getText());
                    task.setDescription(descriptionField.getText());
                    addTask(task);
                }
            }
        });
    }
    protected Label createErrorLabel() {
        Label errorLabel = new Label();
        errorLabel.addStyleName("errorLabel");
        return errorLabel;
    }
    protected boolean validateForm() {
        boolean titleIsValid = titleField.getText().lenth() > 0;
        titleErrorLabel.setText(titleIsValid ? "" : "Required");
        return titleIsValid;
    }
    protected void addTask(TaskInfo task) {
        Window.alert(task.toString());
    }
}
```

As you can see in Listing 4-18, the basic structure of the TaskForm is similar to that of the UserRegistrationForm. A TextBox widget is used for entering the task title. Furthermore, as the title is a mandatory field, the validateForm() method validates that the user indeed entered it in the form. As for the description field, we chose to use a TextArea widget instead of the TextBox. While the latter is appropriate for short text based data, the TextArea widget provides a more convenient way of entering long multiline texts.

When running this version of the TaskForm, you may notice that the description text area is indeed a better fit for large text entries than the text box. That said, in most cases (and in our example) its default size is less than optimal. We can easily fix this by customizing two properties of the TextArea widget. Listing 4-19 shows (highlighted in bold) the snippet of the code required to customize the size of the area.

Listing 4-19. *Customizing TextArea Size*

```
...
descriptionField = new TextArea();
descriptionField.setVisibleLines(10);
descriptionField.setCharacterWidth(50);
descriptionErrorLabel = createErrorLabel();
...
```

Customizing the height of the text area is done by specifying how many lines of text it should display. The width is set by specifying the maximum number of characters each line can contain. One caveat to remember when using the setCharacterWidth(int) method is that the character size varies between browsers and platforms, thus the same text area may appear differently in different environments. To circumvent this problem, you can instead set the size of the TextArea using the more generic setWidth, setHeight, setSize, and setPixelSize methods which are defined in the UIObject class.

Adding the Priority Field

So far we've used simple text widgets as data entry fields for different types of information. We could have chosen to use the TextBox once more to enable the user to enter a task priority. The problem with this approach is that the priority can only hold one of a fixed set of possible values. Letting the user enter this value in a free text manner introduces two issues. First, the user needs to guess which values are valid and acceptable by the system. Second, even if the user knows about the valid values, we introduce extra complexity both for the user (who has to retype the same value over and over again) and for the developer (who needs to validate that the entered text is a valid priority value). Luckily, GWT comes with the ListBox widget, which provides a clean solution to this problem.

The main goal of the ListBox widget is to present to the user a list of options from which she can choose one or more values. Typically, when the user can only choose one option, the list is displayed as a drop-down list. When multiple options can be chosen, it's possible to customize the list box size by specifying how many options should be visible at once.

As a task can only have one priority, a drop-down list of all three possible priorities will suffice. Listing 4-20 shows how this field can be added to our existing TaskForm class (again, highlighted in bold).

Listing 4-20. *Adding the Priority ListBox to the TaskForm*

```java
public class TaskForm extends EntryPoint {
    ...
    private ListBox priorityField;
        public void onModuleLoad() {
        ...
        priorityField = new ListBox(false);
        priorityField.setVisibleItemCount(1);
        priorityField.addItem("LOW");
        priorityField.addItem("NORMAL");
        priorityField.addItem("HIGH");
        priorityField.setItemSelected(1, true);
        RootPanel.get("priorityLabel").add(new Label("Priority"));
        RootPanel.get("priorityField").add(priorityField);
        submitButton.addClickListener(new ClickListener() {
            public void onClick(Widget widget) {
                if (validateForm()) {
                    TaskInfo task = new TaskInfo();
                    task.setTitle(titleField.getText());
                    task.setDescription(descriptionField.getText());
                    TaskInfo.Priority priority = resolvePriority();
                    task.setPriority(priority);
                    addTask(task);
                }
            }
        });
        ...
    }
    protected TaskInfo.Priority resolvePriority() {
        int priorityIndex = priorityField.getSelectedIndex();
        String priorityName = priorityField.getValue(priorityIndex);
        return Enum.valueOf(TaskInfo.Priority.class, priorityName);
    }
}
```

As shown in the listing, the first thing we need to do is define a ListBox class field. In the onLoadModule(), we instantiate this field and initialize its state. Note that the list box is instantiated with false as a constructor argument, which tells the ListBox not to allow the user to select multiple options. We also configure the ListBox to be displayed as a drop-down list using the setVisibleItemCount(int) method. We then add all possible priorities to the list box and configure the NORMAL priority to be displayed by default. The only thing left is to resolve the priority based on the selected option in the list box (using the resolvePriority method) and set it on the new task. Figure 4-4 shows how our final version of the task form looks within the GWT shell.

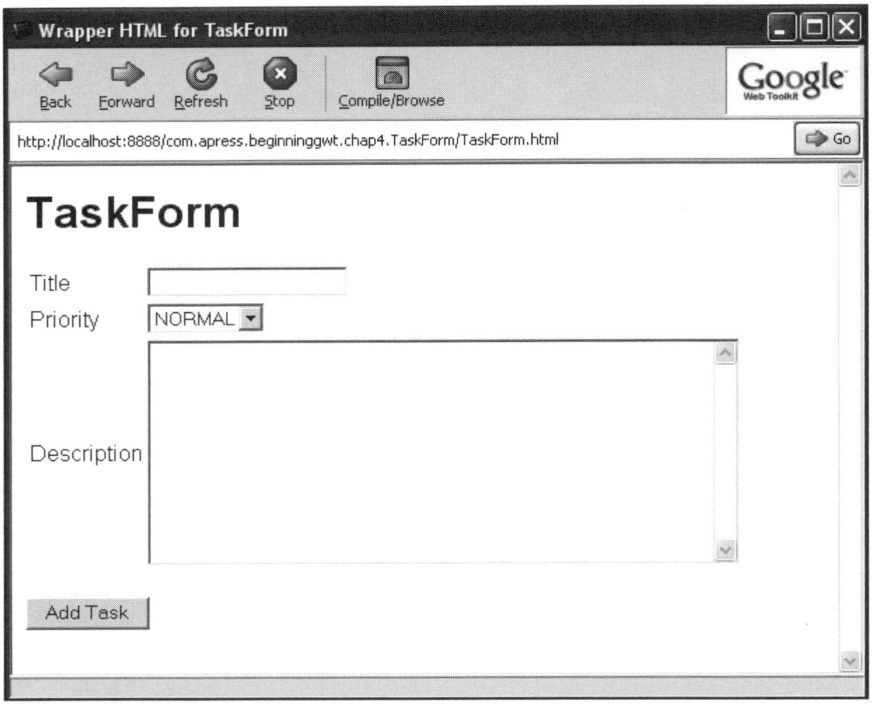

Figure 4-4. *Screenshot of the TaskForm application*

There are quite a few widgets we haven't covered that you might find useful. Some will be dealt with as we build our GWTasks sample application, while we'll leave others for you to explore. As mentioned at the beginning of this chapter, the GWT component model is quite consistent in its public API. A good understanding of the widgets we've discussed is a strong foundation for getting up to speed with all the other available widgets.

Panels

In all the examples so far, we've used the HTML host page and the RootPanel to lay out the widgets and attach them to the screen. Although this approach worked well for our simple forms, it's bound to fail for most real-world applications, as they require more complex layout schemes. This is where panels come into the picture. A GWT panel can be seen as a UI component whose sole purpose is to contain other components (widgets or other panels) and define their layout on the screen. As usual with GWT, you define the panels in your application's Java code base, and work with them just like any other Java object. Looking back at Figure 4-1, you can even see that all the panels are part of the GWT component class hierarchy, and have a well-defined class hierarchy of their own.

In the next few sections, we'll cover some of the more important panels available. We'll continue working on our sample application and show the important role that panels play in the overall architecture of the application.

Creating the Sample Application

Before we move on to showing how to work with panels, we first need to create the sample application project. Learning about panels will finally enable us to create a code base for our sample application. As always, we'll use the `applicationCreator` to create the application, as shown in Listing 4-21.

Listing 4-21. *Using applicationCreator to Create the GWTasks Application*

```
> $GWT_HOME/applicationCreator com.apress.beginninggwt.gwtasks.client.GWTasks
```

■**Note** Don't forget to clean up all the dummy code that's autogenerated by the `applicationCreator` tool. You can find this code in both the hosting HTML file and the `GWTasks` entry point class file.

Designing the Main Look and Feel of GWTasks

When building rich UI applications, we find that UI design usually takes center stage. It's the design that really distinguishes a great application from a good one, and a good one from a bad one. Coming up with that special design isn't as easy as it may seem and it's beyond the scope of this book. Nonetheless, we'll try to use some of the tools and techniques that UI designers use for our sample application. One of these techniques is *wireframes*—a simple sketch that defines the blueprint of the user interface. Using wireframes makes it easier to communicate ideas about the interface and also serve as basic documentation. Figure 4-5 shows an initial wireframe for the general structure of the GWTasks main page.

As you can see in Figure 4-5, the main page in our application is divided into four main parts. The top part is called the *header* and the bottom part is called the *footer*. These two parts are visible in all pages of the application, and as such, serve to display information and expose functionality that the user would be interested in at all times. The other two parts are closely related to the functional purpose of the main page itself.

When entering the application, the user should be able to easily browse his tasks and manage them (for example, create new tasks, update existing ones, or remove tasks). In the wireframe shown in Figure 4-5, the left part of the screen is dedicated to the task categories while the right part is dedicated to the actual tasks. When the user selects a category on the left, all tasks in that category should be listed on the right.

There are several ways in GWT to achieve this layout, one of which is by using a `DockPanel`. This is a simple yet powerful panel that divides the screen into five regions—north, south, east, west, and center (as shown in Figure 4-6).

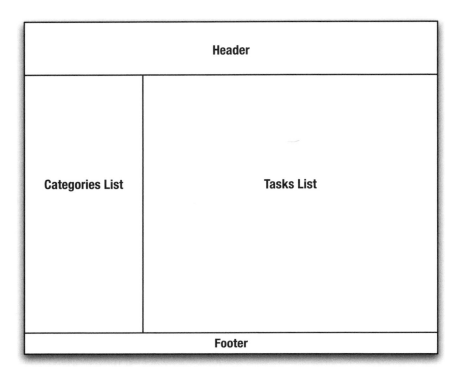

Figure 4-5. *Wireframe for the main page in the GWTasks application*

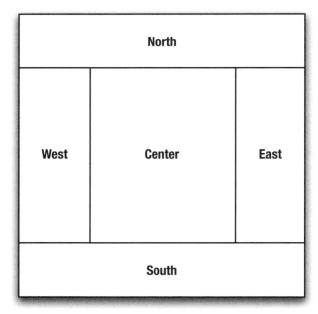

Figure 4-6. *DockPanel regions*

DockPanel provides three main methods for binding widgets to the different regions:

- add(Widget, DockPanel.DockLayoutConstant)—this method adds the given widget and binds it to the region specified by the given layout constant. As there are only five possible regions, DockPanel defines five static fields that can be used as the layout constant argument: DockPanel.NORTH, DockPanel.SOUTH, DockPanel.EAST, DockPanel.WEST and DockPanel.CENTER.

- setCellWidth(Widget, String)—this method enables you to control the width of a region to which the given widget is bound.

- setCellHeight(Widget, String)—this method enables you to control the height of a region to which the given widget is bound.

Listing 4-22 shows how we can create the main page of our application using these three methods.

Listing 4-22. *Setting Up the GWTasks Main Page Layout*

```
public class GWTasks implements EntryPoint {
    public void onModuleLoad() {
        DockPanel mainPanel = new DockPanel();
        mainPanel.setBorderWidth(5);
        mainPanel.setSize("100%", "100%");
        mainPanel.setVerticalAlignment(HasAlignment.ALIGN_MIDDLE);
        mainPanel.setHorizontalAlignment(HasAlignment.ALIGN_CENTER);
        Widget header = createHeaderWidget();
        mainPanel.add(header, DockPanel.NORTH);
        mainPanel.setCellHeight(header, "30px");
        Widget footer = createFooterWidget();
        mainPanel.add(footer, DockPanel.SOUTH);
        mainPanel.setCellHeight(footer, "25px");
        Widget categories = createCategoriesWidget();
        mainPanel.add(categories, DockPanel.WEST);
        mainPanel.setCellWidth(categories, "150px");
        Widget tasks = createTasksWidget();
        mainPanel.add(tasks, DockPanel.EAST);
        RootPanel.get().add(mainPanel);
    }
    protected Widget createHeaderWidget() {
        return new Label("Header");
    }
    protected Widget createFooterWidget() {
        return new Label("Footer");
    }
    protected Widget createCategoriesWidget() {
        return new Label("Categories");
    }
    protected Widget createTasksWidget() {
        return new Label("Tasks");
    }
}
```

In Listing 4-22, we create widgets that represent the different elements in our design (simple labels for now), bind them to their appropriate regions, and fit the region sizes appropriately. The header and the footer are bound to the north and south regions, and the categories and tasks lists are bound to the west and east regions, respectively. To visualize the design better, we further customize the DockPanel itself by setting its border width and alignments.

Showing the Categories and Task Lists

Now that we have the skeleton of the main page ready, we can move on to fill it with data. As mentioned earlier, the functionality of the main page revolves around browsing and managing tasks and categories. Figure 4-7 shows a more detailed version of our original wireframe that illustrates how this functionality will be supported by the UI.

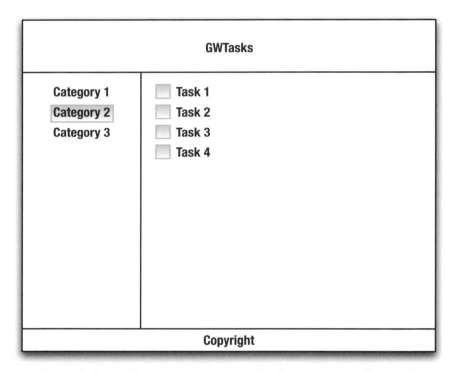

Figure 4-7. *Wireframe of the main page including the categories and tasks lists*

As shown in Figure 4-7, the categories and tasks are presented as lists of rows. The category rows show the name of the categories, and the task rows show the title of each task, with a check box next to it. The tasks list only shows the tasks for the selected category.

To support this layout of categories and tasks, we're going to use two of the most commonly used panels in GWT—HorizontalPanel and VerticalPanel. The HorizontalPanel is a simple panel that enables you to lay out widgets horizontally next to one another. The VerticalPanel, on the other hand, enables you to lay out widgets vertically above (or below) one another.

The Categories List

Let's start by implementing the categories list. Listing 4-23 shows the implementation of the createCategoriesWidget() that creates it.

Listing 4-23. *Displaying the Categories List*

```
...
protected Widget createCategoriesWidget() {
    VerticalPanel categoryList = new VerticalPanel();
    List<Category> categories = getAllCategories();
    for (final Category category : categories) {
        Widget categoryRow = createCategoryRow(category);
        categoryList.add(categoryRow);
    }
    return categoryList;
}
protected Widget createCategoryRow(Category category) {
    return new Label(category.getName());
}
protected List<Category> getAllCategories() {
    List<Category> categories = new ArrayList<Category>();
    categories.add(new Category(1L, "Shopping List", ""));
    ...
    return categories;
}
...
```

The createCategoriesWidget() method creates a row for every category in the system and adds it to a VerticalPanel. When running this example, the names of all categories will be shown on the left side of the page (the west region) in a vertical list.

In this example, the category row is nothing more than a label displaying the category name. We want to change this to allow the user to click a category and select it. Let's reimplement the createCategoryRow(Category) method to support this behavior (shown in Listing 4-24).

Listing 4-24. *Adding Behavior to the Categories List*

```
private Widget selectedCategoryRow;
private Category selectedCategory;
...
protected Widget createCategoryRow(final Category category) {
    final Label row = new Label(category.getName());
    row.setWordWrap(false);
    row.setStyleName("categoryRow");
    row.addClickListener(new ClickListener() {
        public void onClick(Widget widget) {
            if (row.equals(selectedCategoryRow)) {
                return; // do nothing as it is already selected
```

```
            }
            markSelected(selectedCategoryRow, false);
            markSelected(row, true);
            selectedCategoryRow = row;
            selectedCategory = category;
            updateTasksList();
        }
    });
    return row;
}
protected void markSelected(Widget categoryRow, boolean selected) {
    if (categoryRow == null) {
        return;
    }
    if (selected) {
        categoryRow.addStyleName("selectedCategory");
        categoryRow.removeStyleName("unselectedCategory");
    } else {
        categoryRow.addStyleName("unselectedCategory");
        categoryRow.removeStyleName("selectedCategory");
    }
}
protected void updateTasksList() {
    //TODO
}
```

As shown in Listing 4-24, we continue using the standard Label as the category row widget. We also introduce two new global variables to hold the currently selected category and its row. When the user clicks the category row, we first check that the clicked row isn't already selected (in which case nothing should happen) and then we change the currently selected category to the clicked one. The markSelected(Widget, Boolean) method sets the style of the given category row widget appropriately. Note that we also call the updateTasksList() method, which we'll implement next.

The Tasks List

When a category is selected, the relevant tasks should appear on the right side of the page (as shown in Figure 4-7). Listing 4-25 shows how this behavior can be implemented.

Listing 4-25. *Displaying the Tasks List*

```
...
private VerticalPanel tasksWidget;
...
public void updateTasksList() {
    List<Task> tasks = getTasksForSelectedCategory();
    tasksWidget.clear();
```

```
    for (Task task : tasks) {
        Widget taskRow = createTaskRow(task);
        tasksWidget.add(taskRow);
    }
}
public Widget createTasksWidget() {
    tasksWidget = new VerticalPanel();
    return tasksWidget;
}
public Widget createTaskRow(Task task) {
    HorizontalPanel row = new HorizontalPanel();
    CheckBox checkbox = new CheckBox();
    row.add(checkbox);
    row.add(new Label(task.getTitle()));
    return row;
}
public List<Task> getTasksForSelectedCategory() {
    // return the relevant list of tasks
}
```

The createTasksWidget() method is called once when the application is loaded. Its only task is to initialize a shared VerticalPanel that will be used to show the tasks lists. The updateTasksList() method is called when a category is selected. First it retrieves all tasks related to the currently selected category. Then it removes all widgets from the shared vertical panel, creates a task row for each task in the list, and adds each row to the panel. In this example, we use the HorizontalPanel to position a check box next to the task title in the createTaskRow(Task) method.

Figure 4-8 shows a screenshot of the current version of our sample application.

■**Note** At this point, both getAllCategories() in Listing 4-23 and getTasksForSelectedCategory() in Listing 4-25 provide hard-coded dummy data for our sample application. A more appropriate way would be to fetch this data from a central repository where all application data is stored. We'll see how this can be done in the next chapter.

Enhancing the User Experience with HorizontalSplitPanel

As we've previously shown, the DockPanel enables us to implement the main page layout as defined in Figure 4-5. Nonetheless, there's still a small problem with this implementation that might get bigger once the application runs with real-world data. If you look closely at Listing 4-22, we set the width of the categories widget to a fixed size of 150 pixels. This width was large enough to show the name of the categories in our dummy data, but there's nothing stopping the user from creating categories with longer names that wouldn't fit within this fixed width. To solve this problem, we'll need to slightly modify our layout and introduce yet another useful panel—the HorizontalSplitPanel.

The HorizontalSplitPanel is a panel that can lay out two widgets next to each other and separate them with a split bar. The user can extend or reduce the visual space allocated for each widget by dragging the split bar. When a widget doesn't fit in its visually allocated space, a scrollbar will appear.

Since it's impossible to predict the exact length of the category names in our application, we can use the HorizontalSplitPanel to separate the categories list from the tasks lists. This will enable the user to customize the size of the categories list as she sees fit.

Listing 4-26 shows the reimplemented onModuleLoad() method of our application, this time using the HorizontalSplitPanel (changes highlighted in bold).

Listing 4-26. *Using a HorizontalSplitPanel to Separate the Categories and Tasks Lists*

```
...
public void onModuleLoad() {
DockPanel mainPanel = new DockPanel();
    mainPanel.setBorderWidth(5);
    mainPanel.setSize("100%", "100%");
    Widget header = createHeaderWidget();
    mainPanel.add(header, DockPanel.NORTH);
    mainPanel.setCellHeight(header, "30px");
    Widget footer = createFooterWidget();
    mainPanel.add(footer, DockPanel.SOUTH);
    mainPanel.setCellHeight(footer, "25px");
    HorizontalSplitPanel categoriesAndTasks = new HorizontalSplitPanel();
    categoriesAndTasks.setSplitPosition("150px");
    Widget categories = createCategoriesWidget();
    categoriesAndTasks.setLeftWidget(categories);
    Widget tasks = createTasksWidget();
    categoriesAndTasks.setRightWidget(tasks);
    mainPanel.add(categoriesAndTasks, DockPanel.CENTER);
    RootPanel.get("main").add(mainPanel);
}
...
```

■**Tip** The split bar is transparent by default. To fix this, either apply one of the themes that come with GWT or customize its background color and cursor explicitly by setting up the .gwt-HorizontalSplitPanel .hsplitter { } CSS style.

When running the application, you can now dynamically change the sizes of the categories and tasks lists by dragging the split bar. Figure 4-8 shows a screenshot of the current GWTasks application.

There are many other panels that we haven't covered here. Some, such as FlexTable and TabPanel, will be covered in later chapters as we further extend our sample application.

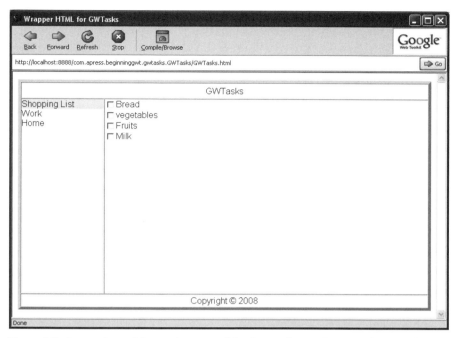

Figure 4-8. *Screenshot of the main page of the GWTasks application showing both the categories and tasks lists*

Summary

In this chapter, you took your first dip in the GWT ocean. We started by introducing elements, layouts, and behavior as the three aspects of UI development. We then discussed the basic concepts of component-based UI development and how they relate to these aspects. We showed how GWT provides a well-thought-out programming model to build web-based applications, and how it can bridge the different worlds of Java, HTML, and JavaScript.

You were introduced to the basic UI widgets that ship with GWT. You've seen how a Label can be used to display static text and the HTML widget to display HTML content. You've also used the Button, ToggleButton, and Hyperlink widgets to enable user interaction in the application.

You learned about form widgets, and together we've implemented two different forms in our GWTasks sample applications. You've seen how simple it is to add form validation and customize the look and feel of forms using CSS styles.

We covered the basics of application design and layout. You saw how the GWT panels provide a powerful way to lay out different widgets on the screen. We used basic panels, such as DockPanel, HorizontalPanel, and VerticalPanel, to define the skeleton of our sample application, as well as more complex panels, such as HorizontalSplitPanel, to enhance the user experience.

■■■

## CHAPTER 5

Building an Advanced UI

In the previous chapter, we introduced you to the world of object-oriented user interface development, and in particular the core GWT constructs for creating rich web applications. In this chapter, we'll continue to explore the GWT API and delve further into the OO nature of GWT applications. We'll introduce some more advanced widgets such as tables, trees, and dialog boxes. We'll show you how to modularize the application code base and create your own generic GWT components as well. What's more, we'll make good use of all these ideas by applying them to our GWTasks sample application. By the end of this chapter, we'll have a full-blown, well-modularized application with built-in infrastructure for data management.

This chapter is quite long and involves a lot of coding on your part. We strongly recommend you work your way through this chapter using the code that accompanies this book as a reference to all the following discussions.

So without further ado, let's start by checking out some of the more advanced widgets in GWT.

Using Tables

Tables have always played a dual role in web application design. On one hand, they served as a mechanism to present information to the user in a tabular form (that is, column-based lists). On the other hand, although this wasn't their original purpose, they also served as a mechanism for laying out different elements on a web page. While the first role is widely accepted, there's some dispute about the second role as layout components. We won't go into this discussion, but just say that with GWT, you can use tables for both purposes as you wish.

GWT comes with two table implementations: `Grid` and `FlexTable`. Both inherit from the same `HTMLTable` base class.

Using Grid

A `Grid` represents a fixed table. By *fixed*, we mean that before you create a new `Grid`, you have to know up front how many rows and columns the table should have. You can, however, change its size after creation by adding rows and/or columns explicitly. This fixed nature of `Grid` makes it appropriate for static layout. Let's take a look at how you can implement a login form using a `Grid`. For this example, you can assume the existence of a `LoginForm`, which is essentially a panel that shows a simple login form. Figure 5-1 shows how this panel should look and how its layout can be achieved using a grid.

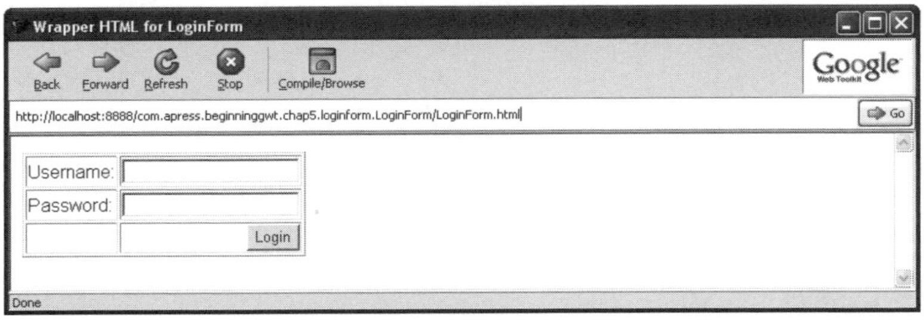

Figure 5-1. *Login form layed out using a Grid*

As you can see, each cell in the grid contains various UI elements. The first row holds the username label and input field in two separate cells. The second row holds the password label and field. The third row contains the Login button. Listing 5-1 shows how you can implement this interface using the Grid widget. As the intent here is to learn about Grid, we dropped all logic related to this screen (we assume that by now you can figure out how to add it yourself).

Listing 5-1. *LoginForm Using a Grid*

```
public class LoginForm implements EntryPoint {
    public void onModuleLoad() {
        Grid grid = new Grid(3, 2);
        grid.setBorderWidth(1);
        grid.setWidget(0, 0, new Label("Username:"));
        grid.setWidget(0, 1, new TextBox());
        grid.setWidget(1, 0, new Label("Password:"));
        grid.setWidget(1, 1, new TextBox());
        grid.setWidget(2, 1, createSubmitButton());
        grid.getCellFormatter()
            .setHorizontalAlignment(2, 1, HasHorizontalAlignment.ALIGN_RIGHT);
        RootPanel.get().add(grid);
    }
    ...
}
```

■**Note** For illustration purposes, we set the border width of the Grid to 1. Normally, when using a grid as a layout mechanism, you want to keep the default, which is set to zero.

As can be seen in the listing, you first create a grid with three rows and two columns. Then you set the widget in each cell of the grid using the setWidget method (try comparing these method calls with Figure 5-1). Also note that the grid enables you to customize each cell using the CellFormatter object. You can retrieve a cell formatter for every cell in the grid and use it to set the cell's style name, size, and alignment properties. In this example, you make sure that the login button is aligned to the right as needed.

Using FlexTable

If the `Grid` is considered to be a static table, the `FlexTable` (as its name suggests) is a more flexible implementation of the `HTMLTable`. This table is meant to be used whenever the size isn't known in advance and is open for dynamic changes. For example, if you need to display a dynamic list of items in tabular form and items can be added or removed at any time, the `FlexTable` is a good candidate. The tasks list in our sample GWTasks application fits this requirement exactly, which makes it an ideal use case to show how the `FlexTable` works.

    If you recall from the previous chapter, you initially implemented the tasks list view using a `VerticalPanel`. When you needed to add a new task to the list, you created a proprietary widget (a `HorizontalPanel`) for it and added it to the vertical panel. You're now going to change this implementation and use `FlexTable` instead. The change is actually so easy to apply that it's a great opportunity to further enhance this list by showing the priority of each task next to its title.

    The basic idea here is simple—the tasks list itself will be a `FlexTable`, and for each new task, we'll dynamically create a new row for it in the table. The table will have three columns: a check box column, a priority column, and a title column. Listing 5-2 shows the changes you need to apply to the existing code.

Listing 5-2. *Implemeting GWTasks Task Lists Using a FlexTable*

```
public class GWTasks implements EntryPoint {
    private FlexTable tasksWidget;
    …
    public Widget createTasksWidget() {
        tasksWidget = new FlexTable(); //CHANGED
        tasksWidget.getColumnFormatter().setWidth(0, "20px");
        tasksWidget.getColumnFormatter().setWidth(1, "20px");
        tasksWidget.getColumnFormatter().setWidth(2, "100%");
        return tasksWidget;
    }
    …
    public void updateTasksList() {
        List<Task> tasks = getTasksForSelectedCategory();
        // removing all rows
        while (tasksWidget.getRowCount() > 0) {
            tasksWidget.removeRow(tasksWidget.getRowCount()-1);
        }
        // adding a row per task (row indices are zero-based)
        for (Task task : tasks) {
            int row = tasksWidget.getRowCount();
            tasksWidget.setWidget(row, 0, new CheckBox());
            String priorityName = task.getPriority().name();
            Label priorityLabel = new Label(priorityName.substring(0, 1));
            String priorityStyle = "PriorityLabel-" + priorityName.toLowerCase();
```

```
            priorityLabel.setStyleName(priorityStyle);
            tasksWidget.setWidget(row, 1, priorityLabel);
            tasksWidget.setWidget(row, 2, new Label(task.getTitle()));
        }
    }
}
```

As can be seen in Listing 5-2, you only need to change the `tasksWidget` field type to `FlexTable` and reimplement two methods. The `createTasksWidget` method creates and initializes the `FlexTable`. Using the appropriate `ColumnFormatter`, you define the width of the expected columns. The first two columns are fixed in size, as they contain the check box and the priority first letter (L for LOW, N for NORMAL, and H for HIGH). The last column is given a width of 100%, by which you tell it to expand as much as it can. The other method you change is the `updateTasksList` method. It first removes all the rows from the table and then adds a row for each task. Also note that you need to customize the style of the priority label based on the priority it represents. This enables you to display the different priority letters in different colors by just adding the code shown in Listing 5-3 to the style section in the GWTasks.html file.

Listing 5-3. *Styling the Priority Letters*

```
.PriorityLabel-normal { color: blue; }
.PriorityLabel-high { color: red; }
.PriorityLabel-low { color: orange; }
```

Now that you have the `FlexTable` displaying all the tasks, you can also enhance it with a nice table header. Strangely enough, none of the tables provided by GWT support customizing the headers directly via their API. That said, it's quite easy to work around this limitation by treating the first row of the table as the header row. Listing 5-4 shows the modified code (highlighted in bold).

Listing 5-4. *Adding a Header to the FlexTable*

```
public Widget createTasksWidget() {
    tasksWidget = new FlexTable();
    tasksWidget.getColumnFormatter().setWidth(0, "20px");
    tasksWidget.getColumnFormatter().setWidth(1, "20px");
    tasksWidget.getColumnFormatter().setWidth(2, "100%");
    Label checkHeaderLabel = new Label();
    checkHeaderLabel.setWidth("20px");
    checkHeaderLabel.setHorizontalAlignment(Label.ALIGN_CENTER);
    tasksWidget.setWidget(0, 0, checkHeaderLabel);
    Label priorityHeaderLabel = new Label("!");
    priorityHeaderLabel.setWidth("20px");
    priorityHeaderLabel.setHorizontalAlignment(Label.ALIGN_CENTER);
    tasksWidget.setWidget(0, 1, priorityHeaderLabel);
    Label titleHeaderLabel = new Label("Title");
    titleHeaderLabel.setWidth("100%");
    tasksWidget.setWidget(0, 2, titleHeaderLabel);
```

```
        tasksWidget.getRowFormatter().setStyleName(0, "TableHeader");
        return tasksWidget;
}
public void updateTasksList() {
    List<Task> tasks = getTasksForSelectedCategory();
    while (tasksWidget.getRowCount() > 1) {
        tasksWidget.removeRow(tasksWidget.getRowCount()-1);
    }
    …
}
```

One feature that neither the Grid nor the FlexTable provides out of the box is selection support. In our example, this is quite important, as we want the user to be able to select tasks from the list.

To add row selection to the task list, you need to add two extra class fields to store the currently selected row and task. You then register a ClickListener with the title label of the task that will update these fields when called. Listing 5-5 shows the required changes in the code to accomplish this.

Listing 5-5. *Adding Row Selection to the taskTable*

```
public class GWTasks implements EntryPoint {
    private FlexTable tasksWidget;
    private Task selectedTask;
    private int selectedTaskRow = -1;
    …
    public void updateTasksList() {
        List<Task> tasks = getTasksForSelectedCategory();
        while (tasksWidget.getRowCount() > 1) {
            tasksWidget.removeRow(tasksWidget.getRowCount()-1);
        }
        for (Task task : tasks) {
            addTask(task);
        }
    }
    public void addTask(final Task task) {
        int row = tasksWidget.getRowCount();
        tasksWidget.setWidget(row, 0, new CheckBox());
        String priorityName = task.getPriority().name();
        Label priorityLabel = new Label(priorityName.substring(0, 1));
        Label titleLabel = new Label(task.getTitle());
        titleLabel.addClickListener(new ClickListener() {
            public void onClick(Widget sender) {
                handleTaskRowClicked(row, task);
            }
        });
        priorityLabel.setStyleName("PriorityLabel-" + priorityName.toLowerCase());
        tasksWidget.setWidget(row, 1, priorityLabel);
        tasksWidget.setWidget(row, 2, titleLabel);
```

```
        }
        public void handleTaskRowClicked(int row, Task task) {
            if (selectedTaskRow == row) {
                selectedTaskRow = -1;
                selectedTask = null;
                tasksWidget.getRowFormatter().removeStyleName(row, "TaskRow-selected");
            } else {
                if (selectedTaskRow != -1) {
                    tasksWidget.getRowFormatter()
                            .removeStyleName(selectedTaskRow, "TaskRow-selected");
                }
                selectedTaskRow = row;
                selectedTask = task;
                tasksWidget.getRowFormatter().addStyleName(row, "TaskRow-selected");
            }
        }
        …
    }
```

For convenience, the code that adds a task to the table is extracted to a separate addTask method. Then, when creating the task, you register the appropriate ClickListener on the titleLabel, which delegates the call to the handleTaskRowClicked method. In this method, you first check whether the clicked row is already selected, in which case you unselect it. Otherwise, you mark it as selected and store it in the dedicated fields. In order to make the selection visible, the style of the selected row should be updated. A simple style configuration will just update the background color of the selected row, as shown in Listing 5-6.

Listing 5-6. *Selected Row Styles*

```
.TaskRow-selected {
    background-color: #fed789;
}
```

Climbing Trees

Well… not really climbing them, but when developing any kind of application, you often need to deal with hierarchical data structures, and in most cases you probably want to display these structures in some sort of a tree. GWT comes with a Tree widget that enables you to do exactly that. It exposes a simple API that's based on TreeItem to represent the tree nodes. Let's see how you can use this widget to enhance the categorization mechanism in our sample application.

The first thing you'll do is change the Category class so it also holds child categories. Listing 5-7 shows the required changes.

Listing 5-7. *The New Hierarchical Category Class*

```
public class Category {
    private Long id;
    private String name;
```

```
    private String description;
    private List<Category> children;
    public Category() {
        this(null, null, null);
    }
    public Category(Long id, String name, String description) {
        this.id = id;
        this.name = name;
        this.description = description;
        children = new ArrayList<Category>();
    }
    public List<Category> getChildren() {
        return children;
    }
    public void addChildCategory(Category category) {
        children.add(category);
    }
    // other gettters and setters
    …
}
```

Now that the Category class is ready, let's apply the necessary changes to the GWTasks class (see Listing 5-8).

Listing 5-8. *Using a Category Tree in GWTasks*

```
public class GWTasks implements EntryPoint {
    …
    protected Widget createCategoriesWidget() {
        Tree categoryTree = new Tree();
        categoryTree.addTreeListener(new TreeListener() {
            public void onTreeItemSelected(TreeItem item) {
                selectedCategory = ((CategoryTreeItem)item).getCategory();
                updateTasksList();
            }
            public void onTreeItemStateChanged(TreeItem item) {
            }
        });
        List<Category> categories = getAllCategories();
        for (final Category category : categories) {
            CategoryTreeItem item = createTreeItem(category);
            categoryTree.addItem(item);
        }
        return categoryTree;
    }
    protected CategoryTreeItem createTreeItem(Category category) {
        CategoryTreeItem item = new CategoryTreeItem(category);
```

```
            for (Category child : category.getChildren()) {
                item.addItem(createTreeItem(child));
            }
            return item;
        }
    protected List<Category> getAllCategories() {
        List<Category> categories = new ArrayList<Category>();
        Category work = new Category(1L, "Work", "Things at work");
        work.addChildCategory(new Category(2L, "Calls", "Make phone calls"));
        work.addChildCategory(new Category(3L, "Meetings", "Meetings to attend"));
        categories.add(work);
        Category home = new Category(4L, "Home", "Things at home");
        home.addChildCategory(new Category(5L, "Shoppings", "Things I need to buy"));
        home.addChildCategory(new Category(6L, "Bills", "Bills I need to sort"));
        categories.add(home);
        categories.add(new Category(3L, "Others", "Other things I need to do"));
        return categories;
    }
    protected class CategoryTreeItem extends TreeItem {
        public CategoryTreeItem(Category category) {
            super(category.getName());
            setTitle(category.getDescription());
            setUserObject(category);
        }
        public Category getCategory() {
            return (Category) getUserObject();
        }
    }
}
```

■**Note** For cleanup purposes, the `createCategoryRow` and `markSelected` methods can now be safely removed, as the category rows were replaced by the tree items and the selection of these items is handled by the tree widget itself.

As Listing 5-8 shows, what used to be a VerticalPanel is now a Tree. The createCategoriesWidget method first creates a Tree and registers a TreeListener on it to pick up the selection events. This enables you to change the displayed tasks whenever a new TreeItem is selected. You then iterate over all categories, and for each one, build the appropriate TreeItem by calling createTreeItem method. This recursive method builds a TreeItem hierarchy that reflects the given Category hierarchy. Note the use of the CategoryTreeItem. This is an extended TreeItem class that associates categories with their representing tree nodes. You also had to change the getAllCategories method, which now generates a hierarchy of categories (instead of the flat category list it used to generate). Figure 5-2 shows the new category tree in action.

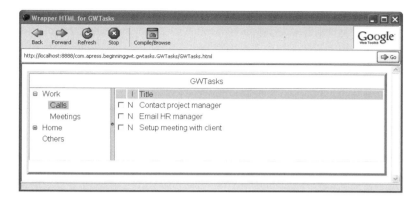

Figure 5-2. *The category tree in action*

■**Tip** By default, the tree doesn't have any UI indication of the currently selected node. You can fix that either by using one of GWT's predefined themes or by explicitly setting the background-color property in the `.gwt-Tree .getTreeItem-selected` CSS class.

Using PopupPanel and DialogBox

Pop-up panels have always played a major role in GUI applications. The simple context menu that appears on the screen when you right-click is one kind of pop-up, and the one that you're probably most familiar with. For many years, although technically possible, this basic UI feature was overlooked in standard web-based applications. But it seems to be making a comeback as part of the Web 2.0 trend. Recognizing this, GWT supports pop-up panels out of the box via the PopupPanel widget.

PopupPanel

A PopupPanel is a panel that's normally hidden and can pop up on the screen when triggered by an event (usually triggered by user action). There are many use cases for such functionality, ranging from customized tool tips to dedicated dialog boxes. To illustrate how a pop-up can be used, we'll create a simple progress indicator.

So what exactly is a progress indicator? It's often the case that a certain action triggered by the user takes some time to complete. Without any indication of this process, the user might be left puzzled as the application has stopped responding. This is where progress indicators enter the picture. In desktop applications, they usually take the form of a progress bar that's displayed as a pop-up. In RIAs, they can have many shapes and forms, and are mostly used to indicate communication with the server. In fact, the asynchronous nature of Ajax requires such an indication, as almost every action taken in the application requires communicating with the server and waiting for its response.

For our example, we'll create a simple progress indicator, named `MessageProgressIndicator`, which will be part of a new sample application named `PopupSample`. It's inspired by the indicators used in most of Google's online applications, and works by showing a small message at the top of the screen. Listing 5-9 shows the implementation of this class.

Listing 5-9. *The MessageProgressIndicator Class*

```
public class MessageProgressIndicator extends PopupPanel {
    private Label messageLabel;
    public MessageProgressIndicator() {
        this("Loading...");
    }
    public MessageProgressIndicator(String message) {
        super(false, true);
        messageLabel = new Label(message);
        messageLabel.setStyleName("Label");
        setWidget(messageLabel);
        setPopupPositionAndShow(new PositionCallback() {
            public void setPosition(int offsetWidth, int offsetHeight) {
                int x = Window.getClientWidth()/2 - offsetWidth/2;
                setPopupPosition(x, 0);
            }
        });
        setStyleName("MessageProgressIndicator");
    }
    public void setMessage(String message) {
        messageLabel.setText(message);
    }
}
```

The `MessageProgressIndicator` extends `PopupPanel`. The constructor accepts a message that this indicator should display. It then calls the superconstructor of the `PopupPanel` with parameters indicating that this pop-up should be modal and shouldn't automatically hide when the user clicks outside its boundaries (which is a typical use case for a context menu). Next, a label is initialized and set as the main wrapped widget of this pop-up. This label will display the message when the pop-up is shown. The `setPopupPositionAndShow` method is used to register a callback with the `PopupPanel` that will be called just before it's shown. Using this callback, it's possible to adjust the position of the pop-up based on its size (here we position it at the center top of the screen). Notice that the style names are also set on both the label and the pop-up panel. This will enable you to customize its look on the screen just by adding the following styles in PopupSample.html (see Listing 5-10). Listing 5-11 shows the `PopupSample` that demonstrates how our indicator works.

Listing 5-10. *The MessageProgressIndicator Styles*

```
.MessageProgressIndicator .Label {
    padding-left: 5px;
    padding-right: 5px;
```

```
        padding-top: 2px;
        padding-bottom: 2px;
        background-color: #ffffcc;
        font-size: 14px;
        color: black;
}
```

Listing 5-11. *The PopupSample Entry Point Class*

```
public class PopupSample implements EntryPoint {
    public void onModuleLoad() {
        Button button = new Button("Show Indicator", new ClickListener() {
            public void onClick(Widget sender) {
                final MessageProgressIndicator indicator =
                        new MessageProgressIndicator();
                indicator.show();
                Timer timer = new Timer() {
                    public void run() {
                        indicator.hide();
                    }
                };
                timer.schedule(3000);
            }
        });
        RootPanel.get().add(button);
    }
}
```

Listing 5-11 adds a button to the screen that, when clicked, creates and shows our indicator. The Timer is a special class provided by GWT that enables you to schedule future events. In our case, we use it to automatically hide the indicator after three seconds (3000 milliseconds).

Using DialogBox

The progress indicator we've just developed, although quite useful, is a somewhat passive popup. Sometimes, you may wish to show more interactive pop-ups through which the user can provide input to the application. This will mostly be the case where the input from the user doesn't fit anywhere else in the application UI design. When such a requirement is encountered, DialogBox should be considered as a good starting point.

A DialogBox is basically a PopupPanel with a title bar, which is usually used to describe its content and also enables the user to drag it on the screen. Apart from that, there's not much difference between DialogBox and PopupPanel. To learn how it can be used, we'll create a dialog box that shows a form to the user where he can create or edit categories. We'll implement a class named CategoryFormDialogBox that extends DialogBox and add all the required form widgets to it as the content. Listing 5-12 shows a snippet of this class. In the interests of brevity, we left out all details related to the actual construction of the form. We encourage you, though, to look at the full version of this dialog, which can be found in the code accompanying this book.

Listing 5-12. *The CategoryFormDialogBox Class*

```
public class CategoryFormDialogBox extends DialogBox {
    ...
    private final Category category;
    private CategoryFormDialogBox(Category category, boolean editMode) {
        super(false, true);
        setText("Category Form");
        this.category = category;
        VerticalPanel main = new VerticalPanel();
        ... // here adding all form elements
        main.setStyleName("DialogContent");
        setWidget(main);
    }
    // called when the submitButton is clicked
    protected void handleSubmit() {
        if (validate()) {
            category.setName(nameField.getText().trim());
            category.setDescription(descriptionField.getText().trim());
            Window.alert("Category: " + category);
            hide();
        }
    }
    // called when the cancelButton is clicked
    protected void handleCancel() {
        hide();
    }
    ...
}
```

The main thing to note about the code in Listing 5-12 is that this custom dialog box is initialized in much the same way as the MessageProgressIndicator pop-up, meaning we call the superconstructor indicating that this dialog should be modal and not hide automatically. The only difference is that we also set the Category Form text to be displayed as the title of this dialog. Also note that we set a style name on its main content widget, which enables us to apply padding around it (for aesthetic reasons). After the form is submitted successfully or canceled, we call the hide method to close the dialog.

To see this dialog in action, you can create a simple sample application like the one shown in Listing 5-13.

Listing 5-13. *The DialogBoxSample Application*

```
public class DialogBoxSample implements EntryPoint {
    public void onModuleLoad() {
        Button button = new Button("Show Form", new ClickListener() {
            public void onClick(Widget sender) {
                CategoryFormDialogBox dialog = new CategoryFormDialogBox();
```

```
                dialog.center();
                dialog.show();
            }
        });
        RootPanel.get().add(button);
    }
}
```

Later on, we'll see how the `CategoryFormDialogBox` can be incorporated into our GWTasks sample application. In fact, in the final version of this application, all forms (except the login form) will be embedded in dialog boxes. We'll also try to use the `MessageProgressIndicator`, but these ideas are all for later on, as we still have a lot of ground to cover before we get there.

Componentizing the Code Base

When we introduced the basic GWT components and panels in the previous chapter, we took the approach of creating a new GWT application for every new component you learned. The main reason for doing that was to keep the code as clean as possible for you to learn from, while still being able to run it and see the appropriate visual results. We finally ended up with multiple applications, where each is responsible for some part of the overall functionality in the GWTasks application.

Naturally, when creating the real application, all this functionality needs to be incorporated within it. In our example, this means that the task form, category form, user registration form, and the main page where the categories and tasks are shown all need to be part of one GWT application. Furthermore, all these distinct parts need to fit into the natural usage flow of the application. For example, when the user enters the application for the first time, she should either log in using her known credentials or alternatively have the option of registering herself. This obviously means that the login screen needs to be in some way associated with the user registration form. The same idea applies to the main categories and tasks views, where the logged-in user should be able to view all her tasks and be able to add new tasks and/or categories using the appropriate forms.

Incorporating all this in one application can be done in many ways. In fact, if we'd really wanted to torture you, we could just have created an application based on one entry point class that would have incorporated all the logic, widgets, and panels of the application. Obviously, a better approach would be to leverage Java as an object-oriented language and split these different pieces of code into the appropriate self-contained components. If GWT provides a set of well-defined components, there's no reason why you wouldn't be able to create a few of your own.

Indeed, there are several ways of writing your own components, two of which we'll cover in the following sections. The first is by directly extending GWT panels, and the second by creating *composites* (don't worry if you don't understand this term; by the end of this chapter you will).

Extending GWT Panels

Extending a GWT panel is as easy as extending any other class in Java. To show how it's done, we'll use the `TaskForm` example application from the previous chapter. If you recall, in the current version of this application, all form elements are directly bound to their appropriate positions in the hosting HTML file using the RootPanel. In the new version, we want to encapsulate all these elements within one panel, namely the TaskFormPanel. Once we achieve that, we'll only need to bind this panel to the host HTML in the proper position. But before we can go ahead and apply changes in the code, we still need to figure out which panel to extend.

As you know by now, GWT comes with many existing panels, each with a different purpose and layout mechanism. In the original application, we applied the layout within the hosting HTML file, and now we need to translate this layout to GWT code using the appropriate panels. As it turns out so often in programming, there are many ways of achieving the same layout—in this case, by using a different set of panels. For our example, we'll keep it simple and use the HorizontalPanel and VerticalPanel, which you're already familiar with. Figure 5-3 shows a hybrid of a wireframe and a screenshot that describes how this can be done.

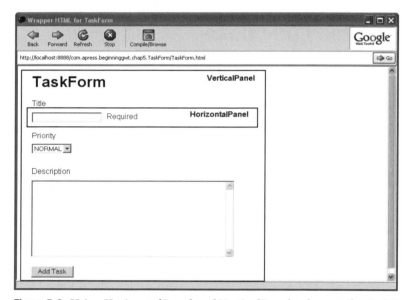

Figure 5-3. *Using HorizontalPanel and VerticalPanel to lay out the TaskForm*

As you can see in Figure 5-3, the top-level panel is a VerticalPanel, which is a good candidate to be the extended panel. To apply the changes to the code, we have to take the following five steps:

1. Create a new TaskFormPanel class that extends VerticalPanel.

2. Move all the code from the original TaskForm class to the TaskFormPanel class.

3. Remove all the RootPanel bindings and instead add the elements to the containing panel.

4. Change the host HTML to only contain a placeholder for the TaskFormPanel.

5. Change the TaskForm class to create a new TaskFormPanel and bind it to the appropriate RootPanel.

First let's look at the `TaskFormPanel` code (shown in Listing 5-14).

Listing 5-14. *The New TaskFormPanel*

```
public class TaskFormPanel extends VerticalPanel {
    private ListBox priorityField;
    private TextBox titleField;
    private Label titleErrorLabel;
    private TextArea descriptionField;
    private Button submitButton;
    public TaskFormPanel() {
        add(new Label("Title"));
        HorizontalPanel titleRow = new HorizontalPanel();
        titleRow.add(titleField = new TextBox());
        titleRow.add(titleErrorLabel = createErrorLabel());
        add(titleRow);
        add(createVGap("10px"));
        add(new Label("Priority"));
        add(priorityField = new ListBox(false));
        priorityField.setVisibleItemCount(1);
        priorityField.addItem("LOW");
        priorityField.addItem("NORMAL");
        priorityField.addItem("HIGH");
        priorityField.setItemSelected(1, true);
        add(createVGap("10px"));
        add(new Label("Description"));
        add(descriptionField = new TextArea());
        descriptionField.setVisibleLines(10);
        descriptionField.setCharacterWidth(50);
        add(createVGap("10px"));
        add(submitButton = new Button("Add Task"));
        submitButton.addClickListener(new ClickListener() {
            public void onClick(Widget widget) {
                if (validateForm()) {
                    TaskInfo task = new TaskInfo();
                    task.setTitle(titleField.getText());
                    task.setDescription(descriptionField.getText());
                    TaskInfo.Priority priority = resolvePriority();
                    task.setPriority(priority);
                    addTask(task);
                }
            }
        });
    }
```

```
    // creates a "hollow" widget with a fixed height
    protected Widget createVGap(String height) {
        Label row = new Label();
        row.setHeight(height);
        return row;
    }
    ...
}
```

As you can see, all fields and most methods were copied unchanged from the original TaskForm class. The main change consists of altering and removing the code from the onModuleLoad method and putting it into the constructor of our new panel. Note, as mentioned previously, that the RootPanel binding was removed and instead the widgets are added as children of the new panel. We recommend that you compare this implementation with Figure 5-1 and see the one-to-one mapping between the two. We even use an empty widget to simulate the appropriate vertical gap between the widgets.

Now that we have our TaskFormPanel ready, the only thing we still need to do is to create it and bind it to the base HTML. This can all be done within the onModuleLoad method of the TaskForm class (see Listing 5-15).

Listing 5-15. *The Narrowed-down TaskForm Class*

```
public class TaskForm implements EntryPoint {
    private TaskFormPanel taskFormPanel;
    public void onModuleLoad() {
        taskFormPanel = new TaskFormPanel();
        RootPanel.get("formPanel").add(taskFormPanel);
    }
}
```

Here we can see that the TaskFormPanel is created and bound to the host HTML under the formPanel element (see Listing 5-16).

Listing 5-16. *The Narrowed-down TaskForm.html*

```
<html>
    ...
    <body>
        <h1>TaskForm</h1>
        <div id="formPanel"/>
    </body>
</html>
```

That's it! When running this application, you'll get the same result as you got with the previous version. You've successfully created your first GWT component.

Although it works well, this approach of extending panels has a slight "smell"[1] in terms of API design. We now have a separate component for the task form panel, but unfortunately it's not self-contained. What does being "self-contained" mean and why is it important? Being self-contained basically means that the component has full control of its internal state, and this can only be achieved by having full control over the API it exposes. It can still be open for extensions, but it should always be aware of these extensions.

Looking at our current implementation of the `TaskFormPanel`, it exposes not only its own public methods but also those of the extended panel, which in our case is the `VerticalPanel`. This means that in theory, someone can use this component wrong (for example, add yet another component to it via the `add(Widget)` method) and thus break it. It's safe to say that the intended abstraction of a task form panel leaked via our concrete implementation.[2] An alternative approach is to prefer object composition to the class inheritance model, for which GWT provides special support.

Using Composites

Composites are core GWT widgets that have only one purpose: to help apply the composition over inheritance model when creating new custom components.

A composite is basically a widget that's composed of other widgets (hence the name). This definition implies that a composite will hold a hierarchy of widgets having one root, which is typically a panel. Because it only has to know about that root component, the API that `Composite` exposes is limited and thus safer to extend without breaking any abstraction.

In practice, creating a composite component is as easy as extending the `Composite` class and initializing its internal state and structure. In the following sections, we'll start by breaking our GWTasks application into separate components by extending each component from the `Composite` class. We'll finish by showing that composites are also a great mechanism for developing generic (application-agnostic) reusable components.

Decomposing GWTasks

Looking at the wireframe diagram from Chapter 4 (Figure 4-5), it's obvious that the GWTasks application can be broken down into four major separate components:

- `HeaderPane`—responsible for displaying the title and potentially exposing other functionality (such as a logout button).

- `StatusBarPane`—responsible for displaying messages to the user.

- `CategoryPane`—responsible for displaying the category tree.

- `TaskPane`—responsible for displaying the tasks of the currently selected category.

Each of these panes has its own responsibilities and roles within the overall application, and our main goal is to break down the `GWTasks` class and move each piece of functionality to its appropriate pane.

---

1. See "CodeSmell" by Martin Fowler—http://martinfowler.com/bliki/CodeSmell.html
2. See "The Law of Leaky Abstractions" by Joel Spolsky—http://www.joelonsoftware.com/articles/LeakyAbstractions.html

Implementing HeaderPane and StatusBarPane

We'll start our breakdown with the HeaderPane and StatusBarPane, as they're quite simple to implement. Listings 5-17 and 5-18 show their implementations.

Listing 5-17. *The HeaderPane Class*

```
public class HeaderPane extends Composite {
    private Label title;
    public HeaderPane(String titleText) {
        title = new Label(titleText);
        initWidget(title);
    }
    public void setTitleText(String titleText) {
        title.setText(titleText);
    }
}
```

Listing 5-18. *The StatusBarPane Class*

```
public class StatusBarPane extends Composite {
    private Label messageLabel;
    public StatusBarPane() {
        messageLabel = new Label();
        initWidget(messageLabel);
    }
    public void setMessage(String message) {
        messageLabel.setText(message);
    }
}
```

When creating a composite, it's necessary to inform the parent Composite class which widget it's composed from. This is done by calling the initWidget method within the constructor (failing to call this method will cause a compile-time error). In both our previous cases, the panes are composed of single Label widgets. Now let's see how these new components can be used within the GWTasks class (see Listing 5-19).

Listing 5-19. *The GWTasks Class Using the HeaderPane and StatusBarPane*

```
public class GWTasks implements EntryPoint {
    ...
    public void onModuleLoad() {
        DockPanel mainPanel = new DockPanel();
        mainPanel.setBorderWidth(5);
        mainPanel.setSize("100%", "100%");
        HeaderPane headerPane = new HeaderPane("GWTasks");
        mainPanel.add(headerPane, DockPanel.NORTH);
        mainPanel.setCellHeight(headerPane, "30px");
        mainPanel.setCellHorizontalAlignment(headerPane, DockPanel.ALIGN_CENTER);
        mainPanel.setCellVerticalAlignment(headerPane, DockPanel.ALIGN_MIDDLE);
```

```
        StatusBarPane statusBarPane = new StatusBarPane();
        mainPanel.add(statusBarPane, DockPanel.SOUTH);
        mainPanel.setCellHeight(statusBarPane, "25px");
        mainPanel.setCellHorizontalAlignment(statusBarPane, DockPanel.ALIGN_CENTER);
        mainPanel.setCellVerticalAlignment(statusBarPane, DockPanel.ALIGN_MIDDLE);
        ...
    }
    ...
}
```

Implementing TaskPane

We'll now move on to implement the TaskPane. This pane is slightly more complex to implement, as it encapsulates a bit more functionality than the HeaderPane and StatusBarPane.
Nonetheless, we already have this functionality implemented within the GWTasks class. Since
the sole purpose of the TaskPane is to show a list of tasks for a specific category, we can start by
drawing a skeleton of the API this pane exposes (see Listing 5-20).

Listing 5-20. *An Initial TaskPane Skeleton*

```
public class TaskPane extends Composite {
    public void reset() {
        reset(null);
    }
    public void reset(Category category) {
        ...
    }
}
```

Besides the concrete implementation of the class, the reset methods are perhaps the most
important ones. All these methods should do is reset the viewed task list to show only the tasks
of the given category, or no tasks at all if the category is null. Later on, you'll see how these
methods are being used by the CategoryPane to reset the view whenever a new category is
selected.

Now that the skeleton is defined, you can start moving all functionality related to the task
table into this new component. Here are the steps that you need to take to complete this task:

1. Define class fields that will hold the FlexTable (which displays the tasks) and the currently selected row and task.

2. Move the code that initializes the FlexTable from the createTasksWidget method in the
   GWTasks class to the constructor of the TaskPane.

3. Call the Composite's initWidget with the FlexTable widget.

4. Move the code from the updateTasksList method in GWTasks class to the reset method
   of the TaskPane class.

5. Move (and slightly modify) the code that generates the dummy tasks for a given
   category.

Listing 5-21 shows the TaskPane class after taking all these steps.

Listing 5-21. *The TaskPane Class*

```
public class TaskPane extends Composite {
    private FlexTable taskTable;
    private int selectedRow = -1;
    private Task selectedTask;
    public TaskPane() {
        taskTable = new FlexTable();
        taskTable.getColumnFormatter().setWidth(0, "20px");
        taskTable.getColumnFormatter().setWidth(1, "20px");
        taskTable.getColumnFormatter().setWidth(2, "100%");
        Label checkHeaderLabel = new Label();
        checkHeaderLabel.setWidth("20px");
        checkHeaderLabel.setHorizontalAlignment(Label.ALIGN_CENTER);
        taskTable.setWidget(0, 0, checkHeaderLabel);
        Label priorityHeaderLabel = new Label("!");
        priorityHeaderLabel.setWidth("20px");
        priorityHeaderLabel.setHorizontalAlignment(Label.ALIGN_CENTER);
        taskTable.setWidget(0, 1, priorityHeaderLabel);
        Label titleHeaderLabel = new Label("Title");
        titleHeaderLabel.setWidth("100%");
        taskTable.setWidget(0, 2, titleHeaderLabel);
        taskTable.getRowFormatter().setStyleName(0, "TableHeader");
        initWidget(taskTable);
    }
    public void reset() {
        reset(null);
    }
    public void reset(Category category) {
        while (taskTable.getRowCount() > 1) {
            taskTable.removeRow(taskTable.getRowCount()-1);
        }
        this.category = category;
        if (category != null) {
            List<Task> tasks = getTasksForCategory(category);
            for (Task task : tasks) {
                addTask(task);
            }
        }
    }
    protected void addTask(Task task) {
        int row = taskTable.getRowCount();
        taskTable.setWidget(row, 0, new CheckBox());
        String priorityName = task.getPriority().name();
        Label priorityLabel = new Label(priorityName.substring(0, 1));
```

```
            priorityLabel.addClickListener(new ClickListener() {
                public void onClick(Widget sender) {
                    handleTaskRowClicked(row, task)
                }
            });

            priorityLabel.setStyleName("PriorityLabel-" + priorityName.toLowerCase());
            taskTable.setWidget(row, 1, priorityLabel);
            taskTable.setWidget(row, 2, new Label(task.getTitle()));
        }
    public void handleTaskRowClicked(int row, Task task) {
        HTMLTable.RowFormatter rowFormatter = taskTable.getRowFormatter();
        if (selectedRow == row) {
            selectedRow = -1;
            selectedTask = null;
             rowFormatter.removeStyleName(row, "TaskRow-selected");
        } else {
            if (selectedRow != -1) {
                rowFormatter.removeStyleName(selectedRow, "TaskRow-selected");
            }
            selectedRow = row;
            selectedTask = task;
            taskTable.getRowFormatter().addStyleName(row, "TaskRow-selected");
        }
    }
    protected List<Task> getTasksForCategory(Category category) {
        // return dummy task list
        ...
    }
}
```

Now you can clean up the GWTasks class from all table related code and instead make it use the new TaskPane (see Listing 5-22).

Listing 5-22. *The GWTaks Class Using the New TaskPane*

```
public class GWTasks implements EntryPoint {
    private Category selectedCategory;
    private TaskPane taskPane;
    public void onModuleLoad() {
        ...
        HorizontalSplitPanel categoriesAndTasks = new HorizontalSplitPanel();
        categoriesAndTasks.setSplitPosition("150px");
        taskPane = new TaskPane();
        categoriesAndTasks.setRightWidget(taskPane);
        Widget categories = createCategoriesWidget();
        categoriesAndTasks.setLeftWidget(categories);
```

```
        mainPanel.add(categoriesAndTasks, DockPanel.CENTER);
        RootPanel.get("main").add(mainPanel);
    }
    ...
    public void updateTasksList() {
        taskPane.reset(selectedCategory);
    }
    ...
}
```

Implementing CategoryPane

The final task in the GWTasks class breakdown is to create the CategoryPane. This can be done in much the same way as the TaskPane. Let's first define the skeleton of this class (see Listing 5-23).

Listing 5-23. *An Initial CategoryPane Skeleton*

```
public class CategoryPane extends Composite {
    private TaskPane taskPane;
    public CategoryPane(TaskPane taskPane) {
        this.taskPane = taskPane;
    }
}
```

As you can see, the CategoryPane needs to know about the TaskPane. This way, whenever a new category is selected, the reset method of the TaskPane can be called to refresh the tasks list.

Next, just as we did with the TaskPane, we'll define the steps needed in order to move the functionality of the category list from the GWTasks class to the CategoryPane class:

1. Create a class field to hold the category Tree.

2. Move the code in the createCategoriesWidget method in GWTasks class to the CategoryPane constructor.

3. Move all related methods and inner classes that the code that was moved depends on (the createTreeItem and getAllCategories methods and the CategoryTreeItem inner class).

Listing 5-24 shows the CategoryPane class implementation after all these steps have been taken.

Listing 5-24. *The CategoryPane Class*

```
public class CategoryPane extends Composite {
    private TaskPane taskPane;
    private Tree tree;
    public CategoryPane(TaskPane taskPane) {
        this.taskPane = taskPane;
        tree = new Tree();
```

```
        tree.addTreeListener(new TreeListener() {
            public void onTreeItemSelected(TreeItem item) {
                Category category = ((CategoryTreeItem)item).getCategory();
                CategoryPane.this.taskPane.reset(category);
            }
            public void onTreeItemStateChanged(TreeItem item) {
            }
        });
        List<Category> categories = getAllCategories();
        for (final Category category : categories) {
            CategoryTreeItem item = createTreeItem(category);
            tree.addItem(item);
        }
        initWidget(tree);
    }
    protected CategoryTreeItem createTreeItem(Category category) {
        CategoryTreeItem item = new CategoryTreeItem(category);
        for (Category child : category.getChildren()) {
            item.addItem(createTreeItem(child));
        }
        return item;
    }
    protected List<Category> getAllCategories() {
        // generate dummy category list
        ...
    }
    protected class CategoryTreeItem extends TreeItem {
        public CategoryTreeItem(Category category) {
            super(category.getName());
            setTitle(category.getDescription());
            setUserObject(category);
        }
        public Category getCategory() {
            return (Category) getUserObject();
        }
    }
}
```

Note how the reset method of the TaskPane is called when a selection event is handled by the registered TreeListener.

And once more, we can clean up the GWTasks class and make it use the new CategoryPane. The GWTasks breakdown process is done, and the final version of this class is shown in Listing 5-25.

Listing 5-25. *GWTasks Class After the Component Breakdown*

```
public class GWTasks implements EntryPoint {
    public void onModuleLoad() {
        DockPanel mainPanel = new DockPanel();
        mainPanel.setBorderWidth(5);
        mainPanel.setSize("100%", "100%");
        HeaderPane headerPane = new HeaderPane("GWTasks");
        mainPanel.add(headerPane, DockPanel.NORTH);
        mainPanel.setCellHeight(headerPane, "30px");
        mainPanel.setCellHorizontalAlignment(headerPane, DockPanel.ALIGN_CENTER);
        mainPanel.setCellVerticalAlignment(headerPane, DockPanel.ALIGN_MIDDLE);
        StatusBarPane statusBarPane = new StatusBarPane();
        mainPanel.add(statusBarPane, DockPanel.SOUTH);
        mainPanel.setCellHeight(statusBarPane, "25px");
        mainPanel.setCellHorizontalAlignment(statusBarPane, DockPanel.ALIGN_CENTER);
        mainPanel.setCellVerticalAlignment(statusBarPane, DockPanel.ALIGN_MIDDLE);
        HorizontalSplitPanel categoriesAndTasks = new HorizontalSplitPanel();
        categoriesAndTasks.setSplitPosition("150px");
        TaskPane taskPane = new TaskPane();
        categoriesAndTasks.setRightWidget(taskPane);
        CategoryPane categoryPane = new CategoryPane(taskPane);
        categoriesAndTasks.setLeftWidget(categoryPane);
        mainPanel.add(categoriesAndTasks, DockPanel.CENTER);
        RootPanel.get("main").add(mainPanel);
    }
}
```

Now it's much easier to see the advantages of breaking the application into components. Not only is the code base cleaner and easier to understand, but the clear separation of responsibilities and roles between the components makes it easier to maintain and extend in future. This separation of responsibilities is commonly referred to as the *Separation of Concerns (SoC) principle*. It's important that you be well familiar with this principle, as it will follow us as we move along with the application refactoring.

But before we do that, let's enhance our application a little more with yet another component. This time, the component isn't tightly related to our application, but rather is generic. We want to show you that it's possible and even desirable to write generic components that can be reused in any GWT application.

THE SEPARATION OF CONCERNS PRINCIPLE

The Separation of Concerns (SoC) principle refers to the need to break complex problems into smaller, less complex and nonoverlapping subproblems, where each deals with well-defined aspects of the original problem. In software development, this is usually applied in the context of system or application architecture, where it's broken into distinct modules and components where each is responsible for specific requirements and/or features. Applying this principle correctly leads to the development of extensible and reusable pieces of software, which eventually account for the robustness, maintainability, and extensibility of the system or application as a whole.

Creating the TitledPanel Component

With our current GWTasks application, when users first see the main screen, they may be a bit puzzled about the purpose of the left and right panes. You, as the developer of this application, obviously know that the left pane shows the categories and the right one shows the tasks, but it would be nice if you could somehow communicate this knowledge to the novice user. This can be done by simply adding a title at the top of each pane describing its purpose. Of course, you could add this directly to the `CategoryPane` and `TaskPane` classes, but this kind of functionality is more generic and is better implemented in a generic manner. This is why we choose to implement a new generic component named `TitledPanel`, which you can then reuse in both panes.

■**Note** GWT already comes with a panel named `CaptionPanel`, which basically represents a `<FIELDSET>` element in HTML. As you'll see, our `TitledPanel` differs quite a bit from it in both its design and functionality.

Let's start off by thinking a bit more about the exact requirements of the new `TitledPanel` component:

- It should be possible to wrap any widget inside it.

- It should be possible to update the title text on demand.

- It should be relatively easy to customize its look.

This set of requirements is enough to get us started. We'll begin by defining the skeleton of the class based on these requirements (just as we did with the `TaskPane` and `CategoryPane` in the previous section). Listing 5-26 shows this initial skeleton.

Listing 5-26. *An Initial TitledPanel Skeleton*

```
public class TitledPanel extends Composite {
    public TitledPanel() {
        this("");
    }
    public TitledPanel(String titleText) {
        this(titleText, null);
    }
    public TitledPanel(String titleText, Widget content) {
    }
    public void setTitleText(String text) {
    }
    public void setContent(Widget content) {
    }
}
```

Defining the skeleton is just the first step to communicating what we want the `TitledPanel` to support. Note also the use of overloaded constructors. When developing reusable components, it's important to make them as simple as possible to use; providing different flavors of constructors is just one way to make the users of the component happy.

The next step is to figure out how to implement this panel internally. Since we want our title to be displayed on top of the main content, the immediate candidate to support this sort of layout is the DockPanel. The problem with this is that the DockPanel has an internal mechanism to manage the size of the different regions. Since we want to have control over it, a better solution would be to use the Grid panel. We can thus define a Grid panel with two rows and one column. The title will be placed in the top cell; the content will be placed on the bottom one. Listing 5-27 shows how this can be implemented.

Listing 5-27. *The TitledPanel Class*

```
public class TitledPanel extends Composite {
    private final static int TITLE_ROW = 0;
    private final static int CONTENT_ROW = 1;
    private Label titleLabel;
    private Grid grid;
    // overloaded constructors
    …
    public TitledPanel(String titleText, Widget content) {
        titleLabel = new Label(titleText);
        grid = new Grid(2, 1);
        grid.setBorderWidth(0);
        grid.setCellPadding(0);
        grid.setCellSpacing(0);
        grid.setWidget(TITLE_ROW, 0, titleLabel);
        grid.getCellFormatter().setWidth(TITLE_ROW, 0, "100%");
        if (content != null) {
            grid.setWidget(CONTENT_ROW, 0, content);
        }
        grid.getCellFormatter().setWidth(CONTENT_ROW, 0, "100%");
        grid.getCellFormatter().setHeight(CONTENT_ROW, 0, "100%");
        initWidget(grid);
    }
    public void setTitleText(String text) {
        titleLabel.setText(text);
    }
    public void setContent(Widget content) {
        grid.setWidget(CONTENT_ROW, 0, content);
    }
    public void setContentVerticalAlignment(
            HasVerticalAlignment.VerticalAlignmentConstant alignment) {
        grid.getCellFormatter().setVerticalAlignment(1, 0, alignment);
    }
}
```

In our current implementation, the TitledPanel simply holds a Label for the title and a Grid with two cell positions, one on top of the other. The width of the label is set so it will spread out as wide as possible. The content cell is also customized so it will try to stretch as much as possible both vertically and horizontally. Also note that using the setContentVerticalAlignment, we enable the user of this component to define the alignment of the content. It's possible that certain scenarios might require the content to be centered while other scenarios require it to be aligned to the top or the bottom. It's important to foresee all the different scenarios in which users will want to use your component.

Although we can now start using our TitledPanel, we're still not quite done with it. We have one more requirement to meet—it should be relatively easy to customize its look.

When developing generic and reusable components, it's important to make them as customizable as possible. The users of your components either can't or don't want to hack into your implementation just to change the background color. This is where CSS styles play a major role. By now, you've seen quite a lot of examples of how you can customize the look of almost any GWT widget. It's time to give the users of your component the same level of flexibility.

The GWT designers really thought through how to support and apply CSS styles to widgets, and they came up with a nice technique that's used by all GWT widgets. The basic idea behind this technique is that when a component is compiled to HTML, its hierarchy of subcomponents is reflected in the generated HTML structure. If we take our TitledPanel as an example, the component itself will be translated to a <DIV> element, under which you'll find a <TABLE> element (the compiled Grid), where the table cells hold other <DIV> elements representing the Label and the content. This enables you to set style names for each component, and customization can be done using nested CSS classes. In our case, we can give the TitledPanel a style named "TitlePanel", the title Label a style named "TitleText", and the grid cell holding the content a style named "Content". Listing 5-28 shows how these style names can be set in our TitledPanel component, and Listing 5-29 shows how you can use these style names to customize the look of the component.

Listing 5-28. *The TitledPanel Class with Customizable Styles*

```
public class TitledPanel extends Composite {
    private final static String STYLE_NAME = "TitlePanel";
    private final static String LABEL_STYLE_NAME = "TitleText";
    private final static String CONTENT_STYLE_NAME = "Content";
    …
    public TitledPanel(String titleText, Widget content) {
        titleLabel = new Label(titleText);
        titleLabel.setStyleName(LABEL_STYLE_NAME);
        grid = new Grid(2, 1);
        grid.setBorderWidth(0);
        grid.setCellPadding(0);
        grid.setCellSpacing(0);
        grid.setWidget(TITLE_ROW, 0, titleLabel);
        grid.getCellFormatter().setWidth(TITLE_ROW, 0, "100%");
        if (content != null) {
            grid.setWidget(CONTENT_ROW, 0, content);
        }
        grid.getCellFormatter().setWidth(CONTENT_ROW, 0, "100%");
        grid.getCellFormatter().setHeight(CONTENT_ROW, 0, "100%");
```

```
            grid.getCellFormatter().setStyleName(CONTENT_ROW, 0, CONTENT_STYLE_NAME);
            initWidget(grid);
            setStyleName(STYLE_NAME);
        }
        ...
}
```

■**Note** When setting the style name on the composite itself, it's required that you call `initWidget` first before actually setting the style. An alternative would be to set the style on the topmost widget of the component (in our case the `Grid`).

Listing 5-29. *Setting the Styles in the GWTasks.html File*

```
.TitledPanel .TitleText {
    padding-left: 5px;
    background-color: #e3dede;
}
.TitledPanel .Content {
    border: 1px silver inset;
}
```

Now we're ready to use our new component. Listings 5-30 and 5-31 show how we can use it within our `TaskPane` and `CategoryPane`.

Listing 5-30. *Using the TitledPanel Within the TaskPane*

```
public class TaskPane extends Composite {
    ...
    public TaskPane() {
        ...
        taskTable.getRowFormatter().setStyleName(0, "TableHeader");
        TitledPanel titledPanel = new TitledPanel("Tasks", taskTable);
        titledPanel.setContentVerticalAlignment(HasVerticalAlignment.ALIGN_TOP);
        titledPanel.setSize("100%", "100%");
        SimplePanel main = new SimplePanel();
        main.setWidget(titledPanel);
        initWidget(main);
        setStyleName("TaskPane");
    }
    ...
}
```

Listing 5-31. *Using the TitledPanel Within the CategoryPane*

```
public class CategoryPane extends Composite {
    ...
    public CategoryPane() {
```

```
    ...
    TitledPanel titledPanel = new TitledPanel("Categories", tree);
    titledPanel.setContentVerticalAlignment(HasVerticalAlignment.ALIGN_TOP);
    titledPanel.setSize("100%", "100%");
    SimplePanel main = new SimplePanel();
    main.setWidget(titledPanel);
    initWidget(main);
    setStyleName("CategoryPane");
  }
  ...
}
```

As you can see, using the new `TitledPanel` has minimal impact on the existing code base. The only changes we had to make were to wrap the main widgets in these panes (the tree of the `CategoryPane` and the table of the `TasksPane`) with new `TitlePanels`, each with the appropriate title text. Note that we then wrap the titled panel with yet another `SimplePanel`. The `SimplePanel` is another GWT panel that just serves as a wrapper around a single widget. This wrapping enables you to set different style names for the different panes. If we hadn't done so (and passed the titled panel as the argument to the `initWidget` method), each titled panel in the different pane would have a different style name, and we would have lost the default styles we've just configured. Now, not only do we still gain from the default styles, but we can still customize each titled pane using nested styles (as shown in Listing 5-32).

Listing 5-32. *Customizing the TitledPanel of the CategoryPane*

```
.CategoryPane .TitledPanel {
    /* custom style */
}
```

Figure 5-4 shows the GWTasks application screenshot using the `TitledPanel` in both panes.

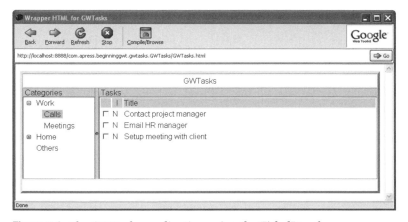

Figure 5-4. *The GWTasks application using the TitledPanel*

Adding a Toolbar

One thing we've ignored so far in our discussion of the GWTasks application is the mechanism by which users will be able to add, remove, and edit categories and tasks. We've seen how using GWT form widgets, it's possible to design forms for these purposes, but we never took the time to see where these forms fit in the UI.

Several approaches can be taken in tackling this issue. One approach would be to define context menus on the category and task panes that will open when the user right-clicks on them. Although an interesting idea in itself, this approach has some limitations when it comes to browser compatibility (Firefox, for example, always likes to open its own context menu on any right-click). Another approach would be to define a menu bar using the GWT MenuBar widget, which we haven't discussed. The approach that we want to take, however, is quite different. In fact, it involves extending our TitledPanel with the ability to hold a toolbar. Once this functionality is in place, you'll be able to add buttons to each pane that trigger any required action.

■**Note** Using a MenuBar is definitely a viable option. Sadly, we don't have space to discuss all the widgets provided by GWT, so it would be great if you tackle this as an exercise to see how the MenuBar can be incorporated within our GWTasks application.

So where does a toolbar fit in our TitledPanel? It can be put in more than one place. But we'll place it on the title, where the text of the title is aligned to the left and the toolbar will be aligned to the right. Figure 5-5 shows a small wireframe diagram of how the title of this panel should look.

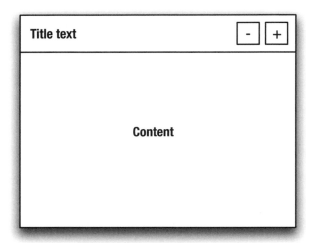

Figure 5-5. *A wireframe of the TitledPanel incorporating a toolbar*

The first thing we need to do is to define the structure of the title using the layout panels we've come to know so well. Here, as in many cases, there are several ways to achieve the same layout using different panels. We chose a HorizontalPanel for the toolbar itself, where each cell in this panel will contain a tool button. A DockPanel will be used for the title as a whole, where the title's Label will be placed on its CENTER part and the toolbar will be placed on its EAST part. Listing 5-33 shows the changes we need to make in order to implement this functionality.

Listing 5-33. *The TitledPanel Class with a Toolbar*

```
public class TitledPanel extends Composite {
    private final static String TOOLBAR_STYLE_NAME = "Toolbar";
    private final static String TITLE_STYLE_NAME = "Title";
    private final static String TOOL_BUTTON_STYLE_NAME = "ToolButton";
    private DockPanel title;
    private HorizontalPanel toolbar;
    ...
    public TitledPanel(String titleText, Widget content) {
        titleLabel = new Label(titleText);
        titleLabel.setStyleName(LABEL_STYLE_NAME);
        toolbar = new HorizontalPanel();
        toolbar.setVerticalAlignment(HorizontalPanel.ALIGN_MIDDLE);
        toolbar.setSpacing(0);
        toolbar.setBorderWidth(0);
        toolbar.setStyleName(TOOLBAR_STYLE_NAME);
        title = new DockPanel();
        title.setStyleName(TITLE_STYLE_NAME);
        title.add(titleLabel, DockPanel.CENTER);
        title.setCellVerticalAlignment(titleLabel, DockPanel.ALIGN_MIDDLE);
        title.setCellWidth(titleLabel, "100%");
        title.add(toolbar, DockPanel.EAST);
        title.setWidth("100%");
        grid = new Grid(2, 1);
        grid.setBorderWidth(0);
        grid.setCellPadding(0);
        grid.setCellSpacing(0);
        grid.setWidget(TITLE_ROW, 0, title);
        ...
    }
    ...
    public PushButton addToolButton(
            String text,
            String title,
            ClickListener clickListener) {
        PushButton button = new PushButton(text, clickListener);
        if (title != null) {
            button.setTitle(title);
        }
        addToolButton(button);
        return button;
```

```
    }
    public PushButton addToolButton(Image image, ClickListener clickListener) {
        PushButton button = new PushButton(image, clickListener);
        addToolButton(button);
        return button;
    }
    public void addToolButton(PushButton button) {
        button.setStyleName(TOOL_BUTTON_STYLE_NAME);
        toolbar.add(button);
        toolbar.setCellVerticalAlignment(button, HorizontalPanel.ALIGN_MIDDLE);
    }
}
```

Not only have we introduced the two panels we discussed; we also added extra methods that enable us to register tool buttons in the TitledPanel's toolbar. These methods come in three flavors:

- addToolButton(String, String, ClickListener)—this method will register a new button with the given caption and title (tool tip), which will trigger the given click listener whenever it is clicked.

- addToolButton(Image, ClickListener)—this method will register a new button with the given Image as its face. Here too, the click listener will be called whenever the button is clicked.

- addToolButton(PushButton)—this is the most flexible method, which enables adding any custom button.

Note the use of the PushButton, which is an extremely flexible implementation of a button. You can customize this button using a set of well-defined faces. For example, you might want to customize its look when it's disabled or when the mouse hovers over it. Each such scenario is associated with a face, which in turn is associated with a style name. To customize our tool buttons, we can set the following styles in the GWTasks.html file (see Listing 5-34).

Listing 5-34. *The Tool Button Styles*

```
.TitledPanel .Title .Toolbar .ToolButton {
    margin-left: 2px;
    vertical-align: middle;
    text-align: center;
    cursor: pointer;
    width: 22px;
    height: 22px;
}
.TitledPanel .Title .Toolbar .ToolButton-up-hovering {
    font-weight: bold;
}
.TitledPanel .Title .Toolbar .ToolButton-up-disabled {
    cursor: default;
```

```
}
.TitledPanel .Title .Toolbar .ToolButton-up-disabled .html-face {
    color: gray;
}
```

Now that our `TitledPanel` has reached its final version, it can be used in the category and task panes to add buttons that trigger some actions. For the `CategoryForm`, we'll add two buttons. The first will show a form to add a new category, and the second will remove the currently selected category (see Listing 5-35).

Listing 5-35. *Adding Buttons to the CategoryPane Toolbar*

```
public class CategoryPane extends Composite {
    …
    private PushButton addButton;
    private PushButton removeButton;
    public CategoryPane() {
        …
        tree.addTreeListener(new TreeListener() {
            public void onTreeItemSelected(TreeItem item) {
                Category category = ((CategoryTreeItem)item).getCategory();
                CategoryPane.this.taskPane.reset(category);
                removeButton.setEnabled(true);
            }
            public void onTreeItemStateChanged(TreeItem item) {
            }
        });
        …
        TitledPanel titledPanel = new TitledPanel("Categories", tree);
        titledPanel.setContentVerticalAlignment(HasVerticalAlignment.ALIGN_TOP);
        titledPanel.setSize("100%", "100%");
        addButton = titledPanel.addToolButton("+", "Add Category",
                new ClickListener() {
            public void onClick(Widget sender) {
                CategoryFormDialogBox dialog =
                    new CategoryFormDialogBox(CategoryPane.this);
                dialog.center();
                dialog.show();
            }
        });
        removeButton = titledPanel.addToolButton("-", "Add Category",
                new ClickListener() {
            public void onClick(Widget sender) {
                CategoryTreeItem item = (CategoryTreeItem) tree.getSelectedItem();
                if (item != null) {
                    Category category = item.getCategory();
                    item.remove();
                    removeButton.setEnabled(false);
```

```
                }
            }
        });
        removeButton.setEnabled(false);
        …

    }
    public void addCategory(Category category) {
        CategoryTreeItem item = (CategoryTreeItem) tree.getSelectedItem();
        if (item == null) {
            tree.addItem(createTreeItem(category));
        } else {
            item.addItem(createTreeItem(category));
        }
    }
}
```

As shown in Listing 5-35, the two buttons are registered with the titled panel. The implementation also makes sure they're enabled and disabled appropriately. More concretely, the removeButton is disabled by default, and will be enabled only when a category is being selected (code highlighted in bold). Of course, it's also possible to register other buttons as you see fit (for example, a button that clears the current category selection). Another thing you might have noticed is that as promised, we finally use the CategoryFormDialogBox we created in an earlier section. We had to make a small modification to this class, however, to make it aware of our category pane. Now when the category is created, it's directly added to the category tree via the newly introduced addCategory method on the CategoryPane class.

A similar approach can be applied to the TaskPane. Basically, the same two buttons need to be added to the TaskPane toolbar. One adds a task to the list (which involves creating a TaskFormDialogBox) and the other removes the selected task from the list. We'll leave this for you as an exercise, but of course you can always refer to the code accompanying the book. Figure 5-6 shows what the end result should look like.

LoginPane and MainPane—The Missing Components

Before moving on to the last part of this chapter where we discuss the application architecture, there are still a few gaps in the current GWTasks application that need to be filled. Somewhere along the way, when we continuously enhanced our application, we overlooked one quite important requirement: security. Having the option to add categories and tasks is all nice and dandy, but if this can't be done within the context of an account session, our GWTasks will be useless as an enterprise application. In this section, you'll see how you can incorporate a login screen with which the user can log in to the application before using it. This will require some changes to the code, but bear with us as we take it one step at a time.

The first thing you need to do is to understand the requirement better. When the user first enters the application, he should see a simple login form. Obviously, new users don't have an account ready for them, so they should be able to register as well. Only after logging in with valid credentials should the user enter the main view of the application (which is what we have right now).

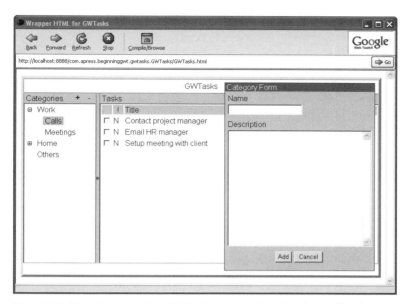

Figure 5-6. *The CategoryFormDialogBox opened using the toolbar button*

To implement this requirement, we'll add two more panes to our application. The LoginPane will contain the login form where the user can enter her credentials. The MainPane will contain all the other panes that we've already defined. In practice, the code that's currently located in the GWTasks class will be moved to the MainPane. The GWTasks will then have a new role, which is to control whether the LoginPane or the MainPane should be displayed.

Let's start with the LoginPane. When implementing this component, we'll try to reuse the TitledPanel we developed in the previous section to give the application a consistent look and feel. Using the title pane will also enable us to add a tool button that will trigger the RegistrationFormDialogBox where the user can register. Listing 5-36 shows the LoginPane class.

Listing 5-36. *The LoginPane Class*

```
public class LoginPane extends Composite {
    private Label messageLabel;
    private TextBox usernameField;
    private PasswordTextBox passwordField;
    private GWTasks gwtasks;
    public LoginPane(GWTasks gwtasks) {
        this.gwtasks = gwtasks;
        VerticalPanel content = new VerticalPanel();
        content.setSize("100%", "100%");
        … // constructing and laying out the form widgets and the message label
        TitledPanel main = new TitledPanel("Login", new CenterPanel(content));
        Image registerImage = new Image("image/edit.gif");
        registerImage.setTitle("Register");
```

```
        main.addToolButton(registerImage, new ClickListener() {
            public void onClick(Widget sender) {
                handleRegister();
            }
        });
        main.setSize("350px", "150px");
        initWidget(new CenterPanel(main));
        setStyleName("LoginPane");
    }
    public void reset() {
        … // clearing the messageLabel and the two fields
    }
    protected Widget createFieldLabel(String text) {
        Label label = new Label(text);
        label.setStyleName("FieldLabel");
        return label;
    }
    protected void handleLogin() {
        clearMessage();
        String username = usernameField.getText().trim();
        String password = passwordField.getText().trim();
        if (authenticate(username, password)) {
            gwtasks.showMainPane();
        } else {
            showErrorMessage("Invalid username and/or password");
            passwordField.setText("");
        }
    }
    protected boolean authenticate(String username, String password) {
        … // authenticating and returning whether it was successful or not
    }
    protected void handleRegister() {
        RegistrationFormDialogBox dialog = new RegistrationFormDialogBox(this);
        dialog.center();
        dialog.show();
    }
    …
}
```

We left out quite a bit in that code snippet, but by now you should feel confident in reading the full version of the class in the accompanying code. The only thing we want to draw your attention to is, once again, the use of the tool button of the TitledPanel along with the RegistrationFormDialogBox. This combination is consistent throughout the whole application, and consistency is valuable in itself. Also note that we use yet another new panel here, the CenterPanel. We created this panel to make it easier to center the login form on the screen. We encourage you to a look at the implementation of the panel to see how it works (remarkably, it's very simple).

The next thing we need to do is to implement the MainPane. This is quite straightforward, as we can just copy the code from the current GWTasks class.

The new GWTasks class will now be responsible for switching the view between the LoginPane and the MainPane. Listing 5-37 shows how it's done.

Listing 5-37. *The New GWTasks Class*

```
public class GWTasks implements EntryPoint {
    private SimplePanel main;
    private LoginPane loginPane;
    private MainPane mainPane;
    public void onModuleLoad() {
        mainPane = new MainPane();
        mainPane.setSize("100%", "100%");
        loginPane = new LoginPane(this);
        loginPane.setSize("100%", "100%");
        main = new SimplePanel();
        main.setSize("100%", "100%");
        main.setWidget(loginPane);
        RootPanel.get().add(main);
    }
    public void showLoginPane() {
        main.setWidget(loginPane);
    }
    public void showMainPane() {
        main.setWidget(mainPane);
    }
}
```

As you can see, we use the SimplePanel as a placeholder for the actual content. Whenever showMainPane or showLoginPane are called, the content is switched appropriately. By default, the LoginPane is shown, as this is the view you need to see when first entering the application.

We're now more or less finished with setting up the user interface of our application. Naturally we couldn't cover all available code at the line level, but we tried to explain at least the important aspects. The code base of GWTasks has grown quite a bit as we went along. We started this chapter with three classes and we now have the following 16 classes: Account, CategoryFormDialogBox, Category, CategoryPane, CenterPanel, GWTasks, HeaderPane, LoginPane, MainPane, MessageProgressIndicator, RegistrationFormDialogBox, StatusBarPane, TaskFormDialogBox, Task, TaskPane, and TitledPanel.

This is already quite a few classes to handle and maintain, and in the next section we'll see how we can add more structure to our code base to help us with that.

GWT Application Architecture

In the previous section, we were introduced to the importance of breaking down the application into separate components. Although important on its own, this is only a small step toward making the code base of the application clear, maintainable, and extensible. In this section, we'll continue in this direction and a look at a higher architecture level of a GWT application. To be precise, many of the ideas we'll cover here apply to application development in general, not only with GWT. But we feel it's important to show how these ideas can be realized in any GWT application, and GWTasks is a good starting point.

Layers and Packages

When developing a large application, one of the first things you need to plan in advance is how you want to structure your code base. In Java, this is done by adopting a packaging strategy.

There are many approaches you can take to packaging, as Java itself doesn't enforce any particular strategy. In fact, you can write a whole application without any packages at all. But there's a good reason why packages exist in the first place, and using them can greatly improve your view of the code. That said, if you don't use them wisely, you might not see much benefit, and their added value might be lost. But what is that added value?

Packages let you group a set of classes together. Without packages, it would be quite hard to find your way around an application code base. With them, you can focus on one group of classes at a time. This is similar to our GWTasks application, where the different tasks are put under different categories (imagine how hard it would be to focus on a group of tasks if they were all shown in one huge list). That said, there's not much use in looking at a group of classes if they don't relate to each other in some way. Which brings us to our first rule of thumb—packages should group together closely related classes and subpackages.

Another thing to consider when packaging your code is the interrelationships between the packages themselves. This issue is closely related to the SoC principle we touched on earlier in the chapter, and also to how your classes are designed. Package A is said to be *dependent* on package B if a class in package A depends on or uses a class in package B. If you also have classes in package B that depend on a class in package A, it's said that there's a *circular dependency* between these two packages.

Circular dependencies are in general considered harmful, and should always be avoided. The main reason for this is that these dependencies reflect the complex relationships between the different classes of the application, and the more complex these relationships are, the harder it is to maintain the code base. For example, optimally you want to make changes to a certain package with minimal effect on the rest of the application. With circular dependencies, this can be quite hard to achieve. Consider a scenario where changes in package A lead to changes in package B, which in turn lead to changes in package C, which then lead to even more changes to package A again. Before you know it, you can find yourself trapped within this vicious refactoring cycle, which can be quite frustrating to break. To help reduce circular dependencies you can adopt one of the following two approaches:

- Top-down approach—a package depends on its subpackages but not vice versa.

- Bottom-up approach—a package depends on its parent packages but not vice versa.

We believe that the clearest and simplest approach is the top-down approach, and so this is the approach we chose for our GWT application.

Now that we know what packages are good for, our next step is to figure out how we want to group the different classes. Here, as well, there are two common approaches:

- Architecture layering—this packaging strategy suggests grouping classes based on the layers they belong to within the overall application architecture. GWT enforces such layering and packaging by making you put all UI-related classes in the client package, the server-side classes in the server package, and all publicly accessible resources in the public package.

- Functional layering—this strategy suggests grouping classes based on their functionality. For example, all security-related classes would be put under a security package.

We believe that the best approach is a hybrid of both strategies. Since GWT already provide the architecture layering, it's our job to define the functional layering. Figure 5-7 shows the layering we chose for our GWTasks application.

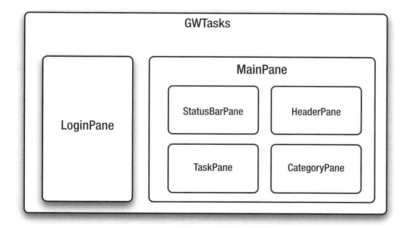

Figure 5-7. *The different UI layers in GWTasks*

The next step is to reflect this layering in the package structure of the application, as you can see in Figure 5-8.

■**Tip** We strongly encourage you at this point to start using an IDE if you haven't already done so. Any decent IDE should have pretty good support for code refactoring. Doing it manually is quite hard and error prone. Check out Appendix A, where we explain how to develop GWT applications with two of the more popular IDEs.

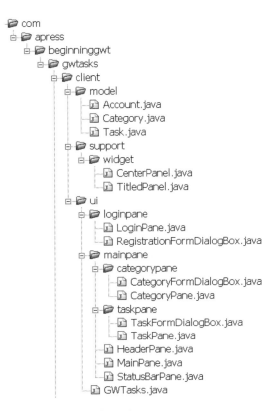

Figure 5-8. *GWTask package structure*

As you can see, we defined three top-level packages. The ui package holds the implementation of the user interface. The support package holds all the infrastructure classes. These are generic and shouldn't be closely tied to the application code. (Who knows, perhaps later you can take these classes out of this code base so you can reuse them in other applications as well.) The last top-level package is the model package, which holds all the domain model classes of the application. These aren't tied only to the UI, either. In fact, in Chapter 6, we'll see that the server also needs to know about them. Apart from these three packages, the rest are quite self-explanatory.

It's clear that by rearranging the classes in an appropriate package structure, we gain much better understanding of the different parts that make up our application. But we're not done yet. In fact, by applying this packaging strategy, we just introduced a huge amount of clutter when it comes to package dependencies. Our current code base clearly has quite a few circular dependencies between its packages. (For example, consider the GWTasks and the LoginPane classes, which have bidirectional dependency between them, while the latter is located in a subpackage of the former). We obviously want to resolve this issue, for all the reasons given previously, but how? This is where application events come to the rescue.

Application Events

We've seen how the different GWT widgets communicate with each other via events and event listeners. The existence of these events makes it easy to write complex applications where different widgets can communicate without being aware of each other. For example, this is why a tree doesn't have to know about a dialog box that's opened when one of its nodes is clicked. Clearly, the nature of this event-driven design promotes decoupling and thus follows the SoC principle.

The different layers and components of an application are no different in this respect, and we encourage you to apply this design methodology at the application level, by using application-oriented events. In the next few sections, we'll create a simple infrastructure to support such application events. We'll then try to define a few application events for GWTasks and see how they help to decouple the different layers of the application.

Application Event Infrastructure

The simple infrastructure we offer here consists of four classes: `ApplicationEvent`, `ApplicationEventListener`, `ApplicationEventSource`, and `ApplicationEventListenerCollection`. These four classes will be placed in our new package structure under a new `org.apress...client.support.event` package.

`ApplicationEvent` is an abstract class that will later serve as a base class for all custom events we'll define in the application. It holds an `ApplicationEventSource`, which represents the source from which the event was fired. It also holds a description, which varies based on the concrete event implementation. This enables us, for example, to listen to all events in the application and show their associated description in the `StatusBarPane`. As the `ApplicationEventSource` can fire events, obviously it should be possible to register `ApplicationEventListeners` with it that will listen to these events. The last class is the `ApplicationEventListenerCollection`. This class serves as a helper class to implement `ApplicationEventSources`. It serves as a collection of event listeners that can fire events to all the listeners it holds.

GWTasks Application Events

There are many application-level events that we can think of that may be of some use in the application:

- `CategoryCreatedEvent`—fired whenever a new category is created and added in the application.

- `CategorySelectionEvent`—fired whenever a category is selected or unselected by the user.

- `TaskCreatedEvent`—fired whenever a new task is created and added to a category.

- `TaskSelectionEvent`—fired whenever a task is selected or unselected by the user.

- `LoginEvent`—fired whenever a user has logged in.

- `LogoutEvent`—fired whenever the user has logged out.

These events are all closely related to our specific application, but it's also possible to create more generic events that can be used in different scenarios:

- MessageEvent—fired to broadcast a generic message in the system.

- CancelEvent—fired whenever an action is canceled by the user.

Obviously the possibilities are endless, but there's no point in defining all possible events in advance, as it may result in code bloat. It's better to define events as the need for them arises.

Now that we have the infrastructure in place, let's see how it can solve our tight coupling and package dependency problems. Let's take the case of the GWTasks class and the LoginPane as an example. Since the LoginPane knows when the user is trying to log in to the application and whether or not she does so successfully, it's only natural to have it fire a LoginEvent in the event of a successful login.

At the moment when the user logs in successfully, the LoginPane directly calls the showMainPane method on the GWTasks class. (Not only does it know about the GWTasks class, but it also knows there's a MainPane somewhere in the application.) If instead, we just make the LoginPane an ApplicationEventSource and have it fire a LoginEvent, the GWTasks class can pick up this event and switch the view on its own. Listing 5-38 shows the LoginEvent class implementation, and in Listing 5-39 you can see the changes required in the LoginPane to support it.

Listing 5-38. *The LoginEvent Class*

```
public class LoginEvent extends ApplicationEvent {
    private final String username;
    public LoginEvent(ApplicationEventSource source, String username) {
        super(source);
        this.username = username;
    }
    public String getDescription() {
        return "'" + username + "' logged in";
    }
}
```

■**Note** We will place all application level events under the ui.event package. We do that because the events are strictly used by the different UI components but don't belong to a specific layer within this package. In practice, any event can be used by any layer.

Listing 5-39. *The LoginPane as an ApplicationEventSource*

```
public class LoginPane extends Composite implements ApplicationEventSource {
    ...
    private ApplicationEventListenerCollection listeners;
    public LoginPane() {
        listeners = new ApplicationEventListenerCollection();
        ...
```

```
        }
        public void addListener(ApplicationEventListener listener) {
            listeners.add(listener);
        }
        public void removeListener(ApplicationEventListener listener) {
            listeners.remove(listener);
        }
        public void clearListeners() {
            listeners.clear();
        }
        protected void handleLogin() {
            clearMessage();
            String username = usernameField.getText().trim();
            String password = passwordField.getText().trim();
            if (authenticate(username, password)) {
                listeners.fireEvent(new LoginEvent(this, username));
            } else {
                showErrorMessage("Invalid username and/or password");
                passwordField.setText("");
            }
        }
    }
}
```

Note that by introducing the LoginEvent, we've managed to completely remove the dependency on the GWTasks class. Instead, whenever there's a successful login, the appropriate LoginEvent is fired for any listener who's registered with this pane. To complete this example, we need only modify the GWTasks class to register the appropriate listener on the LoginPane and act accordingly when a LoginEvent is fired (see Listing 5-40).

Listing 5-40. *The GWTasks Handling LoginEvents*

```
public class GWTasks implements EntryPoint {
    ...
    public void onModuleLoad() {
        ...
        loginPane = new LoginPane();
        loginPane.addListener(new LoginPaneListener());
        loginPane.setSize("100%", "100%");
        ...
    }
    ...
    protected class LoginPaneListener implements ApplicationEventListener {
        public void handle(ApplicationEvent event) {
            if (event instanceof LoginEvent) {
                showMainPane();
            }
        }
    }
}
```

As mentioned before, we take the top-down approach, where classes may depend on other classes down the package hierarchy but not vice versa. The GWTasks class depends on the LoginPane class, but the latter is no longer dependent on the GWTasks. Voilà! One circular dependency down.

Our mission, however, is only partially accomplished, as there are still many places in the code where circular dependencies need to be removed. Nonetheless, with the application event infrastructure in place, the same approach can be applied practically anywhere in the code, and bit by bit, all circular dependencies can be removed. For example, the category pane can fire a CategorySelectionEvent, and the MainPane can pick it up and update the TaskPane. Or when a task is selected in the TaskPane, we can fire a TaskSelectionEvent that will be picked up by the MainPane, which in turn will show a message on the StatusBarPane. And last, when the user clicks on a Logout link in the HeaderPane, the MainPane picks it up and "bubbles" it up to be picked by the GWTasks class, which in turn switches the view back to the LoginPane (see Figure 5-9).

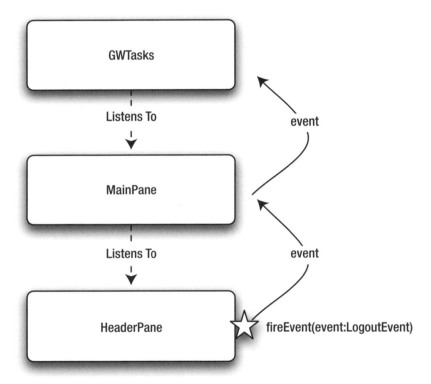

Figure 5-9. *The LogoutEvent bubbling*

When implementing all these events and listeners, you'll notice in general, the different panes of our applications also serve as ApplicationEventSources. This calls for some code refactoring by introducing a common Pane superclass for all these panes to extend that incorporates the event functionality in it (see Listing 5-41). This simplifies the code in all the concrete panes of the applications and certainly makes it easier to introduce new ones when needed.

Listing 5-41. *The Pane Class*

```
public abstract class Pane extends Composite implements ApplicationEventSource {
    private final ApplicationEventListenerCollection listeners;
    protected Pane() {
        listeners = new ApplicationEventListenerCollection();
    }
    public void addListener(ApplicationEventListener listener) {
        listeners.add(listener);
    }
    public void removeListener(ApplicationEventListener listener) {
        listeners.remove(listener);
    }
    public void clearListeners() {
        listeners.clear();
    }
    protected void fireEvent(ApplicationEvent event) {
        listeners.fireEvent(event);
    }
}
```

Managing the Data

In all our examples thus far, we focused on the UI functionality and how you can use different widgets to build the desired user interface. Although GWT is largely about UI, an application that only shows information but can't actually manage it is quite useless as an RIA, and belongs more in the "static web site" category. When the user manipulates data in the application and then logs out, he obviously hopes that next time he logs in, the application will be in the same state as when he left it.

When developing a GWT application, it's essential that you have a clear idea of how the data is going to be managed, and there are several questions that you need to ask yourself:

- What data is being managed?

- Where is the data stored?

- How can we access and manage the data?

- What is the nature of the communication by which the data is being managed?

The first question is quite obvious—you need to know your data. In big enterprise applications, it's likely that the type of managed data is already defined for you by the existing systems you integrate with. Nonetheless, it should be noted that the data your application uses can be only a subset of what the enterprise knows about, and the structure of this data can differ as well. In the next chapter, when we discuss the different GWT remoting strategies, you'll see that in many cases the domain model of your GWT application is located in a completely separate code base from that of your enterprise back-end system. Luckily, in GWTasks, we don't have this problem, and it's quite easy to identify the managed data as being categories, tasks, and accounts (the new package structure makes it even simpler, as all the relevant classes are located under the model package).

The answer to the second question is more interesting and less obvious. There are many places where the data can be stored. It can be stored on a remote server, but it can also be stored locally, on the browser (using cookies or even technologies such as Google Gears). You can even store everything in memory using POJOs (which translate to JavaScript objects at compile time).

■**Note** Google Gears is an open source project that enables tighter integration between web applications and the native desktop. Among other features, it enables a web application to store data on the local machine. This is normally done by installing a special plug-in in your browser. For more information about this project see `http://gears.google.com`.

The answers to the last two questions depend greatly on your answer to the second one. If the data is stored on a remote web server, then different data managers can be used depending on the communication protocol used. The nature of this communication is also a major factor. As we mentioned in Chapter 1, Ajax communication is asynchronous by nature, while communicating natively with the browser is synchronous.

So as you can see, a great deal of thought needs to be put into data management. Whatever approach you choose, there are two clear goals that your solution needs to achieve:

- It should be clear how data is accessed, and this should be consistent throughout the code base.

- Whatever approach you choose, there should be a clear decoupling between the actual implementation and the interface used. If you tie a specific widget to a specific remote implementation, it might be difficult to test the widget without having the remote service available.

In the following sections, we propose a simple and clear abstraction that will enable you to work with any data store and communication protocol. You'll learn how to build an in-memory solution behind this abstraction, and in Chapter 6 you'll see how this abstraction paves the way to using a remote back-end store for the same data.

Managers and ManagerRegistry

Our solution is based on the notion of managers and the manager registry. A *manager* is a conceptual service that lets you manage data. There is no single interface that all managers should implement and no abstract class to extend. The manager is just a concept, and it can be anything you want as long as it manages something. To explain the idea behind it, it's probably best to see what managers we can define in the GWTasks application.

The first manager in our application is the `SecurityManager`. This manages everything related to application security and provides appropriate services that can be called from anywhere at any time. Listing 5-42 shows this interface.

Listing 5-42. *The SecurityManager Interface*

```
public interface SecurityManager {
    void createAccount(Account account, AsyncCallback<Account> callback);
    void login(Authentication authentication, AsyncCallback<Account> callback);
    void logout();
    boolean isLoggedIn();
    Authentication getCurrentAuthentication();
}
```

As you can see, this manager provides methods to create accounts and authenticate, and also holds the currently logged in authentication. Authentication is a simple object that encapsulates an account's username and password. There's also a clear distinction between services that are strictly local and those that might be remote. The latter can only be executed in an asynchronous manner. Must it be asynchronous? Yes! When creating an abstraction layer, you can't make any assumptions about how the concrete implementation will work. Using an asynchronous abstraction allows for both asynchronous and synchronous implementations. Listing 5-43 shows an in-memory implementation of this manager.

Listing 5-43. *The InMemorySecurityManager Class*

```
public class InMemorySecurityManager implements SecurityManager {
    private Authentication authentication = Authentication.ANONYMOUS;
    private Map<String, Account> accountByUsername = new HashMap<String, Account>;
    private long accountIdCounter = 0;
    public void createAccount(Account account, AsyncCallback<Account> callback) {
        Account newAccount = new Account(++accountIdCounter, account);
        accountByUsername.put(newAccount.getUsername(), newAccount);
        callback.onSuccess(newAccount);
    }
    public void login(String username, String password,
            AsyncCallback<Boolean> callback) {
        Account account = accountByUsername.get(username);
        if (account == null || !password.equals(account.getPassword())) {
            callback.onSuccess(false);
        } else {
            String username = account.getUsername();
            String password = account.getPassword();
            authentication = new Authentication(username, password);
            callback.onSuccess(true);
        }
    }
    public void logout() {
        authentication = Authentication.ANONYMOUS;
```

```
    }
    public boolean isLoggedIn() {
        return authentication != Authentication.ANONYMOUS;
    }
    public Authentication getCurrentAuthentication() {
        return authentication;
    }
}
```

As you can see, having an asynchronous interface doesn't stand in the way of implementing a local version of it. Although this seems redundant, there's actually some value in
implementing in-memory versions of the manager interface. Since it's a fully working implementation, when configured right, it enables us to test the UI of our application without
worrying about the availability of remote services.

The second manager we define for our application is the DataManager. As its name suggests,
this manager is responsible for managing the raw data in the application. In GWTasks, we
consider the categories and tasks to be raw data and the DataManager should at least provide us
with CRUD services—Create, Read, Update, and Delete—for these classes. Listing 5-44 shows
this interface.

Listing 5-44. *The DataManager Interface*

```
public interface DataManager {
    void createCategory(
            Category category,
            Long parentCategoryId,
            AsyncCallback<Category> callback);
    void updateCategory(Category category, AsyncCallback callback);
    void removeCategory(long categoryId, AsyncCallback callback);
    void getCategories(AsyncCallback<List<Category>> callback);
    void createTask(Task task, long categoryId, AsyncCallback<Task> callback);
    void updateTask(Task task, AsyncCallback callback);
    void removeTask(long taskId, AsyncCallback<Task> callback);
    void getTasks(long categoryId, AsyncCallback<List<Task>> callback);
}
```

Unlike the SecurityManager, the DataManager has no methods that are strictly defined as
local, and they're all designed to be used asynchronously. Although we won't show it here,
the in-memory version of this manager can be implemented just as easily as we did with the
InMemorySecurityManager.

The last manager that we'll define might come as a surprise to you. We call it the UIManager.
As we mentioned earlier, a manager is a concept, an abstraction of a general service. Some
managers don't necessarily relate to data management or remote calls, and the UIManager is a
great example of that. The services this manager provides are what we call *application-level
UI services*—for example, the MessageProgressIndicator we discussed earlier in this chapter.
There should probably be one such indicator in our application; it would be best if it's exposed
as a service that's accessible from anywhere in the code. Another example would be global error
messages, which need to be standardized across the application. Listing 5-45 shows this interface.

Listing 5-45. *The UIManager Interface*

```
public interface UIManager {
    void showDebugMessage(String message);
    void showErrorMessage(String message);
    void showInfoMessage(String message);
    void showConfirmMessage(String message, AsyncCallback<Boolean> callback);
    ProgressIndicator showProgressIndicator(String message);
}
```

Also in this manager, although completely local, we find an asynchronous call. The showConfirmMessage should present the user with a confirmation dialog. Usually, when using such dialogs, the application needs to wait for user input in order to continue its normal execution. Since this interface should be implementation-agnostic, we can't assume that all implementations will be able to block execution. For this reason, the asynchronous call emulates execution blocking. When the user enters his input, the callback will be called and execution may continue within the callback. Also note that we chose to abstract away the concrete implementation of the progress indicator into a separate ProgressIndicator interface. This will enable you to change its implementation as you see fit without affecting the rest of the code.

The default implementation of this manager is quite straightforward, as it uses the browser's native support for messages via the Window.alert and Window.confirm methods. As for the ProgressIndicator implementation, we'll use the MessageProgressIndicator that we've already developed at the beginning of this chapter.

These three managers are the only ones we need for our GWTasks application. The only thing left to do is to see how we can access them from anywhere in our code.

One quick solution would be to bind the concrete implementations of these managers to their corresponding interfaces and access them via static methods. For example, to get a concrete SecurityManager implementation, we would call SecurityManager.get(). This solution is indeed quick, but it's also dirty. Once we do that, we lose quite a bit of the abstraction behind the interfaces (which are supposed to stay implementation-agnostic). This also makes it hard to test code that depends on these services—during the test phase you probably want the in-memory implementation of the services, while at runtime you need the remote version of them. So what's the alternative?

A better solution would be to use what we call a ManagerRegistry. The manager registry serves as a simple abstraction from which we can access all managers in the application. Listing 5-46 shows this simple interface for the GWTasks application.

Listing 5-46. *The ManagerRegistry Interface*

```
public interface ManagerRegistry {
    SecurityManager getSecurityManager();
    DataManager getDataManager();
    UIManager getUIManager();
}
```

A default implementation of this interface that's configured with all the concrete implementations of the managers can easily be created. The challenging part is to make sure we can access this registry from anywhere in the code.

The solution we chose for this book is to have a single instance of this manager constructed and configured in the topmost layer of the application (in our case, the GWTasks class). Then, propagate this instance down the different layers of the application. The simplest way to do that is to incorporate it in the abstract Pane class, as there more or less seems to be a one-to-one mapping between the different layers and the panes in the application. Listing 5-47 shows the changes in the Pane class that are required to support this.

Listing 5-47. *The Pane Class*

```
public abstract class Pane extends Composite implements ApplicationEventSource {
    private final ApplicationEventListenerCollection listeners;
    private final ManagerRegistry managerRegistry;
    protected Pane(ManagerRegistry managerRegistry) {
        listeners = new ApplicationEventListenerCollection();
        this.managerRegistry = managerRegistry;
    }
    ...
    protected ManagerRegistry getManagerRegistry() {
        return managerRegistry;
    }
}
```

Now, each pane in the application must be explicitly configured (constructed) with a manager registry that implicitly makes it accessible from all layers of the application. The only thing that's left now is to go over the code and call the different managers where appropriate. As an example, Listing 5-48 shows the relevant code that's executed when the reset method is called on the TaskPane, which should update the list of tasks for the selected category.

Listing 5-48. *The TaskPane.reset(Category) Method using the DataManager*

```
public void reset(Category category) {
    while (taskTable.getRowCount() > 1) {
        taskTable.removeRow(taskTable.getRowCount()-1);
    }
    this.category = category;
    if (category != null) {
    getManagerRegistry().getDataManager()
            .getTasks(category.getId(), new Callback<List<Task>>() {
        public void onSuccess(List<Task> tasks) {
            for (Task task : tasks) {
                addTask(task);
            }
        }
    });
}
```

Notice the asynchronous nature of this method call. We first issue the call to get all the tasks for the given category, and we continue execution only when the callback is called.

The Callback class in the listing is just a simplified implementation of the AsyncCallback interface that shows a message onscreen for every failed called. We'll discuss this callback class further in Chapter 6.

Note There are other viable solutions that can be used instead of the ManagerRegistry. A few open source projects aim to bring the power of IoC containers to the GWT world. Although this is beyond the scope of this book, we strongly recommend you to check them out (you can find references to these projects in Appendix B).

Some Last Words on Styles

Although this isn't strictly related to architecture, we believe it's important to apply the same best practices of consistency and well-defined structure to the CSS styles in your application. We've already discussed the techniques the GWT team came up with to maximize the customizability of the GWT widgets. We strongly recommend you follow this technique, not only for the generic components you develop, but also for all components in your application. Apply styles where possible and make sure you document the possibilities in the Javadoc of the relevant class. We also recommend you extract the styles settings from the hosting HTML file into a separate CSS file. This makes it easier to maintain and cleans up the HTML file. In GWTasks, we define all the styles in the GWTasks.css file.

Tip CSS files can be declared within the HTML file using the standard <link> tag, but you can also declare them within the GWT module definition file using the <style> element. In fact, GWT theme support is based on this type of configuration.

Summary

This chapter has been a long ride. We began with a closer look at some of the more advanced widgets GWT has to offer. You saw how you can use Grids and FlexTables for layout and for displaying tabular content. You also learned how to climb Trees and saw how easy it is to incorporate them in our application. The last widgets we covered were the PopupPanel and the DialogBox, which we then used to implement our wonderful MessageProgressIndicator.

We then moved on to a discussion about the importance of componentizing the application code base. This is the first time we introduced the Separation of Concerns principle, which accompanied us until the end of the chapter. You learned two techniques for creating your own components and found that composition is usually preferable to inheritance. This led to a process where we broke down our GWTasks application into separate composites, which we called panes. We then took you on a step-by-step guide for developing your own generic components. You developed the TitledPanel, which was later extended to hold a nifty toolbar. The application decomposition then ended by introducing the LoginPane and the MainPane as two alternating views that are controlled by the GWTasks class.

In the last part of this chapter, we focused more on the architecture of the application. We explained the importance of packaging and the different strategies that can be applied. We then took the top-down approach and applied it to our code base. We also discussed the implications that package dependencies have on the extensibility and maintainability of your code. We concluded that circular dependencies should be considered harmful and showed how application-level events can eliminate and prevent them. We then moved on to discuss how data should be managed within the application and offered a simple way of doing that. Finally, we ended up discussing the importance of using CSS styles properly and consistently.

You were presented with quite a handful of information for one chapter. Don't hesitate to go back and step through it again, just to make sure you're familiar with everything we talked about. If you followed it thoroughly along with the code accompanying this book, you should be well prepared to take advantage of the rest of the book.

In Chapter 6, we'll delve into the world of remote server calls.

■ ■ ■

## CHAPTER 6

Server Integration

As mentioned in the previous chapter, a web application without any persistent data is really just a static web site. Therefore, we want to introduce you to the ways the Google Web Toolkit can support communication between the client-side browser and the server. Using different methods, we'll show you how the sample application can be extended to support a server-side data provider.

For a developer, the easiest way to implement the communication between a client and a server is to develop as if there were no separation. And with today's communication frameworks, the reality comes pretty close. The details of communicating a message between client and server and vice versa can be abstracted away by frameworks, so you only have to concern yourself with the details at hand. GWT provides communication at two levels of abstraction: GWT RPC and Basic Ajax. Both use asynchronous communication to provide the rich UI experience expected from RIAs. GWT RPC is the more abstracted of the two and allows you to program your communication by calling a method on a Java interface. You are, however, limited to communication to a Java server. Basic Ajax is a bit less abstract, and similar to Ajax communication in JavaScript. You'll have to program each message you want to transfer, but you're free to talk to whatever server-side language as long as it supports Ajax communication. In this chapter, we'll first show you how you can communicate using GWT RPC and then show you the details of Ajax communication.

GWT RPC

With GWT RPC, almost all communication details are abstracted away. In short terms, all you need to do is define an interface with methods you want to be able to call on the server. GWT will generate a message broker for the interface, which only needs the address of the server.

Defining the Interface

The Java interface is used to define a contract for the communication. As the interface is shared between client and server, they both know which method can be called and what's expected in return. Listing 6-1 shows a contract for requesting a list of tasks. As you can see, defining the interface is really straightforward. Each service can have as many methods as necessary. There's no limitation on how many methods a service provides. The GWT RPC procedure will make sure the correct method is called at the server side.

Listing 6-1. *Interface for a Task Service*

```
public interface TaskService extends RemoteService {
    List<Task> getTasks();
}
```

For GWT to be able to abstract everything away, there are a couple of conditions that need to be fulfilled by this interface. First of all, as it needs to be available for the client-side application, it needs to be placed inside the client package of your GWT application. Second, it should extend the GWT interface com.google.gwt.user.client.rpc.RemoteService in order for the GWT compiler to understand that it defines an RPC interface. Finally, you can only use classes that GWT knows how to send over a wire. As of GWT version 1.5, a class can be transferred if it matches the following conditions:

- You can use all the primitives (such as char, byte, int, and double).

- You can use the wrapper classes (Character, Byte, Integer, and Double).

- You can use the classes java.lang.String and java.util.Date.

- You can use an array of supported classes.

- Any enumeration can be transferred. It will, however, be reduced to the name only. Any member variables won't be serialized and transferred.

- You can use any serializable user-defined class. A class is considered serializable when it meets the following three conditions:

  - The class or one of its superclasses implements java.io.Serializable.

  - The class has a default constructor (no arguments) or no constructor at all. Since GWT 1.5, the access modifier of the constructor is no longer required to be public.

  - Each member itself is serializable.

There's an exception to the last condition. As GWT takes the transient keyword into consideration, everything marked as transient won't be passed between client and server. Additionally, final variables won't be transported at all, so it's a good idea to mark all final variables as transient by default as an indication of the limitation. Listing 6-2 shows an implementation of the Task class.

Listing 6-2. *The Task Class Definition*

```
public class Task implements Serializable {
    private Long id;
    private String title;
    private String description;
    /* getters and setters */
    ...
}
```

In GWT versions prior to 1.5, there was a fourth condition to be taken into consideration. As stated, for an object to be transferred, it needs to be serializable. The transfer of an instance of java.util.Collections or any of its subclasses (List, Set, and Map) creates a problem. As these collections contain by definition instances of java.lang.Object and Object isn't serializable, the collections wouldn't be eligible for serialization. However, by using the Javadoc annotation @gwt.typeArgs on the methods using the collections, either as arguments or as return value, the GWT compiler could be instructed on how to serialize the collections. This had to be done using Javadoc annotations, because once again, the client side only supported Java 1.4 features. Listing 6-3 shows what the interface looks like for a simple task service with a method to get all task names.

Listing 6-3. *A Simple Task Service Using the @gwt.typeArgs Annotation*

```
public interface TaskService extends RemoteService {
    /**
      * @gwt.typeArgs <com.apress.beginninggwt.gwtasks.client.Task>
      */
    List getAllTasks();
}
```

Since the toolkit reached version 1.5, it now supports Java 5 language features. Among these features is generics. While using generics enables a lot of new features in the Java language, primarily it makes it possible to write stronger typed code. Listings 6-4 and 6-5 show two client-side methods for logging the title of tasks. Listing 6-4 doesn't use generics; Listing 6-5 uses generics.

Listing 6-4. *logTaskTitles Without Generics*

```
/**
  * @gwt.typeArgs <com.apress.begininggwt.gwtasks.client.Task>
  */
public void logTaskTitles(List tasks) {
    for(int i=0;i<tasks.size();i++) {
        Object o = tasks.get(i);
        if(o instanceof Task) {
            GWT.log(((Task)o).getTitle(), null);
        }
    }
}
```

Listing 6-5. *logTaskTitles with Generics*

```
public void logTaskTitles(List<Task> tasks) {
    for(int i=0;i<tasks.size();i++) {
        GWT.log(tasks.get(i).getTitle(), null);
    }
}
```

■**Note** The GWT.log() method is a special method for logging during hosted mode development. As normal client-side logging doesn't exist in a browser, these statements will be ignored by the Java to JavaScript compiler. In fact, the compiler will optimize the code as much as possible, so the methods from Listings 6-4 and 6-5 won't generate any JavaScript code at all. In hosted mode, however, these statements are executed and the messages will be displayed in the GWT Development Shell.

As you can see, the use of generics in Listing 6-5 makes the code more strongly typed. More strongly typed java code implies less type casting, thus the code becomes cleaner and easier to maintain. Java 5 introduces more features to make the code even cleaner, such as the for-each style for loop, which is also supported in the GWT client side as of version 1.5. Listing 6-6 shows an optimized version of the logTaskTitle method, using all features of Java 5.

Listing 6-6. *Optimized Version of logTaskTitles*

```
public void logTaskTitles(List<Task> tasks) {
    for(Task task : tasks) {
        GWT.log(task.getTitle(), null);
    }
}
```

Implementing the Server Side

For the server side of the GWT RPC mechanism, Google uses servlets. Servlets are a part of the Java Enterprise Edition (Java EE) specifications and are used to make dynamic content available on the Web. Usually servlets are used for HTTP communication only, but this is certainly no limitation of the specification. Wikipedia references Jim Driscoll's blog at java.net, where he writes that James Gosling came up with the idea for servlets back in 1995, but pushed it aside for other interests. The first servlet API is dated from 1997, so servlets have been around for quite some time and are considered relatively mature.

A servlet is an extension of a web container, able to receive a request and form an applicable response for it. The most commonly known web containers are Tomcat and Jetty. The web container receives the actual request and passes it on to a servlet based on the configuration of the container. The request is marshaled into a Request object and passed to the servlet. Hence, the servlet has full knowledge of the request's origin and content without the requirement to know how the data is transferred.

A servlet that needs to handle requests from a GWT application extends the com.google.gwt.user.server.rpc.RemoteServiceServlet class and implements your service interface. The RemoteServiceServlet class puts another layer of abstraction on the Servlet class. With the RemoteServiceServlet class, not only is the serialization abstracted away, it even determines the method that needs to be invoked and invokes it. Hence, the only task left to the developer is to implement the methods from the service interface like any other server-side service. Listing 6-7 shows a simple implementation of our TaskService interface.

Listing 6-7. *A Server-side Implementation of the TaskService*

```
public class TaskServiceImpl extends RemoteServiceServlet implements TaskService {
    public List<Task> getTasks() {
        /* ... retrieve a list of tasks
        List<Task> tasks = ...
        return tasks;
    }
}
```

As you can see, the code is clean and simple. All complex details about receiving the request, deserializing it, parsing it, serializing the response, and returning it to the client are filtered out into the `RemoteServiceServlet`.

Implementing the Client Side

The next step is start using the created service. Remember that GWT RPC uses asynchronous communication. To enable the client to use this, we need to define an asynchronous version of the service interface, next to the synchronous one in the package structure. The difference is in the return values. As the client won't block execution on the call to the service, it needs a hook to be able to do something with the result of the call. For this purpose, the asynchronous interface will have a callback hook that gets executed when the call to service method returns. Listing 6-8 shows the asynchronous version of our `TaskService` from Listing 6-1. Instead of a zero-argument method returning a list of strings, the method gets an argument for the callback and a void return type.

Listing 6-8. *Asynchronous Interface of TaskService*

```
public interface TaskServiceAsync {
    void getTasks(AsyncCallback asyncCallback);
}
```

Deferred Binding

Now that we've defined our asynchronous interface, we need a way to use it. You might think you need to create a client-side implementation of this interface. Well, you're almost right. You do need an implementation, but it will get generated by the GWT compiler, for good reason. As the client side can run in a lot of different environments, the implementation of the service should be aware of the different environments. However, GWT should make development easy. So instead of requiring the developer to handle every possible environment, GWT introduces a technique called *deferred binding* to generate this proxy object to our server-side implementation.

The primary reason Google introduced deferred binding is the wide variety of browsers available and used on the Internet. This wouldn't be a problem in itself, if browsers would follow, implement, and support the same standards. This, however, is not the case, as each browser has its own quirks and features. Deferred binding makes it possible to use each feature, while circumventing the quirks. Google used the simplest solution for this problem. It generates

JavaScript specific for each of the supported browsers and serves only the required JavaScript files to the client. So if you're using Firefox, you'll get scripts with Firefox code, while Internet Explorer users will use the Internet Explorer–specific scripts.

Deferred binding is not only used to serve browser-specific JavaScript. Another strong feature it solves is internationalization. Although internationalization is covered in more detail in Chapter 8, we want to point out here that for each language, the GWT compiler generates a separate JavaScript application. As a result, you'll find a lot of files in the output directory of the compiler. For each browser and language combination, a separate file is created. Hence, a client requesting to use the application in Internet Explorer using a French locale will only receive the files needed for that purpose. It might be obvious that this will introduce heavy compile-time calculations and a relatively large number of files as a result. The result, however, is optimized for the environment of the client and requires as few bytes to transfer as possible.

Back to our example. We want to use deferred binding to get a reference to the generated proxy object. All deferred binding is done through the static method `com.google.gwt.core.client.GWT.create()`. This method takes a class as a parameter. This class should be the interface definition for which you need a proxy to be generated. Listing 6-9 shows how to get a reference for a server proxy. As you can see, it requires two steps. First we get the proxy, and then we tell the proxy which server it should talk to using the `com.google.gwt.user.client.rpc.ServiceDefTarget` class.

Listing 6-9. *Code Showing How to Get a Reference to a RemoteService Proxy*

```
TaskServiceAsync service = (TaskServiceAsync) GWT.create(TaskService.class);
((ServiceDefTarget) service).setServiceEntryPoint(GWT.getModuleBaseURL() + "tasks");
```

A number of things need some explaining in this code snippet. First of all, you pass the interface definition to the `GWT.create()` method and then cast it to the asynchronous version. Also note the casting to the `ServiceDefTarget` class. Apparently, this interface is implemented by the proxy as well, and enables us to set the endpoint of the service. This type casting is necessary because otherwise, the compiler doesn't recognize the code as valid, because it has no knowledge of the generated proxy class. In Listing 6-9, we set the endpoint to the path where our servlet is listening; in this case it's set relative to the GWT module, extending the path with `"tasks"`.

Now that we have our reference and have set the endpoint, we're ready to use the service and make the call to the server. Listing 6-10 shows the `onModuleLoad` method of our sample application.

Listing 6-10. *The onModuleLoad Method Loads Task Names from the Server*

```
public void onModuleLoad() {
    TaskServiceAsync service = (TaskServiceAsync) GWT.create(TaskService.class);
    ServiceDefTarget serviceDef = (ServiceDefTarget) service;
    serviceDef.setServiceEntryPoint(GWT.getModuleBaseURL() + "tasks");
    service.getTasks(new TasksCallback());
}
```

As you can see, the call to the service becomes quite easy in the end. The call is made on the asynchronous service definition, so instead of a return value, there should be an argument passed to the method pointing to an implementation of GWT's `AsyncCallback` interface.

Before we explain the details of the `AsyncCallback` interface, we want to show you a good practice concerning deferred binding. If you've run the sample code in hosted mode, you might have noticed the application temporarily stalling. At a certain point, the deferred binding kicks in and the browser needs to do some processing to determine the right implementation. This is a relatively expensive procedure and you want to minimize its usage as much as you can. Therefore, you want to create a proxy only once during the application. This singleton pattern is a common practice; in GWT, however, you need to find a logical place to put the factory method. We think by putting an inner class inside the service interface, we define an easy-to-use factory. Listing 6-11 shows the inner class for our `TaskService`.

Listing 6-11. *Locator Class as a Factory for the Proxy Service*

```
public class TaskService {
    ...
    public class Locator {
        private static TaskServiceAsync taskService;
        public static TaskServiceAsync getInstance() {
            if (taskService == null) {
                taskService = (TaskServiceAsync) GWT.create(TaskService.class);
                ServiceDefTarget serviceDef = (ServiceDefTarget) taskService;
                serviceDef.setServiceEntryPoint(GWT.getModuleBaseURL() + "task");
            }
            return taskService;
        }
    }
}
```

Getting a reference to our service proxy becomes as easy as calling the `static getInstance` method. And, because the method only calls `GWT.create()` once, the time to get the reference is reduced dramatically and the performance is improved. The code from Listing 6-10 would thus result in the code shown in Listing 6-12.

Listing 6-12. *Optimized Code for Getting a List of Tasks*

```
public void onModuleLoad() {
    TaskServiceAsync service = TaskService.Locater.getInstance();
    service.getTasks(new TasksCallback());
}
```

Handling Return Values

The `AsyncCallback` interface defines two methods to implement. One is called when the call to the server returns successfully, not surprisingly named `onSuccess`. The second is named `onFailure` and is executed when an exception occurs somewhere along the line. Listing 6-13 gives a sample implementation of the TaskNamesCallback. It shows how we can process the tasks returned by the server by putting them in a VerticalPanel. In the last line, the VerticalPanel is put into the RootPanel to be generated into the view.

Listing 6-13. *The TaskNamesCallback Class Processes the Result of the Server Call*

```
public class TasksCallback implements AsyncCallback {
    public void onSuccess(Object o) {
        List<Task> tasks = (List<Task>)o;
        VerticalPanel taskPanel = new VerticalPanel();
        for(Task task : tasks) {
            taskPanel.add(new Label(task.getTitle()));
        }
        RootPanel.get().add(taskPanel);
    }
    public void onFailure(Throwable t) {
        Window.alert(t.getMessage());
    }
}
```

Handling Exceptions

The shown onFailure method only displays the received message in an alert box. Typically you want to create a default exception handler to show errors in a concise way to the user. Therefore, a good practice would be to make a default abstract implementation of the AsyncCallback class, only implementing the onFailure method. In there, you could create your own styled ErrorDialogBox to show the error message, and optionally add a hidden stacktrace as well for debugging purposes. Listings 6-14 and 6-15 respectively show the classes for the abstract callback handler and the ErrorDialogBox.

Listing 6-14. *An Abstract Callback Class for Centralized Error Handling*

```
public abstract class MyAsyncCallback implements AsyncCallback {
    public void onFailure(Throwable t) {
        new ErrorDialogBox(t).show();
    }
}
```

Listing 6-15. *A Custom Dialog Box Showing a User-friendly Error Message*

```
public class ErrorDialogBox extends DialogBox {
    public ErrorDialogBox(Throwable t) {
        super(false, true);
        setText("An error occurred.");
        VerticalPanel vp = new VerticalPanel();
        vp.add(new Label(t.getMessage()));
        DisclosurePanel panel = new DisclosurePanel("more details...");
```

```
        VerticalPanel stackTracePanel = new VerticalPanel();
        for(StackTraceElement ste : t.getStackTrace()) {
            stackTracePanel.add(new Label(ste.toString()));
        }
        panel.setContent(stackTracePanel);
        vp.add(panel);
        vp.add(new Button("close", new ClickListener() {
            public void onClick(Widget sender) {
                ErrorDialogBox.this.hide();
            }
        }));
        setWidget(vp);
        center();
    }
}
```

The exceptions thrown from the server can't all be transferred to the client's browser. If an exception isn't a default exception supported by the JRE emulation library, it needs to comply with a small set of rules. Just like other data objects, the exception objects and all their member variables are required to implement the `Serializable` interface. Furthermore, they need to be defined inside the GWT `client` package.

Alternatives to GWT RPC

You've now seen how you can communicate with your server-side Java application using GWT RPC. Basically, this is the simplest method for communication if you're using GWT. But you don't always have a server-side application written in Java. For example, if you're creating a new front end on a legacy system, or if you have a PHP, .NET or CGI server-side application, you're restricted in the ways to implement client-server communication. Fortunately, GWT provides other ways to support communication, thus making GWT available for a much wider audience. In fact, GWT RPC really is only a small abstraction layer. The communication underneath GWT RPC is done using the basic principles of Ajax.

Basic Ajax

Ajax is a set of technologies that make it possible for web applications to give the user a highly interactive experience. Using asynchronous communication, Ajax makes it possible for the application to respond dynamically to user actions by performing background operations. Typically, Ajax calls are made from JavaScript, and using DHTML and DOM, the HTML page is updated to reflect the result. This is the basic form of Ajax, but there are other forms of Ajax that use different technologies for the implementation.

GWT also provides methods for performing simple Ajax calls. Using these methods, you can write your Ajax calls in plain Java, thus allowing GWT to handle the difficulties of the different Ajax implementations available in the different browsers. The first thing to do before you can use the Ajax functionality is enable it. You can enable it by adding an `inherits` statement in your module configuration. The Ajax functionality is available in a separate module called `com.google.gwt.http.HTTP`. Listing 6-16 shows the new module descriptor for our GWTasks sample application.

Listing 6-16. *GWTasks Module Descriptor with HTTP Module Enabled*

```
<module>
    <!-- Inherit the core Web Toolkit stuff.               -->
    <inherits name='com.google.gwt.user.User'/>
    <!—- Enable HTTP stuff support                         -->
    <inherits name="com.google.gwt.http.HTTP"/>
    <!-- Specify the app entry point class.               -->
    <entry-point class='com.apress.beginninggwt.gwtasks.client.ui.GWTasks'/>

</module>
```

Now that the HTTP module is enabled, we can start programming our first basic Ajax call. You'll notice that we're going to program the communication on a much lower level than we did with the GWT RPC mechanism. As a consequence, there won't be any convenient Java interfaces to talk to. We have to create the request all by hand and specify every detail we need. There are some easy defaults, but you have to understand them to decide if they're the defaults you need.

We start by instantiating the `com.google.gwt.http.client.RequestBuilder`. Listing 6-17 shows what the instantiation should look like. This class helps us set up the request and configure its parameters. Its only constructor takes two arguments. The first argument specifies the type of HTTP request and can be either `RequestBuilder.GET` or `RequestBuilder.POST`. The second argument is the URL where the service is listening. This could, for example, be a URL where a basic servlet is listening for requests.

Listing 6-17. *Creating an Instance of the RequestBuilder*

```
RequestBuilder builder = new RequestBuilder(RequestBuilder.GET, requestUrl);
```

Now that we have the builder instantiated, we can specify the details of the request. By default, the content type specified in the request header is `text/plain;charset=utf-8`. You can change this value by making a call to `RequestBuilder.setHeader()`, or extend the values using a call to `RequestBuilder.addHeader()`. Both methods take a header name and value as arguments. Other methods of `RequestBuilder` allow you to specify username and password for authentication purposes and configure a timeout for when executing the method takes too long.

When the builder is configured, we can send our request to the server. Based on whether you're using a GET or a POST, you can pass arguments with the request in two different ways. With a GET request, the body of the message remains empty. Therefore, any argument you want to pass to the server must be encoded into the request URL as query parameters. You can recognize query parameters in a URL using a question mark. Multiple query parameters can be placed after the question mark as name-value pairs separated by ampersands. For example, the query `?firstname=bram&lastname=smeets` contains two parameters as name-value pairs. Keep in mind that the URL doesn't allow all characters to be used in these name-value pairs. Special consideration should be taken when using a small set of characters. Some characters, for example the space, should be encoded for the URL to remain valid. Fortunately GWT provides a convenience class to perform this encoding called com.google.gwt.http.client.URL. This class provides an encode() and a decode() method so you don't have to bother yourself with escaping the special characters.

Going back to our GWTask example, there are some methods that could easily be implemented using the basic Ajax functionality. Listing 6-18 shows as an example how the login method of the SecurityManager could be implemented. The username and password are for sake of the example passed as query parameters.

Listing 6-18. *Example of an Ajax Call Using the RequestBuilder*

```
public class BasicAjaxSecurityManager implements SecurityManager {
    ....
    public void login(String name, String password, ➥
            AsyncCallback<Boolean> callback) {
        String requestUrl = URL.encode("login?username=" + username ➥
                            + "&password=" + password);
        RequestBuilder builder = new RequestBuilder(RequestBuilder.GET, requestUrl);
        builder.setTimeoutMillis(5000);
        builder.setCallback(new RequestCallback() {
            public void onError(Request request, Throwable exception) {
                callback.onFailure(exception);
            }
            public void onResponseReceived(Request request, Response response) {
                if(response.getStatusCode() == 200) {
                    callback.onSuccess(true);
                } else {
                    callback.onSuccess(false);
                }
            }
        });
        try {
            builder.send();
        } catch(RequestException re) {
            callback.onFailure(re);
        }
    }
}
```

JSON

For authenticating a user, only a little data needs to be sent between client and server. However, if we implement the rest of the interfaces, we soon realize that the data sent between client and server becomes more and more complex. We could define some XML schema for the communication and use some client-side marshaller to convert our data structures, but this becomes cumbersome and isn't easy to maintain. Our alternative is the JavaScript Object Notation (JSON). JSON is an easy-to-use data format that can be used to exchange data between systems of different origin. JSON uses a subset of the JavaScript types to define structured data. By no means does it provide any way to transport the data; its only purpose is to structure the data so that it can be easily read and interpreted both by men and machine. At the moment, there are a wide range of JSON implementations available for just as wide a set of languages. So no matter whether you're a C# developer or work with Ruby, Python or Java, there are libraries available that allow you to work with the JSON data format.

The Principles of JSON

So now you're wondering what the deal is with this data format. Well, the designers of JSON kept it real easy. Only the basic types are available. Besides the values null, true, and false, you can have string values and number values. Furthermore, you can create data structures of these values by using an array or an object. The array is like a list of elements, but it isn't type restricted. So there isn't a constriction on putting both string values and number values inside the same array. The object data structure is like a java.util.Map; it consists of key-value pairs. It's ideal for mapping a plain Java object, which Listing 6-19 shows for our Category object. Although this is the real representation, it isn't easy to read and interpret for human beings. However, if we make it pretty and give it some structure, as seen in Listing 6-20, the contents of this JSON data object become much clearer.

Listing 6-19. *JSON Representation of our GWTasks Category Object*

```
{id:372,name:"work",description:"all tasks related to work",subCategories: ➥
[{id:491,name:"Calls",description:"telephone calls",subCategories:[]},{id: ➥
284,name:"Meetings",description:"Upcoming meetings",subCategories:[]}]}
```

Listing 6-20. *Pretty-printed JSON Representation of our GWTasks Category*

```
{
    id : 372, name : "work",
    description : "all tasks related to work",
    subCategories : [
        {
            id : 491,
            name : "Calls",
            description : "telephone calls",
            subCategories : []
        },
        {
            id : 284,
            name : "Meetings",
            description : "Upcoming meetings",
            subCategories : []
        }
    ]
}
```

Now that we know what the data looks like, the next step is to actually work with the data. The basic principle behind the JSON data format is that it can be interpreted by machines. In JavaScript, this is realized using the `eval()` function. Note that this function is basic JavaScript; it isn't an addition to the language. The `eval()` function interprets a string value and executes it as if it were a piece of code. As JSON has its origin in JavaScript, the JSON format complies with the code structure of JavaScript. Therefore, the result of a call to the `eval()` function with a JSON string as an argument results in a variable with the interpretation of the data structure as its value. Listing 6-21 shows exactly what we could do if we parse the JSON string value of Listing 6-19.

Listing 6-21. *Working with JSON Objects in JavaScript*

```
var category = eval(JSONString);
alert(category.name);
```

JSON and GWT

Because GWT is primarily written in Java, the guys at Google have written some specific classes to cover the JavaScript support, like the `eval()` function, which is needed for JSON. Introducing these classes makes compiling the classes to JavaScript easy. Again, the JSON support is a separate GWT module and needs to be inherited in the GWT module descriptor to be able to use JSON support. We can extend our descriptor as shown in Listing 6-22.

Listing 6-22. *GWTasks Module Descriptor with JSON Support*

```
<module>
    <!-- Inherit the core Web Toolkit stuff.                 -->
    <inherits name='com.google.gwt.user.User'/>
    <inherits name='com.google.gwt.json.JSON'/>
    <inherits name='com.google.gwt.http.HTTP'/>
    <!-- Specify the app entry point class.                  -->
    <entry-point class='com.apress.beginninggwt.gwtasks.client.ui.GWTasks'/>
</module>
```

We're now able to start using JSON in our GWT client code. The wrapper class for the `eval` function is `com.google.gwt.json.client.JSONParser`. This class has one static method called `parse` that interprets the JSON data structure passed as a string. The result of the `parse` method is an instance of the abstract class `JSONValue`. GWT comes with a set of JSON-specific classes to represent the limited data types allowed in JSON. The `JSONValue` class is the abstract parent of all of these classes. The classes available are `JSONBoolean`, `JSONString`, `JSONNumber`, `JSONNull`, `JSONArray`, and `JSONObject`. The `JSONValue` object contains test methods for each possible type. These methods return the type-specific value if one is applicable, or otherwise `null`. With this knowledge, we can go back to our GWTasks application and create a new implementation for our `DataManager`. The first method we're going to implement is `getCategories`. Listing 6-23 shows a first try at implementing this method. Remember that we get back a JSON structure consisting of an array of categories with subcategories.

Listing 6-23. *JSON Implementation of getCategories*

```
public void getCategories(final AsyncCallback<List<Category>> callback) {
    // make some call to the server and capture the response in a String
    String response = ...
    List<Category> categories = new ArrayList<Category>();
    JSONValue responseValue = JSONParser.parse(response);
    JSONArray responseArray = responseValue.isArray();
    if(responseArray != null) {
        for(int i=0;i<responseArray.size();i++) {
            JSONObject responseCategory = responseArray.get(i).isObject();
            Category category = parseCategory(responseCategory);
            categories.add(category);
        }
    }
    callback.onSuccess(categories);
}
private Category parseCategory(JSONObject cat) {
    Category category = new Category();
    category.setId(((Double)cat.get("id").isNumber().doubleValue()).longValue());
    category.setName(cat.get("name").isString().stringValue());
    category.setDescription(cat.get("description").isString().stringValue());
    JSONArray subCategories = cat.get("subCategories").isArray();
    if(subCategories != null) {
        for(int i=0;i<subCategories.size();i++) {
            Category subCategory = parseCategory(subCategories.get(i).isObject());
            category.addChildCategory(subCategory);
        }
    }
    return category;
}
```

What's left is sending the request to the server. Note in Listing 6-22 that we've also included the HTTP module, and remember that JSON only defines data structures. For the transport, we still need other technologies. Fortunately, we can easily combine JSON with the basic Ajax functionality of GWT. For convenience, we define a new class to handle the communication specifics. Listing 6-24 shows this Server class. It contains one static method and can be used to send JSON structures to the server and back.

Listing 6-24. *Simple Server Class for Handling Ajax Transport Between Server and Client*

```
public class Server {
    public static void post(String url, String requestData,
            final AsyncCallback<String> callback) {
        RequestBuilder builder =
            new RequestBuilder(RequestBuilder.POST, URL.encode(url));
```

```
        try {
            builder.sendRequest(requestData, new RequestCallback() {
                public void onError(Request request, Throwable throwable) {
                    callback.onFailure(throwable);
                }
                public void onResponseReceived(Request request, Response response) {
                    if (response.getStatusCode() != 200) {
                        callback.onFailure(
                            new RequestException( response.getStatusText()));
                    }
                    callback.onSuccess(response.getText());
                }
            });
        } catch (RequestException re) {
            callback.onFailure(re);
        }
    }
}
```

Only a small adjustment to our DataManager is necessary to make it use the new transport service. Listing 6-25 shows our final implementation for the getCategories() method.

Listing 6-25. *The Final Version of the DataManager.getCategories() Method*

```
public void getCategories(final AsyncCallback<List<Category>> callback) {
    Server.post("categories", "", new AsyncCallback<String>() {
        public void onFailure(Throwable caught) {
            callback.onSuccess(new ArrayList<Category>());
        }
        public void onSuccess(String response) {
            JSONValue responseValue = JSONParser.parse(response);
            JSONArray responseArray = responseValue.isArray();
            if(responseArray != null) {
                List<Category> categories = new ArrayList<Category>();
                for(int i=0;i<responseArray.size();i++) {
                    JSONObject responseCategory = responseArray.get(i).isObject();
                    Category category = parseCategory(responseCategory);
                    categories.add(category);
                }
                callback.onSuccess(categories);
            }
        }
    });
}
```

Summary

In the previous chapter, you saw how we created a complex user interface. The final step was to organize the service methods in three classes and create in-memory implementations. At that point, the application was usable, but nothing was persisted. The next step was communication with a remote system, so data could be stored in a central place.

Continuing from the previous chapter, we've shown how you can interact with a remote system in GWT. We explained how the asynchronous character of GWT delivers a highly interactive experience to the user, as expected from a rich Internet application. Using GWT RPC, communication with a remote system becomes as easy as calling a method on a Java interface. We've shown you how to define such an interface, create a server-side implementation, and use it from the client-side code. Unfortunately, there are some limitations to GWT RPC. First of all, it can only be used if the server-side application is written in Java and supports servlets. Furthermore, GWT RPC only supports a limited set of the classes from Java Runtime Environment. However, knowing these limitations is as good as solving them, because you can easily extend the class support by adding your own classes.

As an alternative, you can use GWT's basic Ajax support GWT to talk to any other system that supports Ajax. Thus, even though the complexity of the code goes up due to the lower level of communication, GWT still provides clean support for communicating with the server, independent of the language in which the server-side code is written.

Even communicating complex data structures can easily be implemented using the JSON data format. This language-independent standard is by definition ideal for communicating between two systems if the implementation languages are different. This is because of the real simplicity by which the data can be parsed at the client side, in comparison with other options such as XML.

CHAPTER 7

■■■

Testing GWT Applications

This book shows you how to develop GWT applications. As testing has become an integral part of the software development process, we feel that a book about building GWT applications wouldn't be complete without a chapter on testing.

In this chapter, we'll first explore what testing actually is and what types of testing we can distinguish. Then we'll go into more detail on unit testing, introducing JUnit, the unit test tool that comes with GWT. Next, we'll focus on a tool for doing functional testing, Selenium. Then we'll end the chapter by discussing the support GWT provides for benchmarking code developed using GWT.

What Is Testing?

A great deal of misunderstanding surrounds testing. Many developers consider it to be something that should be done by a separate testing department. We consider testing to be an integral part of software development. But before discussing that in more detail, let's first take a closer look at testing and what it constitutes.

Testing can be roughly divided into three main types:

- **Unit testing**—tests the minimal software component, or module. Each unit (basic component) of the software is tested to verify that the detailed design for the unit has been correctly implemented. In an object-oriented environment, this is usually at the class level, and the minimal unit tests include the constructors and destructors.

- **Functional testing**—exposes defects in the interfaces and interaction between users and the system. On this level, we no longer test single units of work, but focus on functionality and verify that it actually works as expected.

- **System/integration testing**—tests a completely integrated system to verify that it meets its requirements.

The third type of testing is typically done by a separate QA department or at least dedicated testers. However, the first two, unit and integration testing, are considered an integral part of software development, and should therefore be done by the developers themselves. In particular, unit testing is valued highly, as it provides developers with more confidence over the correct functioning of their code. Writing unit tests also encourages programmers to write code in small chunks that can be tested independently. There is a large amount of literature on testing, and why it's important to consider it part of the software development process. More information about unit testing using JUnit can be found in *Test-Driven Development: A J2EE Example* by Russell Gold, Thomas Hammell, and Tom Snyder (Apress, 2004).

As this book is aimed at software developers who want to build robust GWT applications, we should discuss the types of testing most appropriate to them. Therefore, we'll focus on unit and functional testing in the remainder of this chapter. System and integration testing, important as they are, fall outside the scope of this book.

Unit Testing

As mentioned earlier, unit testing is the procedure of verifying that individual units of source code work properly, where a unit is the smallest testable part of an application. In object-oriented programming, the smallest unit consists of a method, which in turn belongs to a class. So in the context of developing GWT applications, unit testing is about testing individual methods of specific classes.

Unit testing is usually done by writing several *test cases* and combining them into *test suites*. A test case is a test instance where one set of conditions or variables will be used to determine whether a requirement or use case of a unit is (partially) satisfied. It usually takes several test cases, at least, to determine whether a requirement is fully satisfied. An important aspect of unit testing is the need to test each unit in isolation. To ensure this, ideally each test should be independent of other units.

Basic Unit Testing

In order to get a more detailed picture of unit testing, assume a `BasicCalculator` class (see Listing 7-1) that offers the four basic arithmetic operations `add`, `subtract`, `multiply`, and `divide`.

Listing 7-1. *The BasicCalculator Class*

```
public class BasicCalculator {

  public int add(int num1, int num2) {
    return num1 + num2;
  }
  public int subtract(int num1, int num2) {
    return num1 - num2;
  }
  public int multiply(int num1, int num2) {
    return num1 * num2;
  }

  public int divide(int num1, int num2) {
    return num1 / num2;
  }
}
```

Now, let's start by writing one or more test cases for this BasicCalculator class. For the sake of this example, the divide method is the most interesting, so let's focus on writing a test case for that method.

Listing 7-2. *The BasicCalculatorTests Class Skeleton*

```
public class BasicCalculatorTests extends TestCase {
  private BasicCalculator calculator;
  protected void setUp() throws Exception {
    calculator = new BasicCalculator();
  }
  // actual tests go here
}
```

The code in Listing 7-2 illustrates a basic test case skeleton for the BasicCalculator class's divide method. Actually, the BasicCalculatorTests class will encompass multiple test cases, as it will test several scenarios with different variables and checks, hence the plural name Tests. Important to note in Listing 7-2 is that the class extends from the TestCase base class provided by JUnit (see sidebar "JUNIT") and that its setup method is overridden in order to provide all test case instances with an already-instantiated BasicCalculator instance.

JUNIT

JUnit is the most widely used testing framework for the Java language at the time of writing. JUnit was originally created by Kent Beck and Erich Gamma.

Writing unit tests usually involves extending a certain base class, central to JUnit: the TestCase class. You then add methods to the class, named according to a certain convention. Each method that starts with test will automatically be run by the JUnit test runner. It's important to know that for each test method, the test class is reinstantiated. In addition to test cases, JUnit provides support for grouping test methods into distinct test suites.

How the testing process works is you can use assertions to validate whether the outcome or result of a method under test is actually what you expect it to be. So, for instance you can use the method assertNotNull() to make sure that the invoked method doesn't return null. These assertion methods are provided by the TestCase base class (see Table 7-1).

So let's start by writing a test to establish whether the divide method works as we expect it to work. In order to do this, we need to write a test case; in JUnit terms, this translates to a method in the TestCase class named testXXX(). Unless configured otherwise, by default JUnit and most build tools such as Ant and Maven will run all methods whose names start with test. In this case, we want to write a method to test the divide method of the BasicCalculator, so we add a method named testDivide() to the BasicCalculatorTests class (see Listing 7-3).

Listing 7-3. *The testDivide() Method Implementation*

```
public void testDivide () {

  int result = calculator.divide(10, 1);
  assertEquals(10, result);
  result = calculator.divide(10, 2);
  assertEquals(5, result);
  result = calculator.divide(10, 3);
  assertEquals(3, result);
  ...
  result = calculator.divide(10, 10);
  assertEquals(1, result);
  result = calculator.divide(10, 11);
  assertEquals(0, result);
}
```

As you can see, the implementation of the test case consists of multiple calls to the already-instantiated calculator instance. The divide method is called several times, each time with arguments to the method that are considered valid. Of course, calling the method is one thing, but making sure that the result of the calculation is as expected is just as important. Luckily, the TestCase base class, through the Assert base class, provides several convenience methods for doing just that. In this case, we use the assertEquals method to test whether the actual result is the same as the result we expected. The most important other convenience methods for asserting the results of method calls are displayed in Table 7-1. Note that all methods listed come in two variants, one basic variant and one where the user can customize the detail message of the AssertionFailedError that's thrown if the assertion fails.

Table 7-1. *Convenient Assertion Methods Provided by JUnit's Assert Class*

Method name	Description
assertEquals	Asserts that two values are equal. Several convenience methods are provided for different types of objects and primitives, such as int, double, String, Object, and many more.
assertTrue	Asserts that a specific condition is true.
assertFalse	Asserts that a specific condition is false.
assertNull	Asserts that an object is null.
assertNotNull	Asserts that an object is not null.
assertSame	Asserts that the two arguments refer to the same object instance.
assertNotSame	Asserts that the two arguments do not refer to the same object instance.

So far we've created a test case to verify that the calculator behaves as expected when provided with valid arguments. However, another important part of unit testing is to verify the expected behavior in case of arguments that might cause problems, such as null arguments or, in the case of the divide method, providing zero as the second argument. As you probably know, division by zero isn't allowed. Therefore, let's add a method to verify the expected behavior when we call the `divide` method with 0 as a second argument (see Listing 7-4).

Listing 7-4. *The testDivideByZero Method Implementation*

```
public void testDivideByZero() {
  try {
    calculator.divide(10, 0);
    fail("An arithmetic exception was expected");
  } catch (ArithmeticException e) {
    // do nothing, was expected
  }
}
```

As you can see, this is a bit more complicated. We call the divide method with zero as the second argument. In this test case, we expect an exception to be thrown by the calculator. So we surround the method call with a try-catch block and ignore the expected exception. But please note the `fail()` statement that's called if, and only if, the exception is not thrown. The `fail` method is another convenience method provided by the `Assert` base class and allows the developer of test cases to programmatically make a test fail.

GWT JUnit Integration

In the previous section, you saw how to unit-test specific features that are part of our application. However, as we'll see in this section, it gets more complicated when we want to apply this technique to some of GWT's client code, such as widgets. Obviously it's just as important to test our logic and server-side classes as it is to test the UI code of our GWT applications.

Let's assume the basic widget shown in Listing 7-5.

Listing 7-5. *The HelloWorldLabel Class*

```
public class HelloWorldLabel extends Label {
  public HelloWorldLabel() {
    super("Hello World!");
  }
}
```

Let's assume we want to write a unit test to verify that this widget really behaves the way we expect it to. In order to do this, we might write the test case in Listing 7-6, similar to the one we wrote in Listings 7-2 through 7-4.

Listing 7-6. *The Incorrect HelloWorldLabelTests Class*

```
public class HelloWorldLabelTests extends TestCase {
  public void testText() {
    HelloWorldLabel widget = new HelloWorldLabel();
    assertEquals("Hello World!", widget.getText());
  }
}
```

However, if we run the test in Listing 7-6, the test case will fail with output similar to the following:

```
java.lang.ExceptionInInitializerError
    at ...HelloWorldLabelTests.setUp(HelloWorldLabelTests.java:10)
    ... 5 more
Caused by: java.lang.UnsupportedOperationException: ERROR: GWT.create() is only
usable in client code!  It cannot be called, for example, from server code.  If
you are running a unit test, check that your test case extends GWTTestCase and
that GWT.create() is not called from within an initializer, constructor, or
setUp()/tearDown().
    at com.google.gwt.core.client.GWT.create(GWT.java:68)
    at com.google.gwt.user.client.ui.UIObject.<clinit>(UIObject.java:126)
    ... 19 more
```

As you can see from the output, the creation of the widget in the setup method fails. This is because the Label, or more specifically one of its superclasses UIObject, relies on the GWT.create() method. This method is used by GWT to accomplish deferred binding (discussed in more detail in Chapter 8), but only works in real client-side code. This effectively means that you can't unit test client-side GWT application code by extending the standard JUnit TestCase class. Note that this only applies to code that directly or indirectly depends on GWT-specific code such as GWT.create().

However, as you can see from the output of the previously failing test case, there's a work-around for this. GWT provides its own base class for test cases that verify things such as widgets. This base class, GWTTestCase, itself extends from the JUnit TestCase class, but what it does internally is start its own test runner, which starts an (invisible) hosted browser to run the widget. However, in order to do this, we need to tell the test case which module to load to test the widget in. So to test widget code, we need have a separate module just for testing. Note that you only need one module that's used by multiple client code tests.

In order to run our HelloWorldLabelTests, we first need to define a module to be run by the test case (see Listing 7-7).

Listing 7-7. *The DefaultModule.gwt.xml Module Definition*

```
<module>
  <inherits name="com.google.gwt.user.User"/>
</module>
```

And of course we need to rewrite the previously introduced test case, in this case to extend the GWTTestCase base class (see Listing 7-8).

Listing 7-8. *The Rewritten and Correct HelloWorldLabelTests Class*

```
public class HelloWorldLabelTests extends GWTTestCase {

  public String getModuleName() {
    return "com.apress.beginninggwt.ch07.DefaultModule";
```

```
  }
  public void testText() {
    HelloWorldLabel widget = new HelloWorldLabel();
    assertEquals("Hello World!", widget.getText());
  }
}
```

■**Caution** Make sure you put the test module descriptor in the parent package of the client package where the unit test and the code under test reside. If you get this wrong, the test will fail with an error indicating that the compiled test class can't be found.

It's important to get two things from the code in Listing 7-8. First, note that instead of extending directly from JUnit's TestCase base class, HelloWorldLabelTests extends from GWT's GWTTestCase base class. This leads to the second difference, namely the added implementation of the abstract method provided by the superclass, the getModuleName method. It's called by the GWT test runner to determine which module it needs to load. In this case, we instruct it to load the module specified in the file with the name DefaultModule.gwt.xml. This file is placed inside the corresponding package.

The junitCreator Utility Script

Instead of creating the test and corresponding module manually, you can use the script that's provided by GWT. This script, junitCreator, is provided by the default distribution of GWT and is part of the package of scripts introduced in Chapter 3. The junitCreator script generates a test case as described previously, and also generates convenient scripts for running the test in both hosted and web mode.

Calling the script with no arguments will display the argument options. Note that because we've added the GWT installation directory to our PATH environment variable, we don't have to refer to the installation directory. Instead, we can just call the script directly:

```
>junitCreator
Google Web Toolkit 0.0.2415
JUnitCreator -junit pathToJUnitJar -module moduleName [-eclipse projectName]
 [-out dir] [-overwrite] [-ignore] className
where
  -junit     Specify the path to your junit.jar (required)
  -module    Specify the name of the GWT module to use (required)
  -eclipse   Creates a debug launch config for the named eclipse project
  -out       The directory to write output files into (defaults to current)
  -overwrite Overwrite any existing files
  -ignore    Ignore any existing files; do not overwrite
and
  className  The fully-qualified name of the test class to create
```

As you can see, the script takes three mandatory arguments: the path to the JUnit jar, the module name, and the class name of the test. All other script arguments are optional, and the preceding code supplies some explanation on how to use them.

So let's run the script to generate a skeleton for the test comparable with what we created earlier. Please note that we use another class name for the test class in order to avoid a collision with the already-created test. Also note that we reuse the module that we've already created:

```
> junitCreator -junit lib\junit-3.8.1.jar
 -eclipse HelloWorldLabel
 –module com.apress.beginninggwt.ch07.DefaultTest
 com.apress.beginninggwt.ch07.HelloWorldLabel2Tests
Created file test\com\apress\beginninggwt\ch07\HelloWorldLabel2Tests.java
Created file HelloWorldLabel-hosted.launch
Created file HelloWorldLabel-web.launch
Created file HelloWorldLabel2Tests-hosted.cmd
Created file HelloWorldLabel2Tests-web.cmd
```

Please note that running the generated `HelloWorldLabel2Tests-hosted.cmd` script will result in the test being run as Java bytecode in a JVM. Running `HelloWorldLabel2Tests-web.cmd` will run the test as compiled JavaScript. The launch configurations do the same thing in Eclipse.

This section has shown that GWT provides support for testing your client-side UI code that you can't test due to dependence on the `GWT.create()` method. The next section will compare the default unit testing with the mechanism introduced in this section and will provide pointers on when to use which.

Comparing Basic and GWT Unit Testing

So far we've seen basic unit testing using JUnit as well as the unit testing support provided by GWT. It's important to know that the GWT unit testing starts a hosted-mode browser for each test case. Therefore, tests written using the unit-test support provided by GWT tend to run slowly when compared to basic unit testing using JUnit.

So as a very important rule of thumb, only use the unit-test support provided by GWT as a last resort. Also, because the startup time of the hosted mode is the biggest bottleneck, try to do as much testing as possible in one test method, without sacrificing too much in the way of test granularity. If you have a choice, always favor fast, basic unit testing over the slow alternative.

Functional Testing

As discussed earlier, functional testing is a way to test the functionality provided by a piece of software. Therefore, functional testing can be used to perform integration, system, and system integration testing. But as mentioned earlier, we consider system and integration testing to be outside of the scope of this book, so we'll focus solely on functional testing in this section.

The means of testing that we've discussed so far are useful when testing individual parts of an application. However, if we want to functionally test an application, we have to resort to other mechanisms. So we'll now look at Selenium, a more comprehensive tool that can be used for extensive functional testing.

An important aspect of functional testing and more specifically testing using Selenium is that it lets you test the application as part of a larger environment. In the case of GWT applications, it's important to test the developed application in different browsers to avoid running into problems later due to browser incompatibilities.

Introducing Selenium

Selenium is a test tool that allows you easily to functionally test your web applications. It's far from specific to GWT applications; it enables testing of all web applications. Selenium is open source and was originally developed by ThoughtWorks.

As mentioned in the introduction to this section, to correctly test a web application, we need to test it in a browser (actually multiple browsers). This is what Selenium allows us to do. Selenium works by letting you define test scripts that Selenium can run in a browser for you. Depending on your needs, you can choose different browsers and platforms to run your script on. You can even include these tests as part of your continuous build/integration environment. But before we go into these more advanced topics, let's first look at the different ways you can use Selenium. Selenium itself distinguishes four separate ways of using it:

- **Selenium IDE**—a plug-in for the Firefox browser that allows you to record and run Selenium tests from within the browser environment.

- **Selenium Core**—this encompasses the core libraries to run the tests as part of your web applications.

- **Selenium Remote Control (RC)**—a more advanced Selenium setup that requires more technical knowledge to set it up, but also allows you to perform more advanced tests because it allows you to write your tests in your preferred language (in our case, Java).

- **Selenium Grid**—an advanced version of Selenium RC that allows you to speed up tests by running them in parallel on different machines. This setup is only interesting when you want to run code on different platforms as part of one test. However, the setup is similar to Selenium RC, so we aren't going to deal with it in this book. More information on how to use Selenium Grid can be found at the Selenium Grid web site: `http://selenium-grid.openqa.org`.

In order to provide you with the most gentle and pragmatic introduction to functional testing with Selenium, it's easiest to look at the Selenium IDE first.

Selenium IDE

As mentioned earlier, the Selenium IDE is a Firefox plug-in that allows developers to record and play back Selenium test scripts in the browser. The most important feature of the IDE is the ability to record test scripts easily and make them part of your functional testing setup. The main advantage of using this plug-in is that even nontechnical people can record test scripts. This allows a nontechnical user or customer to record test scripts and then hand them off to the developers to include them as part of the test suite. However, in the context of this book, starting off with the Selenium IDE provides a gentle introduction to using Selenium in general.

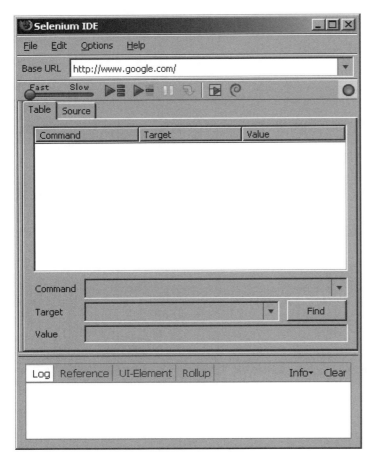

Figure 7-1. *The Selenium IDE (as a separate window)*

In order to start using the Selenium IDE, you first need to install it. We assume you already have Firefox installed; if not, go to the Firefox download site to get it: `http://getfirefox.com`. First, go to the Selenium IDE download page (`http://selenium-ide.openqa.org/download.jsp`) to download the latest version of the IDE. Allow the web site to install the necessary plug-in if your security settings dictate. You may need to restart Firefox to finish the installation.

Once you have the plug-in installed, you can either use it as a separate window or as a sidebar, depending on your preference. In order to use a separate window to view the Selenium IDE, go to the Extra menu and select the Selenium IDE menu item (see Figure 7-1). To use it as a sidebar, go to View > Sidebar and check the Selenium IDE menu item. It will then show as a sidebar item (see Figure 7-2). In the remainder of this chapter, we'll use the sidebar, but there's really no difference in terms of usage.

As mentioned earlier, Selenium isn't limited to just GWT or Ajax applications. You can use Selenium (and therefore its IDE) to test any web application. So let's just take another web site that you might know: `www.google.com`. In this section, we'll pretend to be the QA department of Google that's responsible for functionally testing Google's search application. Let's start off by writing a simple test case using the Selenium IDE.

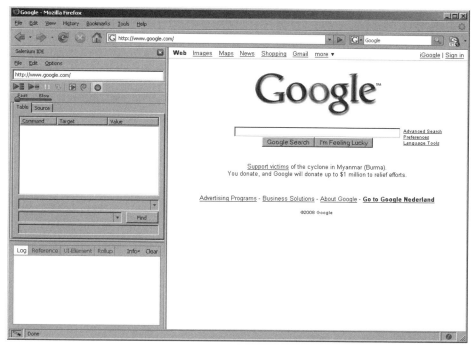

Figure 7-2. *The Selenium IDE (as a sidebar)*

First, go to the Google home page and make sure the Now Recording button (the red, round button) is pressed/active. Now, let's type in a search query in order to test the search functionality. In line with the topic of this book, let's search for "gwt".

As you can see in Figure 7-3, the content panel (the right part) shows the normal Google search results page, while in the Selenium IDE sidebar, some items have been added to the Command list. This command list is visualized as a table with three columns:

- **Command**—the action that was performed

- **Target**—the target to apply the command on

- **Value**—the value (if any) for the command

After issuing the "gwt" search query, you can see that the Selenium IDE has added three actions to the command table. Let's go over each of these commands one by one to introduce them individually.

The open Command

The open command is primarily used as the first command of every test case, but you can have several open commands in the same test case. As the name suggests, this command opens a specific URL, which you provide as the `target` argument. This can be either an absolute or a relative URL. In this case, it's a relative URL pointing to the root URL specified in the top of the Selenium IDE: `http://www.google.com`. Note that this command will force the IDE to wait until the page is completely loaded before continuing to issue the next command.

Figure 7-3. *The Google result page and the first command in the IDE*

The type Command

The next command when issuing the Google search query is the `type` command, which as the name suggests types a certain value in a certain target. In this case, the value "gwt" is typed into an element that can be located using q. We'll discuss element locators later in this chapter, but in this case, the target is an element with the name q, which happens to be the main input field of the Google home page.

The clickAndWait Command

The last command that is issued is the `clickAndWait` command that, again as the name suggests, clicks on something and waits. In this case, it clicks on an element that can be located by the string "btnG", which happens to be the Google Search button on the Google home page. The "wait" part refers to the fact that the command will wait for the resulting page to load completely.

So far, we've seen how to issue some sample commands and record them using the Selenium IDE, but this doesn't really constitute a test case. In order to test, we need to verify that the result of the commands is something we expected. Luckily, the Selenium IDE provides convenient support for this as well. In order to illustrate how this verification works, let's assume the following two test cases that might be interesting from a Google QA department perspective:

1. We want to make sure that the first result page returned by Google actually contains a link to the official home page of the Google Web Toolkit project.

2. We want to check that the query that was issued by the user is reflected in the result page, and more specifically that it's prefilled in the query input field of the result page.

These two test cases are just simple examples of things a QA department wants to test, but they provide a convenient introduction to the assertion support offered by Selenium and more specifically the Selenium IDE.

The verifyTextPresent Assertion

In order to check that the official home page of the GWT project is listed when querying Google for the term "gwt", we want to verify that the returned result page contains a link to the specific page `http://code.google.com/webtoolkit`. Luckily, the Selenium IDE provides easy support for this. The only thing we have to do is select the text we want to assert and bring up the context-sensitive pop-up menu (see Figure 7-4).

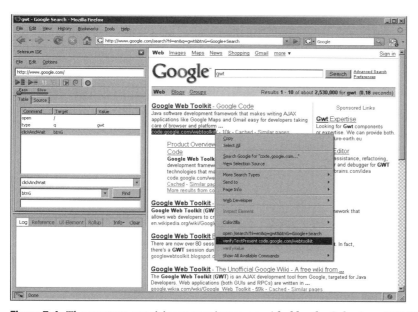

Figure 7-4. *The context-sensitive menu items provided by the Selenium IDE (1)*

In the context-sensitive menu, the bottom menu items are assertions and actions provided by the Selenium IDE. As you can see from the screenshot, one of the assertions is `verifyTextPresent`, with the selected text already added as an argument. If we select this menu item from the pop-up menu, the assertion is added to the Selenium IDE in the command table. Note from Figure 7-5 that the assertion was added to the Selenium sidebar. Also note that the actual text to verify is added to the target column and not to the value column, which might be conceptually better.

That's all we need to do in order to add a simple assertion to our test case that verifies that a certain piece of text is present on the result page.

The verifyValue Assertion

Now, let's do the same thing to verify that the search term is correctly prefilled in the search query field of the result page. In this case, we don't just want to check whether the term is actually present in the page, but take it a little further. We want to check if the value of the input field is what we expect. Again, the Selenium IDE helps us a lot. By doing the same thing as previously, bringing up the context-sensitive pop-up menu, we can select the appropriate assertion (see Figure 7-5).

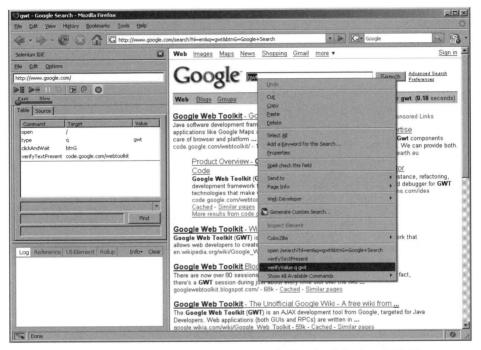

Figure 7-5. *The context-sensitive menu items provided by the Selenium IDE (2)*

In this case we select the verifyValue item, which subsequently is also added to the Selenium sidebar. As you can see from Figure 7-6, the verifyValue assertion has two arguments, the target, in this case an element that can be located by q, and the value "gwt".

Now that we've created our simple test case, let's verify that it works. To do this, all we need to do is click the Play button (the first button containing a green arrow). This forces the IDE to jump out of recording mode and replay the script. As you can see if you look closely (it will probably happen very fast), the script performs all recorded actions: load the root page, type in the search query, and click the Search button. Then it will also run the assertions that we added. As you can tell from Figure 7-7, the assertions are run and the result of each assertion is indicated by coloring the assertion (in this case green because they succeeded).

Now, to verify that it actually works, let's deliberately break the test. In the Source tab of the command table, let's change the value of the last assertion into something else (in this case "flex") and rerun the test. The assertion is now colored red and the test fails (see Figure 7-8).

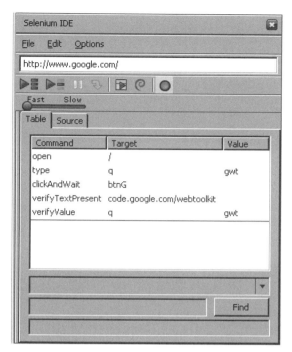

Figure 7-6. *The resulting command table of the Selenium IDE*

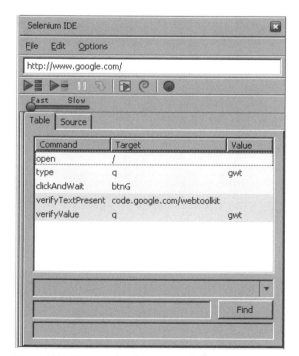

Figure 7-7. *The result of running the test case (success)*

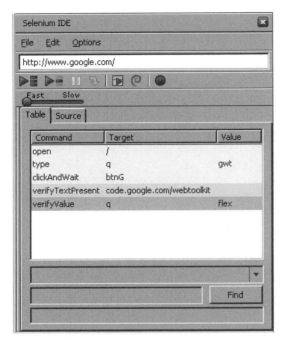

Figure 7-8. *The result of running the test case (fail)*

Just a couple pointers before we move on to a more detailed description of using Selenium. First, as you can see from Figure 7-5, below the commands table there's an area that contains several tabs. If you ran the test cases, you'll notice that the Log tab fills up with log entries that result from running the test. However, a far more interesting tab is the Reference tab. When you click on a command in the command table, the Reference tab shows some reference documentation on the command and its usage. This often contains interesting and useful information.

Another thing to note, as you can see in Figure 7-5, is that the context-sensitive pop-up menu described earlier also contains a submenu item labeled Show All Available Commands. This option (as the name suggests) opens a menu listing all available commands for the current selection and/or position in the document (see Figure 7-9).

Saving the Test Case

So far we've used the Selenium IDE to record a test case and use its built-in support for adding assertions to the test. But now we also want to keep the test for later reference. As we'll see in the next section, we can easily reuse the test cases that were recorded using the Selenium IDE when we start working with the Selenium Core and more advanced parts. So let's look at how we can save the test case that we previously created.

First of all, we need to know that the default format the Selenium IDE uses is HTML. As we'll see later, other formats are also supported, but for the next section, HTML will do fine. To make sure we're saving the test case as HTML, please check the format under Options > Format. If another format is selected, please check HTML.

Figure 7-9. *The Show All Available Commands context-sensitive submenu*

Now, actually saving the generated test case is easy. Just select the Save Test Case menu item, select a location, and type a file name (make sure to use the .html suffix). Now to conclude this section, let's look at the output of the save action, the generated HTML version of the test case (see Listing 7-9).

Listing 7-9. *The Generated Test Case (in HTML Format)*

```
<?xml version="1.0" encoding="UTF-8"?>
<!DOCTYPE html PUBLIC "-//W3C//DTD XHTML 1.0 Strict//EN"
                      "http://www.w3.org/TR/xhtml1/DTD/xhtml1-strict.dtd">
<html xmlns="http://www.w3.org/1999/xhtml" xml:lang="en" lang="en">
  <head profile="http://selenium-ide.openqa.org/profiles/test-case">
    <meta http-equiv="Content-Type" content="text/html; charset=UTF-8" />
    <link rel="selenium.base" href="" />
    <title>selenium_test</title>
  </head>
  <body>
    <table cellpadding="1" cellspacing="1" border="1">
      <thead>
        <tr><td rowspan="1" colspan="3">selenium_test</td></tr>
      </thead>
```

```
    <tbody>
      <tr>
        <td>open</td>
        <td>/</td>
        <td></td>
      </tr>
      <tr>
        <td>type</td>
        <td>q</td>
        <td>gwt</td>
      </tr>
      <tr>
        <td>clickAndWait</td>
        <td>btnG</td>
        <td></td>
      </tr>
      <tr>
        <td>verifyTextPresent</td>
        <td>code.google.com/webtoolkit</td>
        <td></td>
      </tr>
      <tr>
        <td>verifyValue</td>
        <td>q</td>
        <td>gwt</td>
      </tr>
    </tbody>
  </table>
  </body>
</html>
```

Selenium Core

So far we've seen how to use the Selenium IDE to record and play back test cases. This is convenient, but it has one fairly large limitation: it only allows you to test your application in Firefox. There's no version of the Selenium IDE for other browsers (yet). Luckily, Selenium Core comes to the rescue.

Selenium Core provides a mechanism that allows you to run the same test case we created in the previous section as part of your web application. As we'll see in a second, in order to use this mechanism, you need to have control over the application that you want to test and you need to know how to deploy the application (including the test runner and accompanying test cases). But before we go into the specifics of using the Selenium Core mechanism, let's first look at the element locator mechanism, the commands and built-in assertions provided by Selenium in general.

Element Locators

Element locators are strings that tell Selenium which HTML element a command refers to. In the previous section, we touched on element locators twice. Both the `type` and the `verifyValue` commands used a basic element locator to locate the element the command applied to. In both cases, it referred to an element with the name q. But let's look at some more sophisticated element locators provided by Selenium (see Table 7-2).

Table 7-2. *Element Locator Types Provided by Selenium*

LocatorType	Description
`identifier=id`	Select the element with the specified `id` attribute. If no match is found, select the first element whose `name` attribute is `id`.
`id=id`	Select the element with the specified `id` attribute.
`name=name`	Select the first element with the specified `name` attribute. The name may optionally be followed by one or more element filters (see below), separated from the name by whitespace.
`dom=expr`	Find an element using JavaScript to traverse the HTML Document Object Model. DOM locators must begin with `document`. Example: `dom=document.forms['myForm'].myDropdown`
`xpath=expr`	Locate an element using an XPath expression. Example: `xpath=//img[@alt='The image alt text']`
`link=pattern`	Select the link (anchor) element that contains text matching the specified pattern.

The default element locator is the `identifier` (like the ones we discussed earlier), so when a `locatorType` prefix is missing, the `identifier` is used. Please note that the table of element locators isn't exhaustive; it only lists the most important and most widely used locators. Also note that Selenium provides more sophisticated mechanisms, such as so-called element filters and built-in string-match patterns, but those are considered out of scope for this book, as they're generally not needed.

Commands

Commands are the instructions that tell Selenium what to do. Selenium commands come in three specific flavors: actions, accessors, and assertions. As illustrated in the previous section, they all come in the form of command, target, and value.

Actions Actions are commands that directly manipulate the state of the application under testing. So the `open`, `type`, and `clickAndWait` commands are all actions. Other actions include `goBack`, `dragdrop`, `close`, `keyPress`, `refresh`, `select`, and so on. All are pretty straightforward; for a full description, look at the Selenium reference.

Accessors Accessors are used to examine the state of the application under test. They typically store the results in variables that can later be used for assertions. Accessors include things such as storeTitle, storeBodyText, storeAlert, and storeValue. Typically, these aren't the ones used directly while creating simple test cases. But they're used by Selenium to automatically generate the corresponding assertions.

Assertions Before we go into the assertions that Selenium provides, we should note that assertions come in three modes: assert, verify, and waitFor (see Table 7-3).

Table 7-3. *The Three Different Modes of Assertions*

Mode	Description
assert	When an assert fails, the test is aborted.
verify	When a verify fails, the test will continue to execute.
waitFor	Will cause the test to wait for a certain condition to become valid. Note that the test will fail and halt when a certain timeout is reached before the condition becomes valid.

Taking these three modes, the storeTitle accessor automatically generates six assertions: assertTitle, assertNotTitle, verifyTitle, verifyNotTitle, waitForTitle, and waitForNotTitle. The same goes for the storeAlert accessor, leading to assertAlert, assertNotAlert, and so on. The pattern should be clear by now.

Using the Selenium Core

The mechanism provided by Selenium Core depends heavily on using iframes and JavaScript for its internal workings. Because JavaScript is restricted inside a browser environment by the so-called Same Origin Policy, you can only use this mechanism to test applications that you host yourself. So we can't use it to test, for instance, the Google web application, as we previously did using the Selenium IDE. This is because we can't ask (or at least don't expect to get) Google to add Selenium and our test cases to their hosted application. But that's okay, as we want to use Selenium to test our own web application anyway. So let's look at how we can use Selenium Core to test our own application.

Installing Selenium Installing Selenium Core is easy: the only thing you have to do is to navigate to the Selenium download page (http://selenium-core.openqa.org/download.jsp) and download the latest distribution of the Selenium Core. Next, just unpack the core folder of the downloaded zip file to the root of your web server or servlet runner (depending on your setup). That's all you have to do to get Selenium Core installed.

Running Selenium Once installed, using your favorite web browser, just navigate to the TestRunner.html page in the core folder on your web site. You should see something that closely resembles the picture depicted in Figure 7-10. Please note that your screen might look slightly different depending on the exact version of Selenium Core.

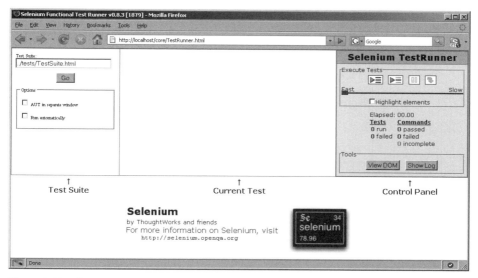

Figure 7-10. *The TestRunner.html page in Firefox*

As you can see, the screen is divided into four sections:

- **Test Suite**—the part where the test suite is managed. In Figure 7-10, this shows the selector for choosing the test suite to open, but as we'll see in a later section, this part can also show the content of a test suite.

- **Current Test**—the part that shows the test that's currently being run.

- **Control Panel**—the control panel part that allows you to control Selenium and how it actually runs your test. The control panel will be discussed in more detail next.

- **Main Application**—the part where the actual application being tested will show.

Before we continue to show how to actually create a test suite and add a test to it, let's first take a more detailed look at the Control Panel of the Selenium test runner page (see Figure 7-11).

As you can see, it closely resembles the Selenium IDE in the sense that it allows you to run individual tests (but also all tests) and provides feedback about the result of the tests.

Creating a Test As mentioned before, we can't use Selenium Core to test applications that aren't under our control, so we need to create a different test case for our own application. Let's go back to the UserRegistrationForm application introduced in Chapter 4. If we create a test manually or using the Selenium IDE, the end result will be something like Listing 7-10. Be sure to save that test in a folder named tests in the root of your web application, under the name UserRegistrationFormTests.html.

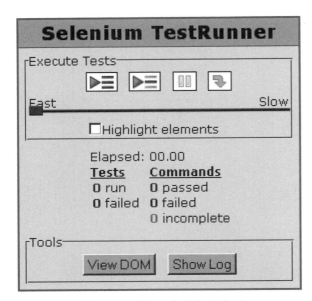

Figure 7-11. *The Control Panel of the Selenium test runner*

Listing 7-10. *A Selenium Test Case for the UserRegistrationForm Application*

```
<?xml version="1.0" encoding="UTF-8"?>
<!DOCTYPE html PUBLIC "-//W3C//DTD XHTML 1.0 Strict//EN"
                      "http://www.w3.org/TR/xhtml1/DTD/xhtml1-strict.dtd">
<html xmlns="http://www.w3.org/1999/xhtml" xml:lang="en" lang="en">
  <head profile="http://selenium-ide.openqa.org/profiles/test-case">
    <meta http-equiv="Content-Type" content="text/html; charset=UTF-8" />
    <link rel="selenium.base" href="http://localhost/" />
    <title>UserRegistrationFormTests</title>
  </head>
  <body>
    <table cellpadding="1" cellspacing="1" border="1">
      <thead>
        <tr><td rowspan="1" colspan="3">UserRegistrationFormTests</td></tr>
      </thead>
      <tbody>
        <tr>
          <td>open</td>
          <td>/...chap4.UserRegistrationForm/UserRegistrationForm.html</td>
          <td></td>
        </tr>
        <tr>
          <td>type</td>
          <td>//input[@type='text']</td>
          <td>bram</td>
        </tr>
```

```
      <tr>
        <td>type</td>
        <td>//input[@type='password']</td>
        <td>lullo</td>
      </tr>
      <tr>
        <td>type</td>
        <td>//td[@id='retypePasswordField']/input</td>
        <td>lullo</td>
      </tr>
      <tr>
        <td>click</td>
        <td>//button[@type='button']</td>
        <td></td>
      </tr>
      <tr>
        <td>assertAlert</td>
        <td>username: 'bram', password: 'lullo'</td>
        <td></td>
      </tr>
    </tbody>
  </table>
 </body>
</html>
```

Adding a Test to the Test Suite Now that we've added the specific test to the `tests` folder of our web application, we need to add it to a test suite. Selenium uses test suites to group individual test cases together. Creating a test suite and adding tests to it is simple when using Selenium Core. Test suites, like individual test cases, are represented by HTML pages, each containing a table. In the case of test suites, the table in the HTML document contains all tests to run. So a test suite that contains only the test we created for our application will have only one entry in its table referencing that one test case (see Listing 7-11).

Listing 7-11. *A Selenium Test Suite Containing Only One Test Case*

```
<?xml version="1.0" encoding="UTF-8"?>
<!DOCTYPE html PUBLIC "-//W3C//DTD XHTML 1.0 Strict//EN"
                      "http://www.w3.org/TR/xhtml1/DTD/xhtml1-strict.dtd">
<html xmlns="http://www.w3.org/1999/xhtml" xml:lang="en" lang="en">
  <head profile="http://selenium-ide.openqa.org/profiles/test-case">
    <meta http-equiv="Content-Type" content="text/html; charset=UTF-8" />
    <link rel="selenium.base" href="http://localhost/" />
    <title>My Test Suite</title>
  </head>
  <body>
    <table cellpadding="1" cellspacing="1" border="1">
      <thead>
```

```
      <tr><td rowspan="1" colspan="3">My Test Suite</td></tr>
    </thead>
    <tbody>
      <tr>
        <td>
          <a href="UserRegistrationFormTests.html">
            UserRegistrationFormTests
          </a>
        </td>
      </tr>
    </tbody>
  </table>
</body>
</html>
```

Just save the code using the default Selenium test suite name `TestSuite.html`. Then navigate back to the test runner page.

Running the Test Suite If you now click on the Go button of the test runner, it opens the selected, default test suite and shows its contents. It also shows the current test as the first test of the test suite (see Figure 7-12).

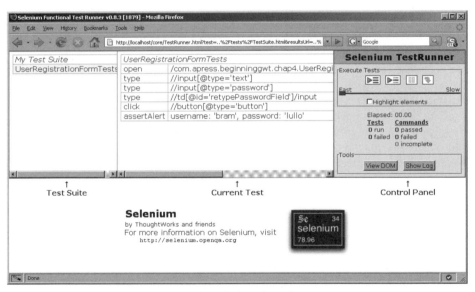

Figure 7-12. *The Selenium test runner with the selected test suite*

Now, the only thing we need to do is run the test suite, by clicking the Run All Tests button. The result (shown in Figure 7-13) looks much like what we saw earlier using the Selenium IDE. But in this case, we can navigate to the test runner page using any browser on any platform to test the application and still verify that it functions correctly in that browser.

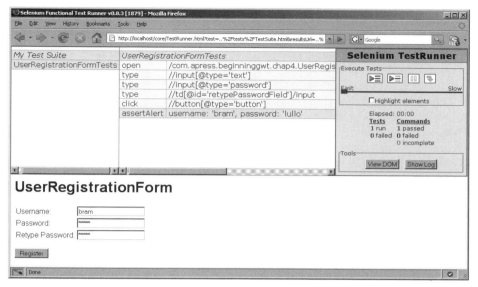

Figure 7-13. *The result of running the test suite in the test runner*

Advanced Features You can also do more advanced things in test cases and test suites, such as using setup and teardown hooks similar to the hooks in JUnit. You can also make the test runner run all tests in the specified suite by specifying an extra parameter (auto=true) when opening the test runner page. This is useful when you want to include Selenium testing as part of your automated test environment and/or continuous integration. For this and other more advanced features, consult the Selenium Core home page (http://selenium-core.openqa.org).

Selenium Remote Control

Selenium Remote Control (RC) is another extension of Selenium Core that allows you to use a much more powerful mechanism to describe your test cases. We found that the most effective way to write our tests was in Java, but Selenium RC has support for other languages as well, including C#, Perl, PHP, Ruby, and JavaScript.

The setup of Selenium RC is also slightly different, in that it uses a remote control server, which acts as a proxy server between the remote test runner and the application under test. It would be tedious to describe this setup in detail. But with the information you've read so far about Selenium, you should easily be able to use Selenium RC if you wish. The main advantage of Selenium RC is that it allows you to orchestrate the same test on different browsers and different platforms. For more information on Selenium RC, have a look at the Selenium RC home page (http://selenium-rc.openqa.org).

Benchmarking

In addition to being able to unit test your normal Java code, GWT's support for testing UI code, and using Selenium for functional testing and testing for browser incompatibilities, GWT also provides out-of-the-box support for benchmarking. This section will describe that support and how it may benefit you as an application developer.

What Is Benchmarking?

In computing, benchmarking is running a program or operation to assess its relative performance. You usually do this by running multiple trials with different input data to see what effect the changes in data have on performance.

When developing GWT applications, it's interesting (and for some operations even essential) to do some benchmarking. Because the entire GWT application is eventually compiled into JavaScript, benchmarking becomes important. Overall, but in some browsers even more than in others, JavaScript tends to run far slower than normal Java code. Therefore, being able to trace and fix performance bottlenecks is truly important.

Luckily for us, GWT comes with some built-in support for benchmarking. It enables you to write benchmarks easily and then run them on different platforms and browsers to compare their performance.

Writing a Benchmark

Writing a benchmark using GWT's built-in support is easy (see Listing 7-12). It's just like writing a normal unit test, only we need to extend from another base class: Benchmark.

Listing 7-12. *The BasicCalculatorBenchmark Class*

```
public class BasicCalculatorBenchmark extends Benchmark {
  private BasicCalculator calculator;
  protected void setUp() throws Exception {
    calculator = new BasicCalculator();
  }

  public String getModuleName() {
    return "com.apress.beginninggwt.ch07.DefaultModule";
  }
  // actual benchmark methods go here
}
```

As you can see from the sample benchmark skeleton, there's not much difference between this benchmark class and the unit test that uses GWT's unit test support. We just need to extend the Benchmark class and implement the getModuleName() method. But now, let's write the actual benchmark.

Let's first write a simple benchmark for the multiply() method of the BasicCalculator class (see Listing 7-13). We just add a method called testMultiply() as we would do using JUnit. Only in this case, we want to provide the test method with different input on each run, so we need to provide it with an argument to the method. We give the method a single argument, so it takes a single integer as argument.

Listing 7-13. *The testMultiply Method with One Argument and Without Arguments*

```
public void testMultiply(@RangeField("testRange") Integer arg) {
  calculator.multiply(arg, 2);
}
```

```
public void testMultiply() {
  // just placeholder for junit
}
```

As you can see, the first test method just calls the calculator `multiply` method with one variable argument and one fixed argument. The main thing to get from this code listing is that the `testMultiply` method takes one argument, an integer that's annotated with a range (which we'll discuss in a moment). So, this test method will be called with a specific range of input variables. Also note that we need to provide an empty placeholder method with the same name and no arguments. This is because of JUnit's test runner, which doesn't run if there are no test methods, as the method with arguments doesn't count as a real test method according to JUnit. So every benchmark method should have a corresponding test method with no arguments.

Now, in order to perform a benchmark, we need to define the range of input variables to use as input. This is conveniently done by creating a field that defines a range and then referencing it using the corresponding annotation (see Listing 7-14). There are other ways to do it, but this is by far the easiest.

Listing 7-14. *Defining the testRange Field to Use for the Benchmark*

```
protected IntRange testRange =
    new IntRange(0, 1000000, Operator.ADD, 200000);
```

We just define a range of integers to use as input data. We start the range at 0 and work our way up to 1,000,000 by adding 200,000 for each test run, so we complete in five steps. We can now run the benchmark, which will write an output report (using the naming convention: `report-<timestamp>.xml`).

The next step is to view the generated report. Luckily, GWT provides a basic tool to view the generated report. This utility script called `benchmarkViewer` can be used by just specifying the path where the report resides. Starting the viewer will bring up a tool that resembles the hosted mode and lists all known reports. Please note that the appearance and content of the report viewer may differ from those shown in Figure 7-14, depending on the specific version of GWT that you're using.

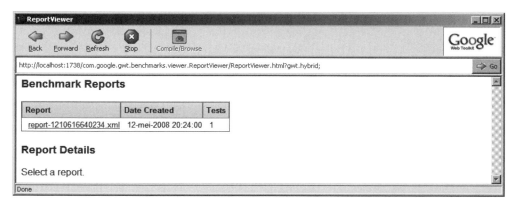

Figure 7-14. *The benchmark report viewer after the initial benchmark run*

If you now click on the single report that's presented, the viewer will show the details of the selected benchmark report, as shown in Figure 7-15.

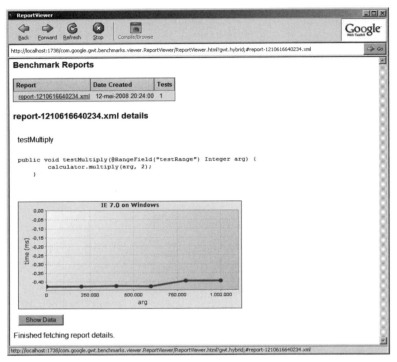

Figure 7-15. *The benchmark report viewer showing the detailed report of the benchmark*

The graph that's part of the report shows how long it took to complete the `multiply()` operation, relative to the value of the argument that was passed in. As you can see from the detailed report, the time taken to complete the operation doesn't fluctuate much based on the input. The small fluctuations are more because of JavaScript's inability to measure small amounts of time. So in order to provide us with a better example, we have to add a more convenient benchmarkable method to the `BasicCalculator`. Let's assume for some reason that `BasicCalculator` also contained the method shown in Listing 7-15.

Listing 7-15. *The slowMultiply Method on the BasicCalculator Class*

```
public int slowMultiply(int num1, int num2) {
  for (int i = 0; i < num1; i++) {
    for (int j = 0; j < num2; j++) {
      multiply(i, j);
    }
  }
  return multiply(num1, num2);
}
```

Although probably not very useful for calculating, it comes in handy from a benchmark perspective. Now, let's assume we want to benchmark this method, using the same range. You might expect the graph to look a little different, because of the way the slowMultiply() method is implemented. But, let's add the method (and corresponding no-argument method) shown in Listing 7-16 to the BasicCalculatorBenchmark class.

Listing 7-16. *The Methods to Benchmark the slowMultiply Method*

```
public void testSlowMultiply(@RangeField("testRange") Integer arg) {
  calculator.slowMultiply(arg, 2);
}
public void testSlowMultiply() {
  // just placeholder for junit
}
```

As you can see, the benchmark method does exactly the same thing as the previous benchmark method, only it calls the slow version of the multiply method.

Now, let's run the benchmark once more and start the report viewer to view the outcome (see Figure 7-16 for the overview and Figure 7-17 for the details). Note that you can also just click Refresh in the report viewer after the benchmark has finished.

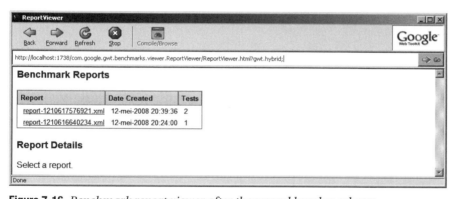

Figure 7-16. *Benchmark report viewer after the second benchmark run*

In the last part of the detailed report—the testSlowMultiply part—the graph shows an obvious trend in that each increment in the argument passed in leads to a large increment in time taken to complete the test method.

There's a lot more to be said about benchmarking and the support GWT provides for it. But as far as this book is concerned, our discussion of benchmarking is now complete. If you want to know more about the features GWT provides for doing more complex benchmarking, take a look at the Javadoc documentation in the Benchmark class of GWT.

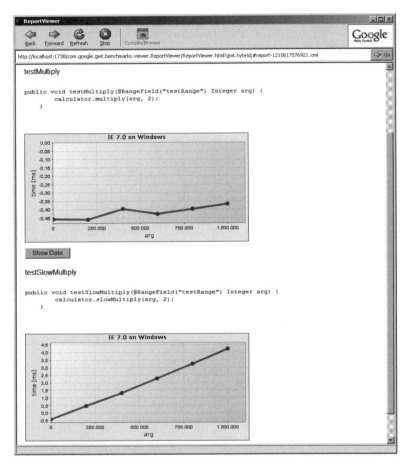

Figure 7-17. *The benchmark report viewer showing the detailed report of the second benchmark*

Summary

This chapter introduces different kinds of testing and goes into some detail on unit testing and functional testing. For unit testing, the chapter introduced JUnit as a tool to easily unit test your code, including client-side code, without dependencies on GWT's deferred binding mechanism.

When you need to test client UI code that depends heavily on the deferred binding mechanism, JUnit is insufficient. In that case, we resort to the unit testing support provided by GWT out of the box. However, this testing tends to be a lot slower than basic unit testing. So when offered a choice, basic unit testing should be favored over GWT's unit test support.

Next, the chapter introduced Selenium and showed how you can leverage its power to test your application functionally and hunt for browser incompatibilities. Selenium allows you to test your application in every conceivable browser on every platform.

Last, the chapter discussed benchmarking, why it's important, and how GWT provides out-of-the-box support for it, including a graphical report viewer to view the result of the benchmark.

CHAPTER 8

■ ■ ■

Advanced Topics

In previous chapters, we walked you through the process of building a rich web-based application using the most basic features GWT has to offer. But there's more to building a real-world RIA than what we've covered so far—issues such as performance, localization, and browser history support need to be considered. Moreover, no framework can be considered complete if it doesn't provide a flexible and nonrestrictive extension mechanism.

This chapter will introduce some of the more advanced features in GWT that will help you tackle these issues. It's structured differently compared to its predecessors, as each section is dedicated to a specific topic and therefore can be read independently from the others.

Internationalization (i18n)

When developing any type of application, one of the most important factors to keep in mind is your target user. The importance of the user increases even more when developing RIAs, as they're potentially open to vast numbers of users around the globe. This multicultural and multilingual nature of modern web applications requires extra care in the design and development phases. RIAs need to be written in such a way that their presentation logic (and sometimes even their functional logic) can adapt to the country and language of their users. Obviously, when writing such applications, you want to avoid manually rewriting the same code over and over, each time targeting a different language and/or locale. Support for i18n[1] is usually built in to the web application framework that you use, and GWT is no exception in this regard.

When it comes to presentation logic, there are two main obstacles to good i18n support—string literals and data formats. String literals are all those static strings that you normally use in your application. In UI applications, they're often used as labels onscreen or captions on top of widgets (for example, button captions). The term *data formats* refers to the different ways a given piece of data can be displayed on the screen. GWT helps overcome these obstacles through a special technique built on top of its deferred binding mechanism.

Deferred binding was introduced in Chapter 6 in the context of remoting. You saw how, through this mechanism, GWT can maximize its cross-browser compatibility by compiling the same Java code to multiple versions, each corresponding to a different browser type. The nonintrusive nature of this mechanism (it has minimal influence on your Java code base) also makes it an ideal way of supporting i18n. Without getting into too much detail, suffice it to say

---

1. *i18n* is short for "internationalization." The first and last letters (*i* and *n*) are taken from the word itself, and the number *18* represents the 18 characters between these two letters.

that when you use GWT's i18n support, the GWT compiler compiles your code into multiple versions, one for each country and/or language you configure. In practice, there are three main ways of using this support; we cover them all in the following sections.

A Few Words on Java Resource Bundles

GWT i18n is based on the same concepts as Java resource bundles. A resource bundle in Java is an abstraction of localized text message lookup, and is the standard mechanism that Java applications use to support i18n. The default and most commonly used implementation of this is the PropertyResourceBundle class, which is based on properties files. With this implementation, messages are associated with unique keys, and multiple properties files can be defined, one for each supported locale. Each file maps the key to a localized version of the message. The properties files are differentiated using a well-defined naming convention. For example, Figure 8-1 shows three resource bundles, one for common English, another for American English, and a third for Dutch. All these resource bundles map the "color" key to the appropriate localized message.

Figure 8-1. *Resource bundles for three different locales*

Note how the names of these files indicate the locales they represent. All the resource bundles in Figure 8-1 have the same base name but differ in their suffixes. The filename suffixes indicate which locales they represent. The message lookup algorithm takes into account the base name, the current locale, and the key of the message. The algorithm follows these steps (assuming a base name of messages):

1. If a messages_<locale.language>_<local.country>.properties file is found in the classpath, it's loaded and the key is looked up within the file. When found, the associated message is returned. Otherwise (if the key wasn't found or the file doesn't exist), the algorithm moves on to the next step.

2. If a messages_<locale.language>.properties file is found in the classpath, it's loaded and the key is looked up. Again, when found, the associated message is returned. Otherwise, the algorithm continues to the next step.

3. If a messages.properties file is found in the classpath, it's loaded and the key is looked up. If found, the associated message is returned; otherwise an exception is thrown, indicating that no appropriate message could be found for the specified key.

As you can see, there are several levels where messages can be defined. The most basic form of the filename (messages.properties in our case) is often called the *default resource bundle* and used as a fallback when a locale-specific bundle or message key can't be found.

Although GWT doesn't use the actual PropertyResourceBundle, you'll soon see that its i18n support is still heavily based on the lookup algorithm we just described.

The Constants Interface

One way of using resource bundles in GWT is by binding the resource bundle files to a Java interface. This is done by creating an interface, which extends GWT's Constants interface and where each method represents a message key in the resource bundle file. Using deferred binding, you ask GWT to instantiate and return a concrete implementation of this interface in which each method implementation returns the appropriate message as defined by the resource bundle properties files. This may sound confusing, and is probably best explained by a concrete example.

Let's say we want to localize our GWTasks application. We can then create an interface called GWTasksConstants and add methods to it, one per message key. Listing 8-1 shows a narrowed down version of this interface.

Listing 8-1. *The GWTasksConstants Interface*

```
public class GWTasksConstants extends Constants {
    String loginButton();
    String logoutButton();
    String addButton();
    String editButton();
    String cancelButton();
}
```

As you can see, the method defined in the interface actually represents labels we use in the application. For example, the loginButton() method represents the label we used on the login button in the LoginPane.

Next, we need to create a resource bundle with these keys and map them to actual messages. We'll start by creating the default resource bundle; that is, the one that isn't associated with any specific language and/or country. Listing 8-2 shows what this resource bundle looks like.

Listing 8-2. *The GWTasksConstants.properties File*

```
# static messages for the GWTasks application
loginButton=Login
logoutButton=Logout
addButton=Add
editButton=Edit
cancelButton=Cancel
```

▪**Note** As mentioned previously, the Java resource bundle implementation requires that the resource bundle properties files will be located on the classpath. In GWT, however, it's required that these properties files be located in the same package next to the extended Constants class.

It's also possible to customize the mappings between the method names and the actual keys that are used in the resource bundle. This can be done by annotating each method with the @Key annotation, which accepts the name of the message key to look for. This can be useful for making the resource bundle more readable. Listing 8-3 shows such customization for the loginButton method.

Listing 8-3. *Using the @Key Annotation*

```
public class GWTasksConstants extends Constants {
    @Key("button.login")
    String loginButton();

    …
}
# static messages for the GWTasks application
button.login=Login

…
```

Now that we have both the interface and the resource bundle defined, it's time to see how we can bind the two and put them to good use. We'll ask GWT to create an instance of our new interface, which we'll use to access our messages. Listing 8-4 shows a snippet from the LoginPane constructor that uses this technique to localize the login button.

Listing 8-4. *Using GWT.create() with GWTasksConstants*

```
GWTasksConstants constants = GWT.create(GWTasksConstants.class);
Button loginButton = new Button(constants.loginButton(), new ClickListener() {
    public void onClick(Widget sender) {
        handleLogin();
    }
});
```

Note that the only way the code in Listing 8-4 can work is by having GWTasksConstants extend GWT's marker Constants interface. Based on the latter, the GWT compiler knows how to generate the appropriate class implementation at compile time.

In order to support multiple languages and countries, there are two more steps we need to take. First, we need to decide what locales we want our application to support and create the appropriate resource bundles. Then we need to extend the locale property in the application module descriptor and use it to list all the supported locales. Listing 8-5 shows an extra resource bundle that was defined for the Dutch language, and Listing 8-6 shows the extended property that's defined in the GWTasks.gwt.xml module file.

Listing 8-5. *The GWTasksConstants_nl.properties File*

```
# static messages for the GWTasks application
button.login=Aanmelden
button.logout=Afmelden
button.add=Toevoegen
button.edit=Wijzigen
button.cancel=Annuleren
```

Listing 8-6. *The GWTasks.gwt.xml module File*

```
<module>
    ...
    <extend-property name="locale" values="nl"/>
    ...
</module>
```

■**Note** Properties defined in the module files play a key role in the compilation phase. The GWT compiler "decides" what versions of the application should be created based on these properties. Extending the locale property (which is defined by the com.google.gwt.i18n.I18N module) indicates to the GWT compiler which localized versions of the application it should generate.

Before moving on to the next available i18n method, we can apply yet another optimization here. As with the GWT-RPC support, it's sufficient to create the GWTasksConstants instance once and share the same instance within the application. This can be done in several ways. One way we recommend is to treat it as a singleton and provide a public static accessor to it from within the interface itself (as with the GWT-RPC Locator pattern), which creates the concrete instance only once and always returns it for all calls (see Listing 8-7).

Listing 8-7. *GWTasksConstants as a Singleton*

```
public interface GWTasksConstants extends Constants {
    String loginButton();
    String logoutButton();
    String addButton();
    String editButton();
    String cancelButton();
    public static class Impl {
        private static GWTasksConstants instance;
        public static GWTasksConstants getInstance() {
            if (instance == null) {
                instance = GWT.create(GWTasksConstants.class);
```

```
            }
            return instance;
        }
    }
}
```

Although it's a common practice to always provide a default resource bundle as a fallback, this isn't necessary. You can also define default values for every message using annotations, as seen in Listing 8-8.

Listing 8-8. *Using Default Values with Annotations*

```
public interface GWTasksConstants extends Constants {

    @DefaultStringValue("Login")
    String loginButton();
    @DefaultStringValue("Logout")
    String logoutButton();
    @DefaultStringValue("Add")
    String addButton();
    @DefaultStringValue("Edit")
    String editButton();
    @DefaultStringValue("Cancel")
    String cancelButton();
    public static class Impl {
        private static GWTasksConstants instance;
        public static GWTasksConstants getInstance() {
            if (instance == null) {
                instance = GWT.create(GWTasksConstants.class);
            }
            return instance;
        }
    }
}
```

Note that in all the previous examples, we used Strings as the constant values. In practice, you can define any primitive type you want, even a String array. For example, if a requirement should dictate (for whatever reason) that the number of tasks in the system be limited according to the specific locale, we could define a maxTaskCount constant of type int that would hold this value.

The ConstantsWithLookups Interface

In Chapter 6, we explained how a GWT application can interact with a server using asynchronous communication. You've also seen how we can define a common implementation of the AsyncCallback interface that displays any failure in a well-formatted dialog box. Localizing an application often includes localizing the error messages that are displayed to the end user. A common way of doing that is to assign each error a unique code and select the appropriate error message based on this code.

We've seen that when extending the Constants interface, the interaction with the resource bundle is static. It's not possible to dynamically find a message based on a message key without knowing the key up front and hard-coding it by calling the mapped method on the extended interface.

In scenarios such as those previously described, this limitation of the Constants interface renders it useless. Fortunately, GWT provides another interface that can be extended to fix this problem.

The ConstantsWithLookups interface is a special extension to the Constants interface that adds dynamic message lookup. On top of all the mapped methods that you need to provide, you also have more generic access methods that let you look up messages directly using their keys. Listing 8-9 lists these extra dynamic methods.

Listing 8-9. *The Dynamic Lookup Methods on the ConstantsWithLookups Class*

```
public interface ConstantsWithLookups {

    boolean getBoolean(String methodName);

    double getDouble(String methodName);

    float getFloat(String methodName);

    int getInt(String methodName);

    Map<String, String> getMap(String methodName);

    String getString(String methodName);

    String[] getStringArray(String methodName);
}
```

As you can see, there's a dynamic lookup method for each possible data type. This makes it possible to receive an error code from the server and request its localized description by calling the getString method.

Note that the appropriate mapped methods still need to be defined on the extended interface. Calling a lookup method for a message that isn't mapped properly will result in a RuntimeException. For example, if the extended interface doesn't define a method called error001, calling getString("error001") will throw an exception.

■**Note** There's one powerful advantage in using Constants rather than ConstantsWithLookups. Since using Constants is done solely through direct-mapped method calls, the GWT compiler can analyze the code and optimize it by omitting all messages that aren't used by the code. With ConstantsWithLookups, the compiler can't do that, as messages can be retrieved dynamically at runtime based on their keys. Since the compiler can't predict what keys will be used, all messages in the resource bundles will be mapped and compiled with the rest of the code.

The Messages Interface

We've seen how GWT supports localization of messages. This support is most appropriate when the displayed text doesn't depend on any context and therefore is always the same (a Label's caption is a good example). But the text that should be displayed is often context-dependent. For example, the description of the CategorySelectionEvent depends on the selected category. Nevertheless, this description is shown to the user in the StatusBarPane and needs to be localized. Therefore, it can be said that the description of this event is *dynamic* and depends on the context in which it's used (in this case, the context is the selected category).

To support such localized messages, GWT provides the Messages interface. You can use this interface much like the Constants interface, by defining methods that map to messages keys. The main difference is that when using Messages, the methods can accept arguments and the mapped localized messages can define special placeholders where these arguments will go. Listing 8-10 shows the GWTasksMessages interface, which defines the message for the description of the CategorySelectionEvent.

Listing 8-10. *The GWTasksMessages Interface*

```
public interface GWTasksMessages extends Messages {

    @Key("event.categorySelected.description")
    String categorySelectedEventDescription(String categoryName);
    …
}
```

As you can see, the categorySelectedEventDescription method accepts one argument that represents the name of the selected category. Listing 8-11 shows the GWTasksMessages.properties file that defines the mapped message.

Listing 8-11. *The GWTasksMessages.properties File*

```
# Dynamic localized messages for the GWTasks application
event.categorySelected.description=Selected "{0}" category;
```

The format of the localized message is based on Java's MessageFormat. In their simplest form, the placeholders indicate which arguments should replace them by referring to their zero-based indices in the argument list. In our example, the categorySelectedEventDescription method defines only one argument. The message has one placeholder indicating that the first (and in our case, the only) argument should replace it. Check out the MessageFormat class's Javadoc for a more complete explanation. Listing 8-12 shows how the GWTasksMessages can be used within the CategorySelectionEvent to localize its description.

Listing 8-12. *GWTasksMessages Used in CategorySelectionEvent*

```
public class CategorySelectionEvent extends ApplicationEvent {
    …
    public String getDescription() {
        GWTasksMessages messages = GWTasksMessages.Impl.getInstance();
        return messages.categorySelectionEventDescription(category.getName());
    }
}
```

Plural Forms Support

When dealing with dynamic messages, one of the most annoying issues developers face is handling plural forms. Imagine, for example, that when the task form validation fails, we need to show the user a message indicating how many validation errors were encountered. If two or more errors occurred, we want to display the message "Found 2 errors", but in the case of only one error, we would probably want the message "Found one error". To handle such scenarios, we could define two messages, as shown in Listing 8-13.

Listing 8-13. *Supporting Plural Forms Using Multiple Messages*

```
public interface GWTasksMessages extends Messages {
    @DefaultMessage("Found {0} errors")
    String validationErrorCountPlural(int count);
    @DefaultMessage("Found one error")
    Stirng validationErrorCountSingle();
}
```

Since version 1.5, this is no longer the case, as the Messages interface has built-in support for handling these scenarios. This support is based on the @Plural annotation and works as shown in Listing 8-14.

Listing 8-14. *Supporting Plural Forms Using the @Plural Annotation*

```
public interface GWTasksMessages extends Messages {

    @DefaultMessage("Found {0} errors")
    @Plural("one", "Found one error")
    String validationErrorCount(int count);
}
```

The advantage of using the @Plural annotation is that, from the code perspective, there's only one message. GWT displays the proper message based on the value passed in (in our case, the error count). The @Plural annotation accepts an array of strings that represent alternative messages to use in the special value cases of "one" and "none". Listing 8-15 shows the same interface, which also supports providing a special message in case no errors are encountered.

Listing 8-15. *Supporting Plural Forms Including "None"*

```
public interface GWTasksMessages extends Messages {

    @DefaultMessage("Found {0} errors")
    @Plural("none", "No errors found", "one", "Found one error")
    String validationErrorCount(int count);
}
```

When mapping plural forms in the resource bundles, you still need to provide multiple messages in the form shown in Listing 8-16.

Listing 8-16. *The GWTasksMessages.properties File*

```
# Dynamic localized messages for the GWTasks application
validationErrorCount=Found {0} errors
validationErrorCount[none]=No errors found
validationErrorCount[one]=Found one error
```

Formats

One aspect of localization we haven't discussed yet is the different formats data can have when switching locales. For example, January 2, 2008, is represented as 01/02/08 in American English, but as 02/01/2008 in Dutch. Another example is how numbers are represented. In American English, a dot is used as a decimal separator, while in Dutch a comma is used for the same purpose. To handle these differences, GWT provides two classes—DateTimeFormat and NumberFormat.

These two format classes can be used to create the appropriate representation of dates and numbers. They are both locale-aware—GWT comes with predefined resource bundles for many language/country combinations where default formats are defined. (You can check all these resource bundles in the source code of gwt-user.jar under the com.google.gwt.i18n.client. constants package.) You can also define your own formats and use them explicitly. Listing 8-17 shows how we'd use the DateTimeFormat to display the current date to the user.

Listing 8-17. *The DateTimeFormat Used to Display a Date*

```java
public class DateTimeFormatSample implements EntryPoint {
    public void onModuleLoad () {
        DateTimeFormat format = DateTimeFormat.getFormat("dd/MM/yyyy HH:mm:ss");
        String date = format.format(new Date());
        Window.alert(date);
    }
}
```

If you want to provide your own localized formats, you can take the same approach as shown in Listing 8-17, but instead of hard-coding the format in the class, you can extract it to your own resource bundle as shown in Listings 8-18 and 8-19.

Listing 8-18. *A Custom Localized Date Format*

```java
public class LocalizedDateTimeFormatSample implements EntryPoint {
    public void onModuleLoad () {
        String datePattern = MyConstants.Impl.getInstance().datePattern();
        String date = DateTimeFormat.getFormat(datePattern).format(new Date());
        Window.alert(date);
    }
}
```

Listing 8-19. *The MyConstants.properties Resource Bundle*

```
# Constant messages for the application
datePatter=dd/MM/yyyy HH:mm:ss
```

Generally speaking, GWT's `DateTimeFormat` and `NumberFormat` classes support more or less the same format patterns as their Java counterparts, `java.text.SimpleDateFormat` and `java.text.DecimalFormat`. Furthermore, just like their counterparts, not only do they support formatting dates and numbers to strings, but also the reverse: parsing strings back to their appropriate data type. An example can be seen in Listing 8-20.

Listing 8-20. *Parsing Strings to Dates*

```
…
String datePattern = MyConstants.Impl.getInstance().datePattern();
String date = DateTimeFormat.getFormat(datePattern).format(new Date());
Date now = DateTimeFormat.getFormat(datePattern).parse(date);
…
```

This section showed you how i18n support can easily be added to an existing application. But the decision of whether to support i18n or not should be made as early in the project as possible. In general, we recommend using the i18n support even if you think there's no real need for it. It will make your life much easier if such a need comes up at a later stage. We've discussed the different mechanisms through which i18n can be applied and the role that the standard Java resource bundles play in this support. You've seen that the `Constants` and `ConstantsWithLookups` classes enable the localization of constant values of different types. You also saw how the `Messages` class enables more dynamic localized messages. Finally, we discussed the role of the format classes provided by GWT which help to present data in different formats based on locale.

Image Bundles

So far, when it comes to application design, we've focused mainly on the roles of panels that help lay out the different UI elements on the screen, and on CSS styles that can be used to customize the look of these elements. While extremely powerful, CSS styles take you only so far, and in most cases, external images are required to achieve the desired design. Not only can using images dramatically improve the look of the application, but in many cases, setting the appropriate icons on the various widgets shows their functionality and their role in the UI more clearly. It's not for nothing that they say "A picture is worth a thousand words."

In Chapter 5, we showed how you can use the `Image` class to customize the different faces of a `PushButton` and also to indicate a validation error in input forms. Although the approach we used works, it has one main disadvantage. For every `Image` class that you create, the browser needs to issue a separate request to the server in order to load the image. Even if the images are cached by the browser, it still needs to issue separate requests to verify that the cached images are up-to-date. Obviously, the more requests the browser makes, the longer it takes for the application to load. Moreover, if network latency is high, image display is delayed and application responsiveness falls off, compromising the overall user experience.

To overcome this limitation, the GWT team came up with a creative mechanism that enables you to bundle multiple images together into a single larger image. This bundles images in a single request and so reduces network round trips.

The image bundle support is also based on the deferred binding mechanism. To create an image bundle, all you need to do is extend the `ImageBundle` interface and define methods that represent the different images you want to bundle. At compile time, GWT will pick up the mapped images and generate the appropriate composite larger image. A nice side effect of this approach is that as a developer, you get immediate feedback when certain images are missing (in the traditional approach, you would get this feedback only at runtime). Listing 8-21 shows a simple image bundle definition that bundles three images: a tree, a house, and a car.

Listing 8-21. *A Typical Image Bundle Interface*

```
public interface MyImages extends ImageBundle {

    AbstractImagePrototype tree();
    AbstractImagePrototype house();
    @Resource("automobile.gif")
    AbstractImagePrototype car();
}
```

Each method you define in the interface should return `AbstractImagePrototype` and have a method name that corresponds to an image file. For example, the `tree` method in Listing 8-21 should have an image named "tree" in the same package. This default behavior can be customized by specifying the exact location of the image file using the `@Resource` annotation. In the listing, the `car` method is associated with an image file named "automobile.gif". When using the `@Resource` annotation, the location of the file can be either a relative path to the package of the interface or an absolute path in the classpath.

■**Note** GWT supports all major image formats, including GIF, JPEG, and PNG.

Note that the `AbstractImagePrototype` isn't the actual image, but rather serves as a prototype[2] from which the actual images can be created. It provides methods to create different flavors of the represented image. Listing 8-22 shows the three methods this class provides.

Listing 8-22. *The AbstractImagePrototype Class*

```
public abstract class AbstractImagePrototype {
    public abstract Image createImage();

    public abstract void applyTo(Image image);

    public abstract String getHTML();
}
```

---

2. Prototype is a well-known (creational) design pattern that enables a single object to serve as a prototype from which other objects can be created.

The `createImage` method creates an `Image` instance for the represented image. The `applyTo` method enables you to replace an existing image with the image that the prototype represents. And the `getHTML` method returns the HTML representation of the image, which can sometimes be useful for optimizations, as it avoids the creation of an `Image` instance.

Using Image Bundles Within GWTasks

To show how image bundles can be used within an application, we'll modify our GWTasks application to use them. In the process, we'll replace the current usage of `Images` in the forms and the different panes, and also introduce new images to further enhance the UI. Listing 8-23 shows the single image bundle that will be used in our application.

Listing 8-23. *The GWTasksImages Interface*

```
public interface GWTasksImages extends ImageBundle {
    // image methods should come here

    public static class Impl {
        private static GWTasksImages instance;
        public static GWTasksImages get() {
            if (instance == null) {
                instance = GWT.create(GWTasksImages.class);
            }
            return instance;
        }
    }
}
```

As you can see, our `GWTImageBundle` is currently empty; image methods will be added gradually as we go along. The only thing we did add to this interface (just as in `GWTasksConstants`) is an implementation of the locator pattern to provide easy access to the actual (cached) bundle instance.

We will place this bundle in a new `...gwtasks.client.ui.image` package that will also contain all the appropriate image files.

Form Validation Error Indication

Let's start with the simplest task: using the image bundle to show an error image next to an invalid field in the `RegistrationFormDialogBox`. The current implementation of this feature is also based on `Images`, though every image is loaded on demand when needed. Using the image bundle will greatly improve performance, as fewer round trips to the server will be required.

The first thing we need to do is to add the appropriate image to the image bundle. Listing 8-24 shows the changes to the `GWTasksImages` interface to accomplish that.

Listing 8-24. *The GWTasksImages Interface with the Field Error Icon*

```
public interface GWTasksImages extends ImageBundle {
    @Resource("field-error.gif")
    AbstractImagePrototype fieldErrorIcon();
    ...
}
```

Of course, you'll also need to add the field-error.gif image to the package in which the image bundle is defined.

Next, we change the RegistrationFormDialogBox class to use the image bundle instead of loading the images on demand each time. Listing 8-25 shows the modified code.

Listing 8-25. *RegistrationFormDialogBox Using the Image Bundle*

```
public interface RegistrationFormDialogBox extends DialogBox {
    ...
    protected Image createErrorImage() {
        return GWTasksImages.Impl.get().fieldErrorIcon().createImage();
    }
}
```

As it turns out, the change was quite minimal. We'd already isolated the functionality of creating the image to the single createErrorImage method, so all we had to do was call the appropriate method on the image bundle instead of constructing a new Image class.

Adding Task Priority Images

Our next task in enhancing the UI concerns displaying tasks in the TaskPane. Currently, each task in the list shows its priority as colored text (red H for HIGH, blue N for NORMAL, or orange L for LOW). The UI will look much cleaner if we change these letters to images of the appropriate color.

As with the previous example, the first thing we need to do is to come up with the appropriate images and add them to our bundle (see Listing 8-26).

Listing 8-26. *GWTasksImages with Task Priority Icons*

```
public interface GWTasksImages extends ImageBundle {
    ...
    @Resource("priority-high.png")
    AbstractImagePrototype highPriorityIcon();
    @Resource("priority-normal.png")
    AbstractImagePrototype normalPriorityIcon();
    @Resource("priority-low.png")
    AbstractImagePrototype lowPriorityIcon();
    ...
}
```

Now that we've defined and added the images to our bundle, let's see how we can change the TaskPane class to use these images as an indication for the task priorities (see Listing 8-27).

Listing 8-27. *The TaskPane Using the New Priority Icons*

```
public class TaskPane extends Pane {
    …
    protected void addTask(final Task task) {
        final int row = taskTable.getRowCount();
        taskTable.getRowFormatter().setStyleName(row, "TaskRow");
        final CheckBox checkBox = new CheckBox();
        checkBox.addClickListener(new ClickListener() {
            public void onClick(Widget sender) {
                task.setClosed(checkBox.isChecked());
                DataManager dataManager = getManagerRegistry().getDataManager();
                dataManager.updateTask(task, new Callback() {
                    public void onSuccess(Object result) {
                        fireEvent(new TaskStatusChangedEvent(TaskPane.this, task));
                    }
                });
            }
        });
        taskTable.setWidget(row, 0, checkBox);
        Image priorityImage = resolvePriorityImage(task.getPriority());
        priorityImage.setTitle(task.getPriority().name());
        taskTable.setWidget(row, 1, priorityImage);
        Label titleLabel = new Label(task.getTitle());
        titleLabel.addClickListener(new ClickListener() {
            public void onClick(Widget sender) {
                handleRowClicked(row, task);
            }
        });
        taskTable.setWidget(row, 2, titleLabel);
        fireEvent(new TaskCreatedEvent(this, task));
    }
    protected Image resolvePriorityImage(Task.Priority priority) {
        switch (priority) {
            case HIGH:
                return GWTasksImages.Impl.get().highPriorityIcon().createImage();
            case NORMAL:
                return GWTasksImages.Impl.get().normalPriorityIcon().createImage();
            default:
                return GWTasksImages.Impl.get().lowPriorityIcon().createImage();
        }
    }
    …
}
```

Here, as well, the change is quite minimal. The addTask method is responsible for translating tasks to their appropriate representations within the tasks table. Now, instead of creating a label for the priority, the appropriate priority image is resolved and set in the dedicated cell. The resolvePriorityImage method uses the image bundle to create the appropriate Image for the given priority.

Tree Image Bundles

So far you've seen how to create image bundles from scratch to manage the images used in your application. Because image bundles are so powerful, GWT uses them internally as well in some of its widgets. One of the most common examples is the Tree widget. As you may have noticed, the Tree widget comes with two images by default to represent closed and collapsed nodes. (If you hadn't noticed that yet, try creating a hierarchy of categories in the GWTasks application.) As it turns out, the Tree widget works with the TreeImages interface, which is a proprietary extension of the ImageBundle interface. Listing 8-28 shows this interface.

Listing 8-28. *The TreeImages Interface*

```
public interface TreeImages extends ImageBundle {
    AbstractImagePrototype treeOpen();
    AbstractImagePrototype treeClosed();
    AbstractImagePrototype treeLeaf();
}
```

As you can see, this interface defines three methods, each representing a different state of a tree node. By extending this interface and redefining these methods, you can customize the images the Tree widget will work with. For example, Listing 8-29 shows a custom TreeImages extension we can use for the categories tree in our GWTasks application.

Listing 8-29. *The CategoryTreeImages Extension*

```
public interface CategoryTreeImages extends TreeImages {
    @Resource("open.gif")
    AbstractImagePrototype treeOpen();
    @Resource("closed.gif")
    AbstractImagePrototype treeClosed();
    @Resource("leaf.gif")
    AbstractImagePrototype treeLeaf();
    // locator class and method
    ...
}
```

Adding this interface and its associated images to the image package lets us use it to customize the Tree used in the CategoryPane, as shown in Listing 8-30.

Listing 8-30. *Customizing the Category Tree in CategoryPane*

```
public interface CategoryPane extends Pane {
    …
    public CategoryPane(ManagerRegistry managerRegistry) {
        super(managerRegistry);
        tree = new Tree(CategoryTreeImages.Impl.getInstance());
        …
    }
    …
}
```

As you can see, once the image bundle is created, the only thing left to do is instantiate it and pass it as a constructor argument to the `Tree`. Figure 8-2 shows the category tree with the new images as well as the task priorities images introduced earlier.

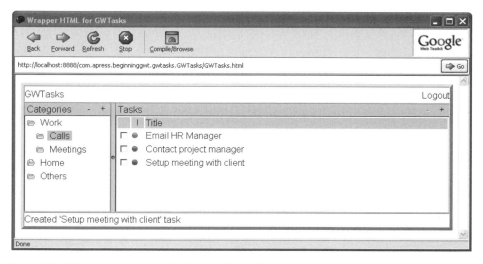

Figure 8-2. *The category tree with the configured images*

Browser History and Back Button Support

When developing any kind of application, one of the most important considerations the UI designer should take into account is the target user's mindset. This mindset is shaped by many factors, such as the specific domain in which the application will be used and the level of expertise users are expected to have. Another important factor is the environment in which the application is running and the way the users are accustomed to working within that environment. Ignoring this can potentially worsen the user experience, even in an otherwise well-designed application.

RIAs are essentially web applications running within a standard web browser. As such, the users of these applications will most likely treat them in the same way as any other web site. An integral part of this mindset is how the different browser buttons work—especially the Back and Forward navigation buttons.

If you're an experienced web developer, this shouldn't come as news to you. You've probably dealt with it in the past and never found it to be much of a hassle (except maybe when dealing with form submission). But when developing Ajax-based applications, giving the user the same navigation experience with browser buttons isn't as trivial as it may seem. The main reason for this is the asynchronous nature of Ajax communication and the fact that it's done behind the scenes without affecting the browser's history.

Take our GWTasks application as an example. We've managed to create a whole application that's referred to by a single URL! Any changes made to the categories or tasks are managed within the application using Ajax calls, while the URL remains untouched, just as the browser's history and navigation buttons remain in the same state. If you entered our application from another site, you can exit the application at any point by clicking on the browser's Back button. This behavior, at times, defies the user's expectations and thus breaks the user interface metaphor. In this section, we'll see how you can leverage GWT's history support to integrate with the browser history and preserve intuitive navigation within the application.

GWT History View

To understand how GWT uses the browser history, you first need to understand how the latter works. Generally speaking, browser history keeps track of all the URLs that are loaded. It can be seen as a dynamic stack of URLs, where the browser always displays the top URL on the stack. Every newly entered URL is added to the top of the stack, and when the user clicks the Back button, the top URL is popped out and the new top URL is loaded. Similarly, when the user clicks the Forward button, the previously popped-out URL is put back on the top of the stack and is reloaded.

This stack-based mechanism, which works well for simple web sites and web applications, doesn't work very well for GWT applications. Each GWT application is invoked through a single URL. Once this URL is entered, the appropriate GWT module is loaded, and from there on operates within this single URL. Of course, it's possible to load other URLs from within the application (for example, using external links as discussed in Chapter 4), but once the GWT module page is unloaded, it loses its internal state, and the next time it's entered, the GWT module will be reloaded from scratch. For this reason, the use of external links within a GWT application is often limited (if not completely absent) and most of the navigation is done within the application itself. This is similar to how GWTasks manages the navigation between the LoginPane and MainPane. It may look as if there's a hopeless conflict between the way GWT internal navigation works and the way browser history is managed. Nonetheless, there's a small exception to the normal operation of browser history, and it relates to internal URLs.

The HTML Anchor specification (which lays down how hyperlinks work) defines two types of links—external and internal. External links refer to other HTML pages. These are the most common links and work with the browser history as described previously. Internal links, on the other hand, are links that refer to sections within pages. These links can refer to sections within the same page (a page that contains the link and the section it refers to) or to sections in other pages. The main difference is that when an internal link refers to a section within the same page, when clicked, the page isn't reloaded by the browser, but rather scrolls to the appropriate section in the page. Internal links also have a special syntax, which is defined by the URL of the appropriate page, followed by a pound sign, and ending with the ID of the section being referred to. For example, the URL http://www.mycoolpage.com/index.html#sec2 refers to section sec2 in the page http://www.mycoolpage.com/index.html.

When an internal URL is entered, it's added to the history stack, even though the browser doesn't actually reload the page. This behavior is the key feature behind GWT history integration. Using internal URLs, GWT is able to manipulate the history without forcing the browser to reload the whole application from scratch. In a sense, you can see a GWT application as a single page with multiple sections. These sections can be anything you like, from different screens (as in the case of the LoginPane and MainPane) to virtual sections that represents user actions. The only constraint a section has is that it must have a unique ID that the application knows how to interpret. This ID is also referred as a *history token*.

The History Class

By default, GWT doesn't do anything with the browser history—not just because it shouldn't, but because it can't. GWT doesn't know what sections or history tokens it should work with and how to react to changes in history, nonetheless it lets you access this functionality via the History class. This class exposes a set of static methods that lets you manipulate the browser history and listen to history change events. Listing 8-31 shows the public interface of this class.

Listing 8-31. *The History Class*

```
public class History {
    public static void addHistoryListener(HistoryListener listener) {…}
    public static native void back();
    public static native void forward();
    public static String getToken() {…}
    public static void newItem(String historyToken) {…}
    public static void removeHistoryListener(HistoryListener listener) {…}
    public static void onHistoryChanged(String historyToken) {…}
}
```

▪**Note** Some of the methods in Listing 8-31 are declared as native. We cover native interfaces later on in this chapter when we discuss JSNI.

Using this class, you can directly access the current history token and add new tokens as you wish (via the newToken method). You can also issue navigation commands by calling the back and forward methods. Last but not least, you can listen to any changes in the history state by registering a custom HistoryListener (see Listing 8-32). This listener is notified whenever the history stack changes (that is, whenever a new token is added to the stack or when the navigation methods are called). It's also possible to notify history listeners explicitly by calling the onHistoryChange method.

Listing 8-32. *The HistoryListener Interface*

```
public interface HistoryListener extends java.util.EventListener {
    void onHistoryChanged(String historyToken);
}
```

To demonstrate how we can use the History class, we'll create a small sample application named HistorySample. This application will present a TabPanel. A TabPanel is yet another GWT panel that can be used to associate different widgets with tabs. When a tab is clicked, its associated widget is displayed. In our example, each tab will be associated with a simple label, and each label will be considered to be a section in the application. When the user clicks on a tab, the browser history will be updated accordingly, allowing the user to navigate between the viewed tabs using the browser's Back and Forward buttons. Listing 8-33 shows the HistorySample class.

Listing 8-33. *The HistorySample class*

```
public class HistorySample implements EntryPoint {

    public void onModuleLoad() {
        final TabPanel tabPanel = new DecoratedTabPanel();
        tabPanel.setSize("100%", "100%");
        tabPanel.add(new Label("Content of Tab 1"), "Tab 1");
        tabPanel.add(new Label("Content of Tab 2"), "Tab 2");
        tabPanel.add(new Label("Content of Tab 3"), "Tab 3");
        tabPanel.addTabListener(new TabListener() {
            public boolean onBeforeTabSelected(SourcesTabEvents ste, int index) {
                return true;
            }

            public void onTabSelected(SourcesTabEvents ste, int index) {
                History.newItem(String.valueOf(index));
            }
        });
        History.addHistoryListener(new HistoryListener() {
            public void onHistoryChanged(String historyToken) {
                if (historyToken.length() > 0) {
                    int tabIndex = Integer.valueOf(historyToken);
                    tabPanel.selectTab(tabIndex);
                }
            }
        });
        RootPanel.get("main").add(tabPanel);
    }
}
```

■**Tip** Using DecorateTabPanel instead of TabPanel results in slick decorated tabs with rounded corners.

In this example, we first create the tab panel and associate different labels with the appropriate tabs. We then register a TabListener to be notified when a tab is selected. When such notification arrives, we update the browser history by adding a new item on its stack. For this example, we decided that the history token will represent the index of the selected tab. We then register a HistoryListener, which will select the appropriate tab based on changes to the history tokens.

To see history integration in action, simply run the application, select a few tabs, and then use the browser's Back and Forward buttons to navigate to the previously viewed tabs.

Revisiting Hyperlinks

In Chapter 4, when we introduced the basic GWT widgets, we briefly discussed the Hyperlink widget and showed how you can use it instead of simple buttons. We also mentioned that there's more to this widget than a simple button replacement. In addition to the normal button-like functionality, it's also specially integrated with browser history. When constructing a Hyperlink, it's possible to associate a history token with it that will be added to the browser history when it's clicked.

In the HistorySample we developed in the previous section, we used a tab listener to listen to tab selection events, based on which we manually updated the browser history using the History class. We can achieve the same results by replacing the tab label with Hyperlinks which will automatically take care of the appropriate history updates. Listing 8-34 shows how this can be done (highlighted in bold).

Listing 8-34. *The HistorySample Class using Hyperlinks*

```
public class HistorySample implements EntryPoint {

    public void onModuleLoad() {
        final TabPanel tabPanel = new DecoratedTabPanel();
        tabPanel.setSize("100%", "100%");
        tabPanel.add(new Label("Content of Tab 1"), new Hyperlink("Tab 1", "0"));
        tabPanel.add(new Label("Content of Tab 2"), new Hyperlink("Tab 2", "1"));
        tabPanel.add(new Label("Content of Tab 3"), new Hyperlink("Tab 3", "2"));
        // we no longer need the tab listener registration
        History.addHistoryListener(new HistoryListener() {
            public void onHistoryChanged(String historyToken) {
                if (historyToken.length() > 0) {
                    int tabIndex = Integer.valueOf(historyToken);
                    tabPanel.selectTab(tabIndex);
                }
            }
        });
        RootPanel.get("main").add(tabPanel);
    }
}
```

In this example, we associated each Hyperlink with a token that represents the index of the tab. When clicked, the Hyperlinks add their associated tokens to the browser history without the need to interact explicitly with the History class.

■**Note** The usage of `Hyperlink` in the `HistorySample` was only to show how it works with the browser history. As it's also possible to select tabs programmatically, without having the user click any tabs, the `TabListener` would be a more appropriate approach for this example.

Bookmark Support

As we saw when integrating with the browser history, the URL changes based on the history tokens that are added to the history stack. It's also possible that your application may be loaded for the first time with a history token already specified. Such scenarios are quite common when using the browser bookmark functionality.

Most, if not all, web browsers support bookmarks. This functionality enables users to save a link to a specific URL so they can easily return to it later. When integrating with the browser history and manipulating the browser URL, you should always keep in mind that the user can save a bookmark at any point. For example, in our `HistorySample`, the user can view a specific tab and then save a bookmark with the intention of loading this tab later on. To support this feature, we need to examine the initial history token when the application loads. If such token exists, we need to reconstruct the view accordingly. Listing 8-35 shows how this can be done.

Listing 8-35. *The HistorySample Supporting Initial History Tokens*

```
public class HistorySample implements EntryPoint {

    public void onModuleLoad() {
        …
        String initialToken = History.getToken();
        if (initialToken.length() != 0) {
            tabPanel.selectTab(Integer.valueOf(initialToken));
        } else {
            tabPanel.selectTab(0);
        }
        RootPanel.get("main").add(tabPanel);
    }
}
```

In the listing, when the application loads, we first check whether an initial history token exists. If so, we select the appropriate tab; otherwise we make sure a default tab is selected.

Integrating GWTasks with History Navigation

Now that we've seen how to work with the browser history, let's integrate it with our GWTasks application. The first thing we need to do is define what kind of navigation we want to offer our users. For the sake of brevity, we'll narrow the navigation feature of our application and only allow the user to navigate between the different categories. More concretely, each selected category should be treated as a section in the application that the user can navigate to using the browser's Back and Forward buttons. The user should also be able to bookmark a specific category and return to it at a later time.

To implement this support, we only need to change the CategoryPane. The first thing we need to do is to make sure the appropriate token is added to the history when a category is selected. This can easily be done by changing the registered TreeListener as shown in Listing 8-36 (highlighted in bold).

Listing 8-36. *Adding History Tokens as Categories Are Selected*

```
public class CategoryPane extends Pane {
…
    public CategoryPane(ManagerRegistry managerRegistry) {
        super(managerRegistry);

        tree = new Tree();
        tree.addTreeListener(new TreeListener() {
            public void onTreeItemSelected(TreeItem item) {
                Category category = ((CategoryTreeItem) item).getCategory();
                String token = String.valueOf(category.getId());
                History.newItem(token);
                fireEvent(new CategorySelectionEvent(CategoryPane.this, category));
                removeButton.setEnabled(true);
                editButton.setEnabled(true);
            }
            public void onTreeItemStateChanged(TreeItem item) {
            }
        });
        …
    }
    …
}
```

As you can see, we chose to use the category IDs as the history tokens. Next, we need to make sure that when the history changes, the appropriate category is selected. For this, we need to implement the HistoryListener and register it with the history when the CategoryPane is loaded (see Listing 8-37).

Listing 8-37. *Registering the Appropriate HistoryListener*

```
public CategoryPane extends Pane {
    …
    public CategoryPane(ManagerRegistry managerRegistry) {
        …
        historyListener = new HistoryListener() {
            public void onHistoryChanged(String historyToken) {
                setStateFromHistoryToken(historyToken);
```

```
            }
        };
        SimplePanel main = new SimplePanel();
        main.setWidget(titledPanel);
        initWidget(main);
        setStyleName("CategoryPane");
    }
    public void reset() {
        tree.clear();
        History.removeHistoryListener(historyListener);
        if (getManagerRegistry().getSecurityManager().isLoggedIn()) {
            DataManager dataManager = getManagerRegistry().getDataManager();
            dataManager.getCategories(new Callback<List<Category>>() {
                public void onSuccess(List<Category> categories) {
                    for (final Category category : categories) {
                        CategoryTreeItem item = createTreeItem(category);
                        tree.addItem(item);
                    }
                    setStateFromHistoryToken(History.getToken());
                    History.addHistoryListener(historyListener);
                }
            });
        }
    }
    ...
    protected void setStateFromHistoryToken(String historyToken) {
        if (historyToken.length() > 0) {
            long categoryId = Long.valueOf(historyToken);
            setSelectedCategory(categoryId);
        } else {
            clearSelection();
        }
    }
    ...
}
```

Note that the history listener is created in the constructor of the CategoryPane but registered only when the reset method is called. This is important, as we want to handle history changes only when the CategoryPane is actually shown. Therefore, when the pane is reset and needs to be cleared (which happens when the user logs out), we need to deregister the history listener from the History. On the other hand, when the CategoryPane is reset and populated with a list of categories (which happens when the user logs in), we register the listener with the History and handle all history changes appropriately. Also note that just before we register the listener, we initialize the state of the CategoryPane based on the initial history token. Just as with our HistorySample application, we want to enable the user to use bookmarks as she pleases. The setStateFromHistoryToken method simply checks whether the token holds a value, and if so, selects the appropriate category. Otherwise, the category selection is cleared.

In this section, we've discussed the importance of understanding the mindset of the users of our applications. We saw that the runtime environment is a major factor in this mindset, and when it comes to web applications, browser history support plays an important role in the overall user experience. We showed how a GWT application can integrate with the browser history and thus enable the user to navigate between different sections of the application using the browser's Back and Forward buttons. You also learned how to support bookmarking and how all these features can be utilized in the GWTasks application to enable more natural navigation between the different categories.

JavaScript Native Interface (JSNI)

Sometimes an application can't be written entirely in Java. For instance, you might have a requirement to integrate with a library that was written in another programming language. In Java, you can declare a method as native and provide its implementation in another language. This is called the *Java Native Interface (JNI)*.

GWT provides an analogous interface called JSNI that allows you to call hand-written JavaScript from within your GWT classes. You can also call GWT methods and access Java fields from within native JavaScript. While JSNI is a powerful technique, it should be used sparingly, because when using it you lose all benefits derived from using GWT, such as the guarantees that your code will work across all browsers and won't leak memory.

Writing Native JavaScript Methods

To declare a JSNI method, you define a method that contains the `native` modifier. The native JavaScript code that will be invoked when the method is called is contained in a specially formatted comment block that directly follows the declaration of the method. See Listing 8-38 for an example.

Listing 8-38. *Native Alert Method*

```
public static native void print(String msg) /*-{
    $wnd.alert(msg);
}-*/;
```

■**Tip** You can't single-step through JSNI methods in a Java debugger. But you can set a breakpoint on the source line containing the opening brace of a JSNI method, allowing you to see invocation arguments.

Listing 8-38 shows a method that, when called, displays a browser alert window containing a user-defined message. The $wnd variable that's referenced is one of two variables automatically created by GWT, the other being $doc. The $wnd variable is a pointer to the current page's browser window; $doc is a pointer to the current page's document object. Because of the internal workings of GWT, you can't directly use the JavaScript window and document objects. These variables are provided as a substitute.

The method defined in Listing 8-38 accepts a `String` as argument. GWT will automatically convert primitive and `String` values to their JavaScript counterparts. So an `Integer` with value 10 will be defined in JavaScript as `var x = 10`. Similarly, a `String` will become `var x = "value"`. For more complex objects, things aren't so simple. Look at Listing 8-39.

Listing 8-39. *Direct Field Access*

```
package nl.jteam;
public class Example {
    public static native void sayHello(Person person) /*-{
        $wnd.alert("hello " + person.@nl.jteam.Person::name);
    }-*/;
}
```

Listing 8-39 shows how you can access fields in complex objects. This example introduces a new notation for directly accessing fields that looks like this:

```
[instance-expression]@class-name::field-name
```

- *instance-expression*—references an instance of the object. For static access to the object, this field needs to be left out.

- *class-name*—the fully qualified class name (package plus class name) of the class that contains the field.

- *field-name*—the name of the field to be retrieved.

JSNI methods can return one of four possible results: a Java primitive, a Java `Object`, a `com.google.gwt.core.client.JavaScriptObject`, or `void`. Primitives and `Strings` translate directly to their Java counterparts, just as arguments to JSNI methods are automatically converted. It's also possible to return an object that GWT itself created, and you can even modify the instance before passing it on. You can construct new objects from within native JavaScript, but these will be have to be mapped to a `JavaScriptObject`. As far as your GWT code is concerned, `JavaScriptObject` is a black box. You can't call any methods on it or view its internal state. You can, however, pass them on to other native JavaScript methods that can call methods on it. Listing 8-40 illustrates this.

Listing 8-40. *All Possible Return Types*

```
package nl.jteam;
import com.google.gwt.core.client.JavaScriptObject;
public class Example2 {
    public static native Person modifyName(Person person, String name) /*-{
        person.@nl.jteam.Person::name = name;
        return person;
    }-*/;
    public static native int sum(int val1, int val2) /*-{
        return val1 + val2;
    }-*/;
    public static native JavaScriptObject createCar() /*-{
```

```
        function Car(name) {
            this.name = name;
        }
        return new Car("Fiat 500");
    }-*/;
    public static native void displayCar(JavaScriptObject car) /*-{
        $wnd.alert(car.name);
    }-*/;
}}
```

The method `modifyName()` accepts a `Person` object and returns the `Person` after it has modified the `name` field. Returning the `person` instance is allowed because it was constructed in Java code. The `sum()` method accepts two integers and returns the sum of these values. Because the result is a primitive, it is automatically converted to a Java `.int`. The third method shows how a `JavaScriptObject` is returned. The `createCar()` method defines a JavaScript class called `Car` and returns an instance of this class. Because this JavaScript class has no GWT counterpart, it can only be mapped to `JavaScriptObject`. GWT can't call any methods on the result, but can pass it to `displayCar()`, which displays the name of the car that was created in `createCar()` when called.

Calling GWT Methods from JavaScript

Just as native methods can be called from within GWT, they can also call back into GWT code, as shown in Listing 8-41.

Listing 8-41. *Calling Back into GWT Code*

```
package com.apress.beginninggwt;
import com.google.gwt.user.client.Window;
public class Example {
    public static native void sayGoodbye(String name) /*-{
        @nl.jteam.Example::say(Ljava/lang/String;)("goodbye " + name);
    }-*/;
    public  static void say(String text) {
        Window.alert(text);
    }
}
```

Listing 8-41 shows a method called `sayGoodbye()` that delegates the displaying of the message to the regular Java method `say()`. The syntax for calling a Java method from within a JavaScript method is

`[instance-expression]@class-name::method-name(param-signature)(arguments)`

- *instance-expression*—references the instance of the Java object. It's left out in Listing 8-33 because `sayGoodbye()` is a static method. Had it been an instance method, `this` would have been used instead.

- *class-name*—the fully qualified class name of the class that contains the method to be invoked.

- *method-name*—the name of the method to be invoked.

- *param-signature*—uses the internal Java method signature notation to define the parameter signature. This notation can appear somewhat cryptic to the uninitiated. Table 8-1 lists all possible signatures.

Table 8-1. *JSNI Type Signatures*

Java Type	Signature
boolean	Z
byte	B
char	C
double	D
float	F
int	I
long	J
Object L	*fully qualified classname separated by forward slashes.* For example, Ljava/lang/String
type[]	[type

When a method accepts more than one parameter, the type signatures should be concatenated into one long string. To make things more concrete, there are a number of examples in Table 8-2 that you can examine.

Table 8-2. *Miscellaneous Examples*

Method	Example Invocation
public static void say(String text)	@com.apress.beginninggwt.Example::say(Ljava/lang/String;)("hello")
public void say(String text)	this@com.apress.beginninggwt.Example::say(Ljava/lang/String;("hello")
public int sum(int val1, int val2)	this@com.apress.beginninggwt.Example::sum(II)(4, 2)
public int f(String text, int value)	this@com.apress.beginninggwt.Example::f(Ljava/lang/String;I)("hello", 123)

Exception Handling

Exceptions can occur both in the Java code and in the native code. When a native JavaScript method throws an exception, it can be caught as an instance of JavaScriptException. JavaScriptException extends from RunTimeException and thus doesn't need to be explicitly defined on every native method. Because JavaScriptException is untyped, the authors of GWT recommend handling JavaScript exceptions in the JavaScript code and Java exceptions in the Java code as much as possible. Despite the lack of typing, it's still possible to find out what the original exception was. By using the methods getName() and getDescription() of the JavaScriptException, more details of the thrown exception can be retrieved.

■**Tip** A common use for JSNI is wrapping existing JavaScript components that would be costly and difficult to rewrite in Java. Many wrappers already exist for popular JavaScript libraries such as Ext JS, Google Maps, and Scriptaculous.

Uploading Files

Many applications allow users to upload files. Imagine a content management system (CMS) that allows content editors to upload images and video files to link to an article. But also imagine a financial application that allows users to import historical data by uploading a comma-separated values (CSV) file.

Of course, this is also possible for applications built using GWT. Regrettably, applications developed using GWT aren't desktop applications in the sense that they provide access to the client's file system. A GWT application still operates within the restricted browser environment. So in order to have access to a file, you need to provide the user with the means to select a file and then upload it to the server for the application to read its contents.

This approach is similar to file uploads in any other web application. If you've already built a web application that allows users to upload files, you know that it's not always trivial to do this. The main problem is that you can only get a handle to a file on the user's local file system by means of a special HTML widget, an input element of type file, that's represented in the browser by the widget in Figure 8-3. Basically, when the form that encapsulates the input element is submitted, the selected file is subsequently uploaded.

Figure 8-3. *The HTML file upload widget*

GWT provides support for forms and form widgets as part of its widget library. Normally we don't recommend using the form widgets, because we prefer to use the RPC mechanism to communicate with the server. But for this specific use case, using form widgets is the only way. In order to use the RPC mechanism to upload files to the server, the application should first have access to the file content. Because it doesn't have this access, we can only use the browser's built-in mechanism to get the file content to the server.

First we need to create a form and add an input element to it. Luckily GWT provides some convenient widgets to do just that. In Listing 8-42, we create a FormPanel and add a FileUpload to it.

Listing 8-42. *File Upload Sample Entry Point*

```
public class FileUploadSample implements EntryPoint {
    public void onModuleLoad() {
        // create a form panel and set its properties correctly for file uploading
        final FormPanel form = new FormPanel();
        form.setEncoding(FormPanel.ENCODING_MULTIPART);
        form.setMethod(FormPanel.METHOD_POST);
        form.setAction("upload");
        // create a panel to hold the upload widget and submit button
        VerticalPanel panel = new VerticalPanel();
        form.setWidget(panel);
        FileUpload upload = new FileUpload();
        panel.add(upload);
        panel.add(new Button("Submit", new ClickListener() {
            public void onClick(Widget sender) {
                form.submit();
            }
        }));
        RootPanel.get("content").add(form);
    }
}
```

We set some properties of the form panel that relate to the form attributes you'd expect in HTML. The first property is the encoding to be used by the form, which should be multipart in all cases where you want to upload files. The second property is the HTTP method to use for the form (in this case POST), and the last one is the action to call on the server when the form is submitted. That's all you have to do to allow users to select a file from their hard drive and submit it to the server (see Figure 8-4).

The next step is to write some server-side code that can handle the form when it gets submitted. The exact approach to this server-side code is heavily dependent on personal preference and more specifically the preferred web framework. To keep it simple and generic, this chapter uses an implementation of HttpServlet as the class that handles the file upload. Listing 8-43 shows the implementation of the server-side code that handles the submitted form. We use the FileUpload package that's part of the Apache Commons project (http://commons.apache.org/fileupload/) to deal with parsing the request, storing temporary files in case of large file uploads, and so forth.

Listing 8-43. *File Upload Servlet*

```
public class FileUploadServlet extends HttpServlet {
    protected void doPost(HttpServletRequest request, HttpServletResponse response)
            throws ServletException, IOException {
        // create a factory for disk-based file items and an upload handler
```

```
        DiskFileItemFactory factory = new DiskFileItemFactory();
        ServletFileUpload upload = new ServletFileUpload(factory);

        // parse the request to retrieve the individual items
        List<FileItem> items;
        try {
            items = upload.parseRequest(request);
        } catch (FileUploadException e) {
            throw new ServletException("File upload failed", e);
        }
        // handle the individual items appropriately
        for (FileItem item : items) {
            // code here to process the file
            System.out.println("item = " + item);
        }
    }
}
```

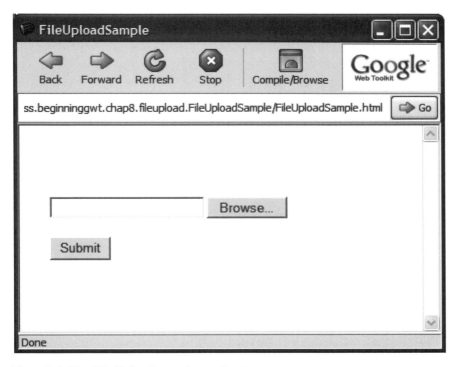

Figure 8-4. *The File Upload sample application*

The next step is to add the servlet to the application. Normally, this would mean defining the servlet inside your web.xml file. If you run your GWT application in hosted mode, there's an embedded Tomcat servlet container instance running behind the hosted-mode application. You can instruct the hosted mode to deploy your servlet inside this container by defining it in the GWT module descriptor. GWT will make sure that the servlet is actually available. As is illustrated in Listing 8-44, this sample will use the second approach.

Listing 8-44. *Module Descriptor of the File Upload Sample*

```
<module>
    <inherits name="com.google.gwt.user.User"/>

    <entry-point class="...beginninggwt.chap8.fileupload.client.FileUploadSample"/>
    <servlet path="/upload"
             class="...beginninggwt.chap8.fileupload.server.FileUploadServlet"/>
</module>
```

Now we're done introducing the file upload functionality provided by GWT. There's really nothing more to it than this. But to make this section more interesting and to show you some more advanced functionality of GWT, we're going to slightly enhance the current implementation. We're going to add a progress indicator to the upload page to indicate the progress of the upload to the user.

Monitoring Progress on the Server

To be able to show the progress of the upload to the user, we first need to monitor it. Luckily the Commons FileUpload package provides support for this through the ProgressListener interface, which you can implement as shown in Listing 8-45. In this case, we keep track of the current number of bytes that are read and store them as a field of the monitor.

Listing 8-45. *File Upload Listener*

```
public class FileUploadListener implements ProgressListener {
    private long kiloBytes = -1;
    private long bytesRead = -1;
    private long contentLength = -1;
    private int items = -1;
    public void update(long bytesRead, long contentLength, int items) {
        long kBytes = bytesRead / 1024;
        if (kiloBytes == kBytes) {
            return;
        }
        kiloBytes = kBytes;

        this.bytesRead = bytesRead;
        this.contentLength = contentLength;
        this.items = items;
```

```
    }
    public long getBytesRead() {
        return bytesRead;
    }
    public long getContentLength() {
        return contentLength;
    }
    public int getItems() {
        return items;
    }

}
```

The next step is to create an instance of the listener each time a form is submitted by a user. Then we store the listener in the session and register the listener with the upload handler, as shown in Listing 8-46.

Listing 8-46. *Adding the Upload Listener to the File Upload Servlet's POST Method*

```
FileUploadListener listener = new FileUploadListener();
session.setAttribute("progress", listener);
upload.setProgressListener(listener);
```

Now that we can track progress on the server and store the current progress in the user session, we also need a way for the user to actually view the current progress. We can easily do this by overriding the servlet's doGet method. For each incoming call to the method, we retrieve the listener from the session, and if it's there we render a message indicating the progress and write it back to the client (see Listing 8-47).

Listing 8-47. *Adding a GET Method to the File Upload Servlet*

```
protected void doGet(HttpServletRequest request, HttpServletResponse response)
throws ServletException, IOException {
    FileUploadListener listener = (FileUploadListener)
            request.getSession().getAttribute("progress");
    if (listener != null) {
        StringBuilder msg = new StringBuilder();
        msg.append(formatSize(listener.getBytesRead()));
        msg.append(" / ");
        msg.append(formatSize(listener.getContentLength()));
        response.getOutputStream().write(msg.toString().getBytes());
    }
}
```

Monitoring Progress on the Client

Because progress is being tracked on the server, the client has to ask the server periodically for the current progress. To do this, we create a class named ProgressTimer that extends the GWT Timer utility class. The ProgressTimer is scheduled to be called (for instance) every second, and this will call its retrieveCurrentProgressFromServer method (see Listing 8-48).

Listing 8-48. *The Implementation of the ProgressTimer Logic*

```
protected void retrieveCurrentProgressFromServer() {
    RequestBuilder builder = new RequestBuilder(RequestBuilder.GET, "upload");
    builder.setCallback(new RequestCallback() {

        public void onResponseReceived(Request request, Response response) {
            StringBuilder builder = new StringBuilder("reponse received: ").
                append(response.getStatusCode()).append(" - ").
                append(response.getStatusText()).append("\n\t content: ").
                append(response.getText());
            System.out.println(builder.toString());
            statusLabel.setText(response.getText());
        }
        public void onError(Request request, Throwable t) {
            GWT.log("Unable to retrieve the current status from the server", t);
        }
    });
    try {
        builder.send();
    } catch (RequestException e) {
        GWT.log("An error occurred while connecting to the file upload monitor", e);
    }
}
```

As you can see from the listing, the statusLabel is updated with the response text. Of course, you can make this more sophisticated by actually showing a progress bar on the client, but we guess you get the picture.

Note that in order to see this progress indicator in action, you have to select and upload a file of considerable size. The larger the file, the better you can see the progress indication in action.

Summary

In this chapter, we covered some of the more advanced GWT topics. You've seen how you can internationalize your application by using constants and messages. Internationalization doesn't just provide localized messages based on the user's preference, but also allows you to bind logic to the locale, for example by using localized formats for dates and numbers.

You now also know how to improve your application's performance by using ImageBundles. This feature combines multiple images into one, enabling the browser to retrieve them with a single request.

One of the hardest problems to solve with RIAs is capturing the Back and Forward buttons of the browser. The history support provided by GWT makes this easy and enables you to define the functionality behind these buttons exactly as you want to.

JSNI lets you use your own or third-party JavaScript libraries. By using the core Java features to write native code, you can program pure JavaScript, saving the extra work of rewriting common operations. A lot of third-party libraries already come with wrapper modules.

We concluded this chapter by showing how you can add file upload functionality using the `FileUpload` widget inside a `FormPanel`. Using the Apache Commons `FileUpload` library on the server side, you can even implement a progress indicator.

And that's as far as this book takes you. We wish you happy coding and good luck with GWT!

IDE Support

Throughout this book, we've built a sample application. You can do this in a plain text editor and use command-line tools to build the code, or start the hosted mode. However, as an alternative, most developers prefer to use an IDE as an easy-to-use working environment. Two of the most commonly used IDEs are Eclipse and IntelliJ IDEA. In this appendix, we'll show how you can configure these IDEs to use with the sample application.

As can be seen in Chapter 3, GWT comes with a set of easy-to-use command-line scripts. Usually, this is also the easiest way to get started. Using the `applicationCreator` script, we can kick off our project. The script creates the `src` directory containing the specified package structure of our module. In the package structure, four files are created that comprise a simple sample application. Furthermore, in the root folder of the project, two batch files are created: one for starting the GWT module in hosted mode, the other for compiling the GWT module into a ready-to-use web application.

Eclipse

Now that you have a basic project set up, you want to start using your IDE. Fortunately, GWT comes with standard support for Eclipse through scripts. At the moment, Eclipse is the most popular IDE among Java developers. Primarily, Eclipse is an open source platform for creating IDEs; the Eclipse IDE is one of its resulting products. Its online community provides tools and frameworks focused on creating the ultimate IDE. As a result, there are already a large set of different Eclipse installations available, each targeted at a specific development environment. We suggest the Eclipse IDE for Java EE Developers installation as a starting point for developing GWT applications. You can download the latest release, called Ganymede, from `http://www.eclipse.org/downloads/packages/`.

The downloaded archive contains a folder with a ready-to-use version of Eclipse. So no installation is necessary; just unpack the archive in a convenient location and start the Eclipse executable. The first time you start up Eclipse, it will ask you for a workspace location. Since you already have your project files created, the workspace location is usually one folder higher in the directory structure than where your project is. In other words, the workspace location is the folder in which your project folder is situated.

The Eclipse welcome screen shows links to samples, tutorials, and other information. You can use these links to get a more thorough understanding of Eclipse. For now, we ignore the welcome screen and continue to set up our project. Close the welcome screen by either clicking the cross on the Welcome tab in the upper left corner or clicking the arrow icon at the right side of the welcome screen. Either option should result in an empty workspace.

Most of the scripts delivered with GWT have optional arguments to perform some Eclipse-specific tasks. To get your project running inside Eclipse, the first step is to make your project folder an Eclipse project. The `projectCreator` script is meant to do just that. By passing in the `-eclipse` argument, you can create the Eclipse project files `.classpath` and `.project` (see Listing A-1).

Listing A-1. *Creating Eclipse Project Files Through the* `projectCreator` *Script*

```
> projectCreator -eclipse GWTasks
Created directory test
Created file .project
Created file .classpath
```

Through the file-import menu, we reach the import pop-up shown in Figure A-1. Here we can choose to import an existing project into our workspace.

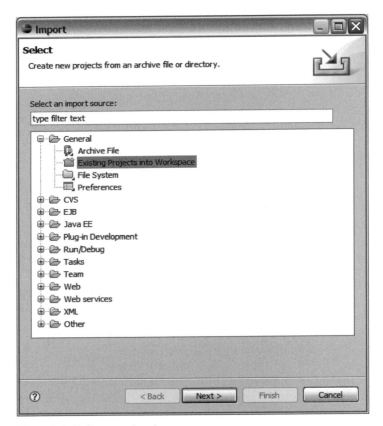

Figure A-1. *Eclipse project import screen*

Click Next to move on to the next window, where you're prompted to select your root folder. After selecting your project folder here, Eclipse recognizes the project files and shows the project in the selection box. Make sure the GWT project is selected and click Finish to open the project in Eclipse. Now you're ready to develop your project in Eclipse. Take a look around in the project explorer to get a feeling of how Eclipse organizes your project files. As you can see in Figure A-2, Eclipse separates the Java files from the resource files in the package folder. Keep this in mind when you start looking for specific files.

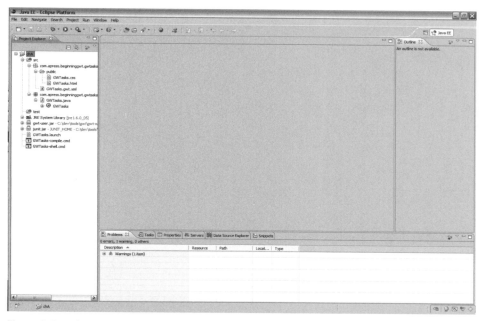

Figure A-2. *Eclipse workspace with open project*

Although you're now ready to use the convenient features of an IDE such as syntax highlighting and code completion, one important feature needs to be discussed in more detail to make your Eclipse experience complete. Using the applicationCreator script, we can generate a launch script through which we can start our GWT hosted mode browser from inside Eclipse. Run the applicationCreator script again, this time adding the -eclipse option as an extra argument. We also have to add the option -ignore to direct the script to not overwrite our existing project. As can be seen in Listing A-2, the script gives clean output, showing us that it didn't overwrite any files and generated a new file called GWTasks.launch.

Listing A-2. *Creating an Eclipse Launcher Using the applicationCreator Script*

```
>applicationCreator com.apress.beginninggwt.client.GWTasks -eclipse GWTasks -ignore
src\com\apress\beginninggwt\GWTasks.gwt.xml already exists; skipping
src\com\apress\beginninggwt\public\GWTasks.html already exists; skipping
src\com\apress\beginninggwt\public\GWTasks.css already exists; skipping
src\com\apress\beginninggwt\client\GWTasks.java already exists; skipping
Created file C:\dev\projects\playground\book\GWTasks.launch
GWTasks-shell.cmd already exists; skipping
GWTasks-compile.cmd already exists; skipping
```

Going back to Eclipse, you need to refresh your project folders for the launcher file to show up in your project explorer. Focusing somewhere in the project explorer and pressing F5 will refresh the list. Now you can start the hosted-mode browser by right-clicking on the new file and choosing the GWTasks option from the Run As menu. Figure A-3 shows the context menu of the launcher file.

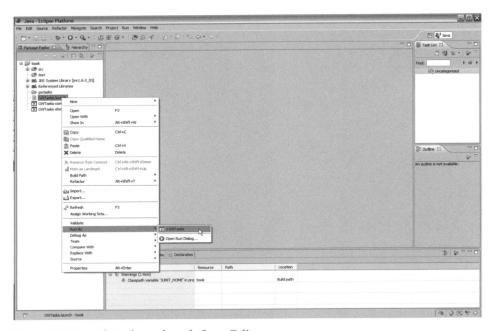

Figure A-3. *Launching hosted mode from Eclipse*

IntelliJ IDEA

As an alternative to the Eclipse IDE, you can use IntelliJ IDEA from JetBrains. This commercial IDE is free to use if you're working on an open source project. But unfortunately, it isn't free for commercial usage. More information about pricing and a 30-day trial version are available from `http://www.jetbrains.com/idea/`.

The GWT support in IntelliJ is rather extensive. As of version 6, the GWT Studio plug-in is available and even installed by default. The Create New Project wizard has a convenient option for selecting the Google Web Toolkit as the technology to be used. However, this option has limited effect on the project, as it only adds the `gwt-user.jar` file to the list of dependencies.

GWT Studio comes with some wizards that can be used to create the different GWT entities in your project. These wizards can be found in the context menu. Figure A-4 shows this context menu, which you can get through different paths. The easiest and shortest path is pressing Alt-Insert when the focus is on the package in which you want to create a GWT entity.

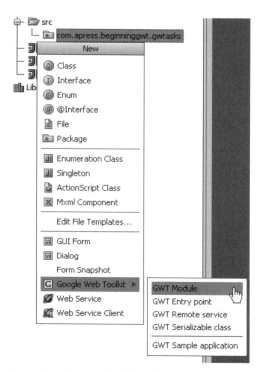

Figure A-4. *Google Web Toolkit context menu in IntelliJ Idea*

The first step for your empty project is creating the GWT module. In contrast to the applicationCreator script, you first have to define a package structure yourself. When you have the package in which the GWT module needs to be created, you can choose to create the GWT module from the package's context menu. So for our GWTasks sample application, you first create the package com.apress.beginninggwt.gwtasks. Then, with the focus on the package, you go to the context menu and select to create a new GWT Module. A pop-up appears, requesting the name for the GWT module. After entering the name (GWTasks), four files are created and our module is ready. Instead of the sample application that is created by the applicationCreator script, you now have an almost empty GWT application.

The second option in the context menu enables you to easily create a second entry point to your GWT application. Not only does this option create the new Java class that inherits the EntryPoint class, it also registers this new EntryPoint inside your GWT module descriptor (.gwt.xml).

Creating a remoting service with GWT-RPC can also be done through a wizard. The third option in the context menu allows you to generate an interface, the corresponding asynchronous interface, and a server-side implementation in the server package. Furthermore, the module descriptor is extended with a servlet definition, enabling you to start up the servlet inside the hosted mode.

The last default option generates a class implementing the IsSerializable interface. This interface is used to mark that your class is intended for use in remoting. However, since implementing this interface is no longer mandatory as of version 1.4, chances are low that you'll ever use this option.

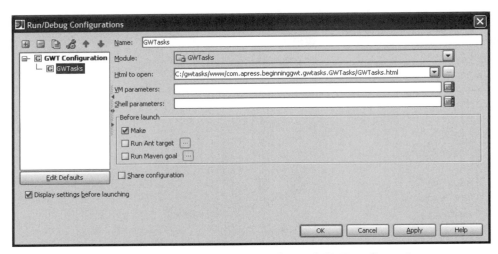

Figure A-5. *The configuration menu with an auto-detected GWT configuration*

Creating a GWT application only scratches the surface of GWT Studio. Just as we showed you in Eclipse, it's also possible to start the hosted mode from within IntelliJ IDEA. This is of course one of the key features, because it allows you to debug your GWT application in Java code instead of digging into the generated JavaScript. In IntelliJ IDEA, you first have to configure a runnable environment. Using the Run menu, you can access the configuration for your project. Using the add button in the top left corner of Figure A-5, you can add a new configuration for your project. In the menu, choose a GWT configuration and you're as good as done. If your project is already set up for GWT, the configuration will auto-detect all the necessary settings, so all that's left is to give the configuration some arbitrary name. Afterward, you can start the configuration in either run or debug mode using the Run menu.

APPENDIX B

■ ■ ■

Resources

There are a lot of GWT resources on the Internet. For your convenience, here are some of our favorites. There are three major Google sites:

- http://code.google.com/webtoolkit—the GWT home page.

- http://google-web-toolkit-doc-1-5.googlecode.com/svn/javadoc/1.5/index.html—API reference.

- http://groups.google.com/group/google-web-toolkit—user forum. Useful to get help or provide help to other users.

There are also some independent resources:

- http://www.ongwt.com—the latest GWT-related news.

- http://www.gwtsite.com—the unofficial GWT blog.

As mentioned in Chapter 3, Google hosts a lot of third-party projects on their portal. Here's a small summary of open source projects related to GWT.

- http://gwt-widget.sourceforce.net—GWT Widget Library.

- http://code.google.com/p/gwt-hibernate/—GWT & Hibernate.

- http://code.google.com/p/gwittir/—code generators, scaffolding, utilities, and a basic MVC framework.

- http://code.google.com/p/gwtoolbox/—a collection of modules to help developers create robust GWT applications. Includes support for JavaBean binding and validation. It also brings inversion of control (IoC) to GWT, by enabling GWT to read Spring-like configurations.

- http://code.google.com/p/rocket-gwt/—also provides IoC. Other components support drag and drop, extended JSON support, and logging.

Index

You Need the Companion eBook

Your purchase of this book entitles you to buy the companion PDF-version eBook for only $10. Take the weightless companion with you anywhere.

We believe this Apress title will prove so indispensable that you'll want to carry it with you everywhere, which is why we are offering the companion eBook (in PDF format) for $10 to customers who purchase this book now. Convenient and fully searchable, the PDF version of any content-rich, page-heavy Apress book makes a valuable addition to your programming library. You can easily find and copy code—or perform examples by quickly toggling between instructions and the application. Even simultaneously tackling a donut, diet soda, and complex code becomes simplified with hands-free eBooks!

Once you purchase your book, getting the $10 companion eBook is simple:

❶ Visit **www.apress.com/promo/tendollars/**.

❷ Complete a basic registration form to receive a randomly generated question about this title.

❸ Answer the question correctly in 60 seconds, and you will receive a promotional code to redeem for the $10.00 eBook.

2855 TELEGRAPH AVENUE | SUITE 600 | BERKELEY, CA 94705

Offer valid through 03/09.